I0810523

CELEBRATING PALATINE

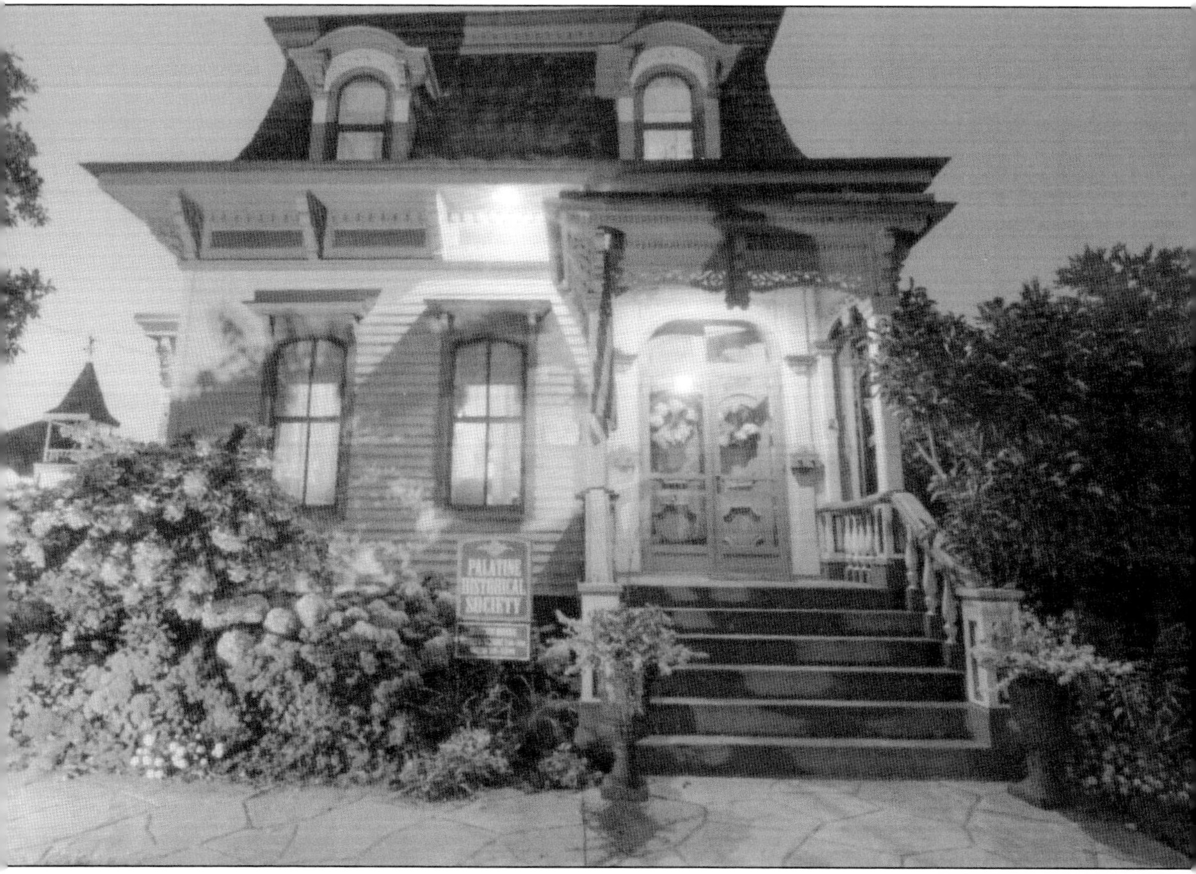

1873 George H. Clayson House Museum and Historical Library, Home of the Palatine Historical Society. The Palatine Historical Society is located at the George H. Clayson House Museum and Historical Library. (Courtesy of the Palatine Historical Society.)

Front Cover: A World War I homecoming parade is pictured in Palatine on August 29, 1919. (Courtesy of Palatine Historical Society.)

Upper Back Cover: The Palatine Historical Society float is pictured in the 1999 Fourth of July parade. (Courtesy of Palatine Historical Society.)

Lower Back Cover: The Palatine Military Band marches in the 1918 Fourth of July parade. (Courtesy of Palatine Historical Society.)

CELEBRATING PALATINE

Palatine Historical Society

ARCADIA PUBLISHING

Copyright © 2017 by Palatine Historical Society
ISBN 978-1-4671-2688-5

Published by Arcadia Publishing
Charleston, South Carolina

Printed in the United States of America

Library of Congress Control Number: 2017938470

For all general information, please contact Arcadia Publishing:
Telephone 843-853-2070
Fax 843-853-0044
E-mail sales@arcadiapublishing.com
For customer service and orders:
Toll-Free 1-888-313-2665

Visit us on the Internet at www.arcadiapublishing.com

Contents

Acknowledgments

It was a pleasure to know that people enjoyed the 150 vignettes in the *Palatine Herald* about the village of Palatine. There have been many suggestions that we reprint them in book form. I enjoyed compiling them and am delighted to present 117 of them in this volume.

I was able to research the extensive Frank Regan Archival and Photograph Collection of the Palatine Historical Society. Through the generosity of Palatine residents and the dedicated Palatine Historical Society members who pursued the materials and preserved them, these records are housed in the Florence Parkhurst Library.

I made use of the following printed and digital materials written by society members: Connie Rawa's *Hillside Cemetery*, David Hammer's *Paddock Publications Index*, my own Then & Now: *Palatine, Illinois*, four PowerPoint presentations, articles from earlier editions of the *Palaver*, and scripts from History Crawls and Cemetery Walks. The wonderful world of the Internet was also helpful.

I thank Marg Plank for the four articles she wrote and Nancy Cairns as editor. Unless otherwise indicated, all images used are property of the Palatine Historical Society.

—Alice Rosenberg

INTRODUCTION

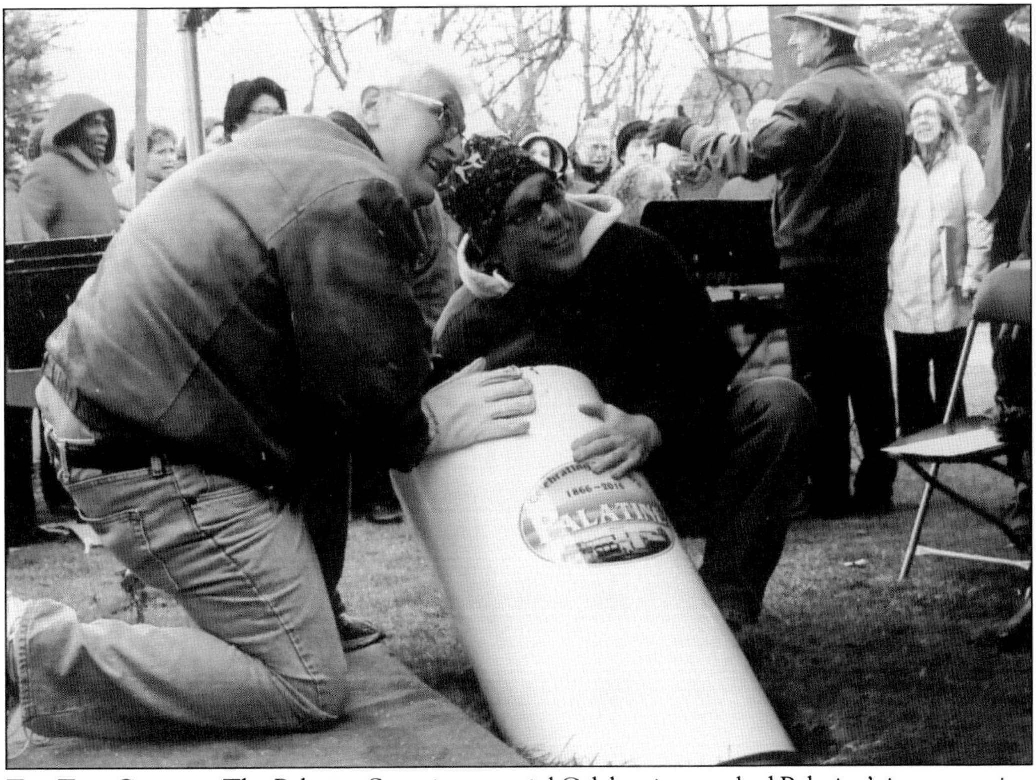

THE TIME CAPSULE. The Palatine Sesquicentennial Celebration marked Palatine's incorporation as a village. On April 2, 1866, a group of 73 farmers, carpenters, blacksmiths, and merchants met and voted to incorporate Palatine. One hundred fifty years later, on a snowy April 2, 2016, residents kicked off the village's anniversary celebration on the grounds of the Clayson House Museum.

The event included the relating of village stories. The Allegro Choir sang a song written for the occasion by David Reiser, a former Palatine High choral teacher. A time capsule, courtesy of the Palatine Lions Club, was buried, to be unearthed in 2066.

The Palatine 150 Core Committee members were Deb Danecki, Marilyn Petersen, Susan Minnott, Melanie Santostefano, and Joe Petykowski. Our thanks go to the many volunteers who gave freely of their time over the course of the year. We appreciate your efforts.

Seen here, Terry Kelly and Paul Pioch from the Palatine Lions Club get ready to bury the time capsule to be unearthed in 2066. (Courtesy of Joseph Petykowski.)

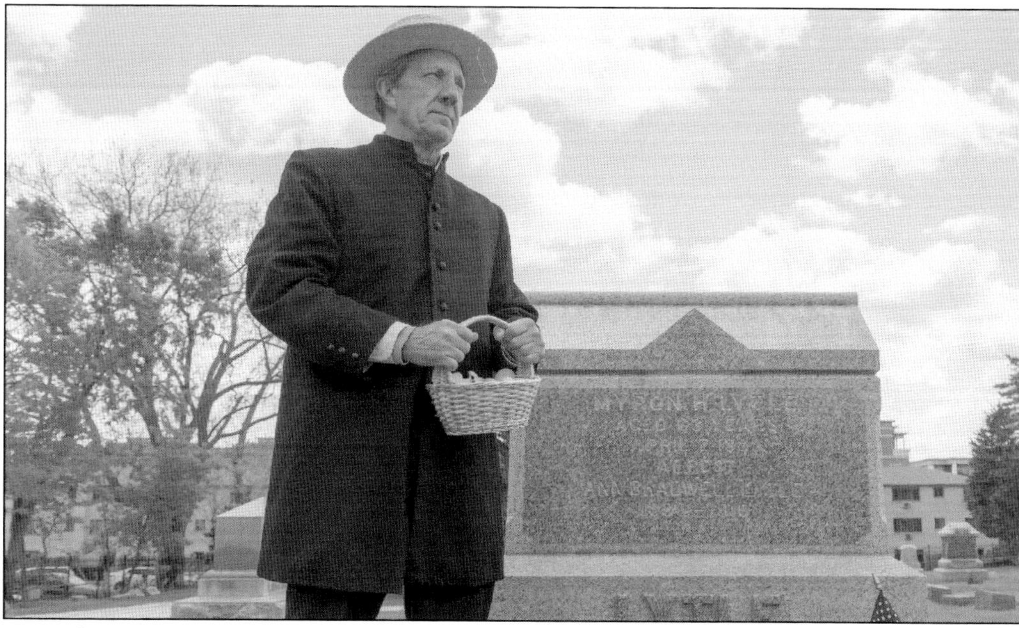

1866 Cemetery Walk. The annual Cemetery Walk at Hillside Cemetery on May 15, 2016, featured people who lived in Palatine in 1866. Tom Landeck portrays Myron Lytle, the first mayor of Palatine. The cemetery is maintained by Palatine Township, and the Palatine Historical Society donates 100 percent of the walk's proceeds to maintenance of the facility and headstones. (Courtesy of Joseph Petykowski.)

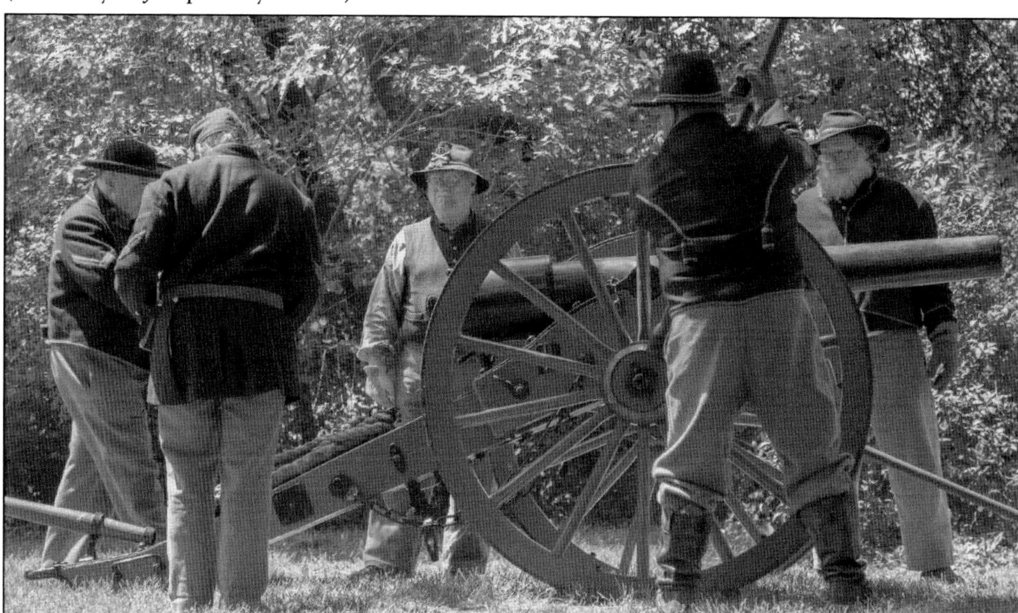

Good Ol' Summertime Festival. Hundreds of people attended a Good Ol' Summertime Festival at the Clayson House Museum on June 5, 2016. The historical society scooped ice cream, and there was a variety of activities and booths for all to enjoy. The original 129-year-old fire pumper was wheeled out and attracted much attention. During the event, the vintage cannon featured here was shot off several times by Taylor's Battery. (Courtesy of Joseph Petykowski.)

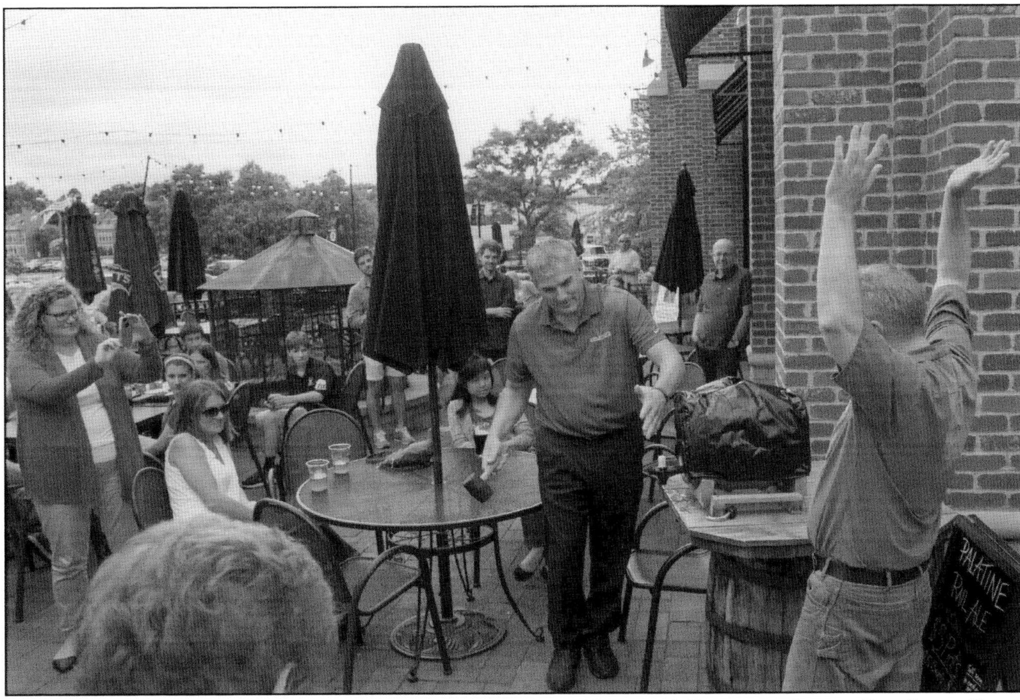

150 Rail Ale. There was a great turnout on June 16 at Emmett's Brewing Co. on Brockway Street for the unveiling of the once-in-a-lifetime Palatine 150 Rail Ale. The limited beer was created especially for the sesquicentennial. Mayor Jim Schwantz opened the ceremony by tapping the first keg. (Courtesy of Joseph Petykowski.)

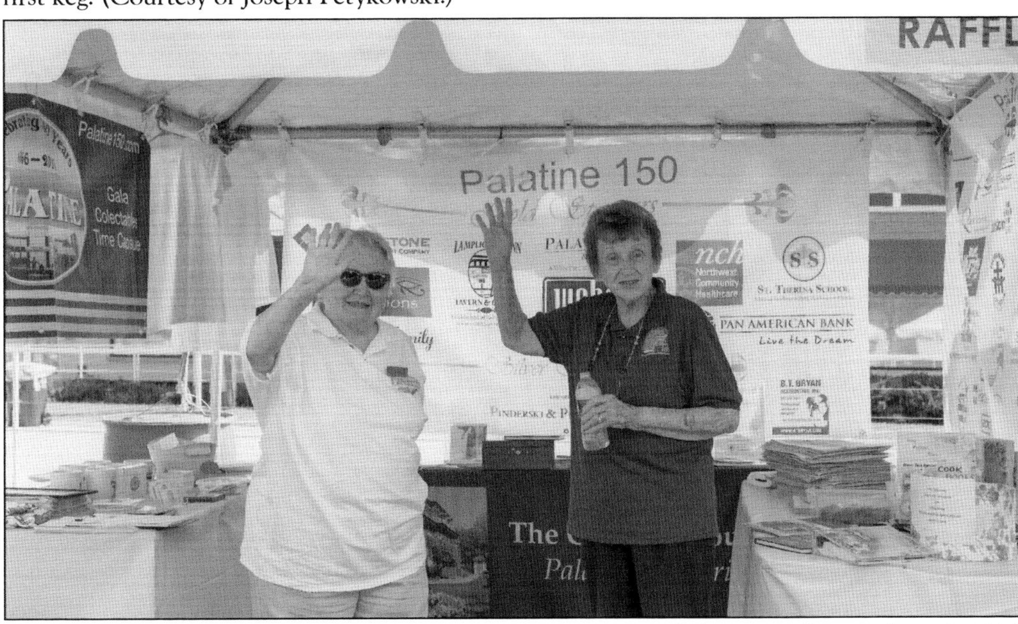

Palatine Streetfest. Throughout the year, volunteers spread the news about Palatine's 150th anniversary at the Palatine Farmer's Market, family days, and local fairs. Nancy Cairns (left) and Marilyn Petersen at the Palatine Historical Society's booth greet attendees at the Downtown Streetfest, held August 27–29. (Courtesy of Joseph Petykowski.)

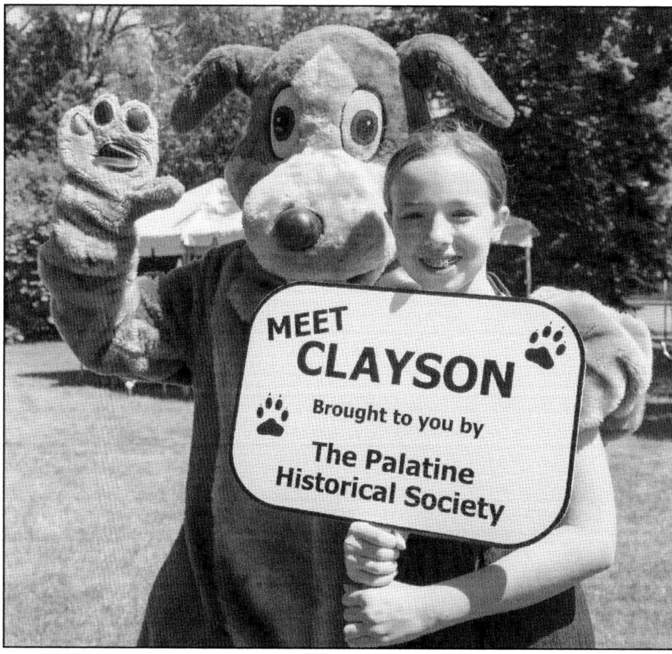

Palatine Historical Society Mascot. Clayson the Family Dog was introduced as part of the 150th celebration. Clayson was adopted in 2016 by the Palatine Historical Society and made many friends during the year. Clayson continues to be present when there are events in the village. MacKelvie Ocheltree introduced Clayson at the Good Ol' Summertime Festival. (Courtesy of Joseph Petykowski.)

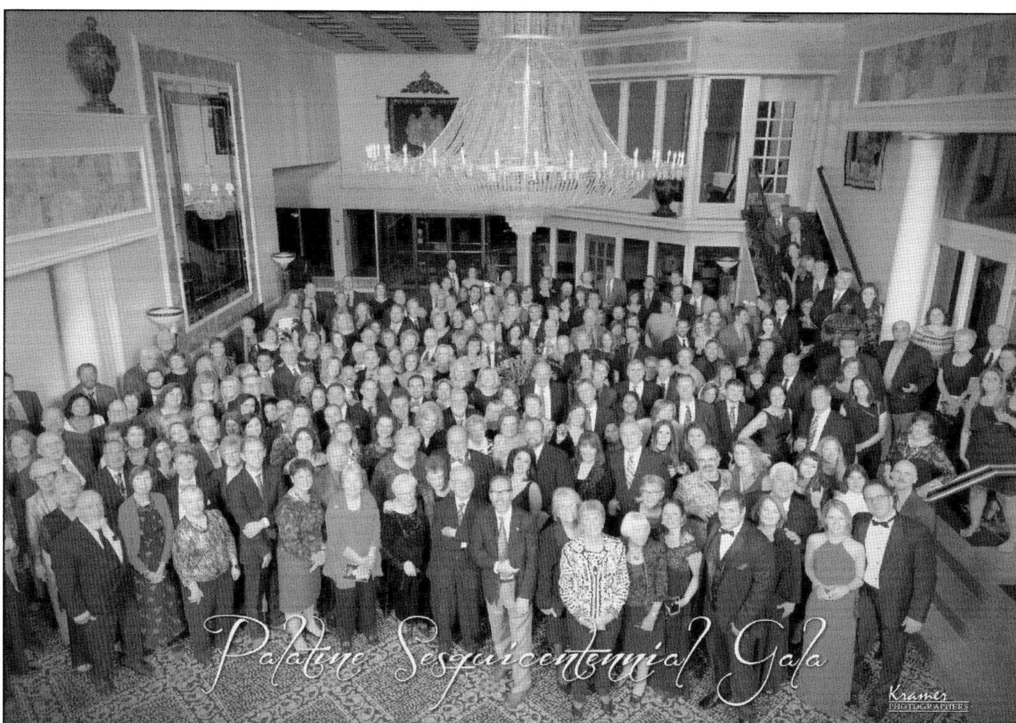

Palatine Sesquicentennial Gala. The 150-year celebration wrapped up with a gala at the Cotillion in Palatine on October 22. Almost 500 people, including 150 event sponsors, danced to the music of the Bluewater Kings Band. A video produced by Michael Noens of the Palatine Park District was accompanied by David Resier's original Palatine song. Thanks go to Kramer Photography for capturing this wonderful shot of the attendees.

One

Early Palatine

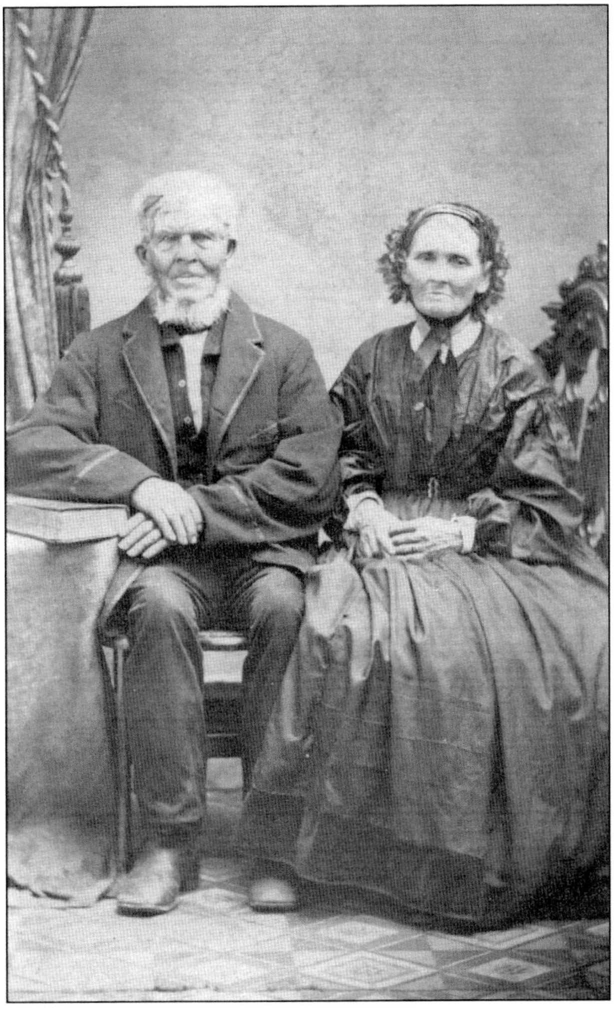

Ezekial and Adeline Cady. Ezekial and Adeline Cady came from Utica, New York, by wagon in 1837 and settled on 240 acres in the southwest part of Deer Grove. They started their journey with horses, a wagon, and a cow. On arriving at Lake Michigan, they traded the horses for a yoke of oxen.

Ezekial Cady built a cabin of logs and bark to shelter his wife and seven children while he made the two-day trip (one-way) to Chicago for supplies. He took his flintlock gun with him as protection, leaving his wife with no way to start a fire. The first night, a severe storm blew up, so Adeline stayed up all night to keep the fire going. Their cabin later became the first schoolhouse in Palatine Township.

In 1838, their daughter, Clarinda, was the first white child born in the township. In 1853, at the age of 15, she married Martin Pinney, "a handsome railroad conductor," who came to build the railroad. She remained a resident of Palatine until her death at the age of 92.

Cady Cemetery in Deer Grove, the first cemetery in the township, was started by the family in 1841 when their son Wilbert died.

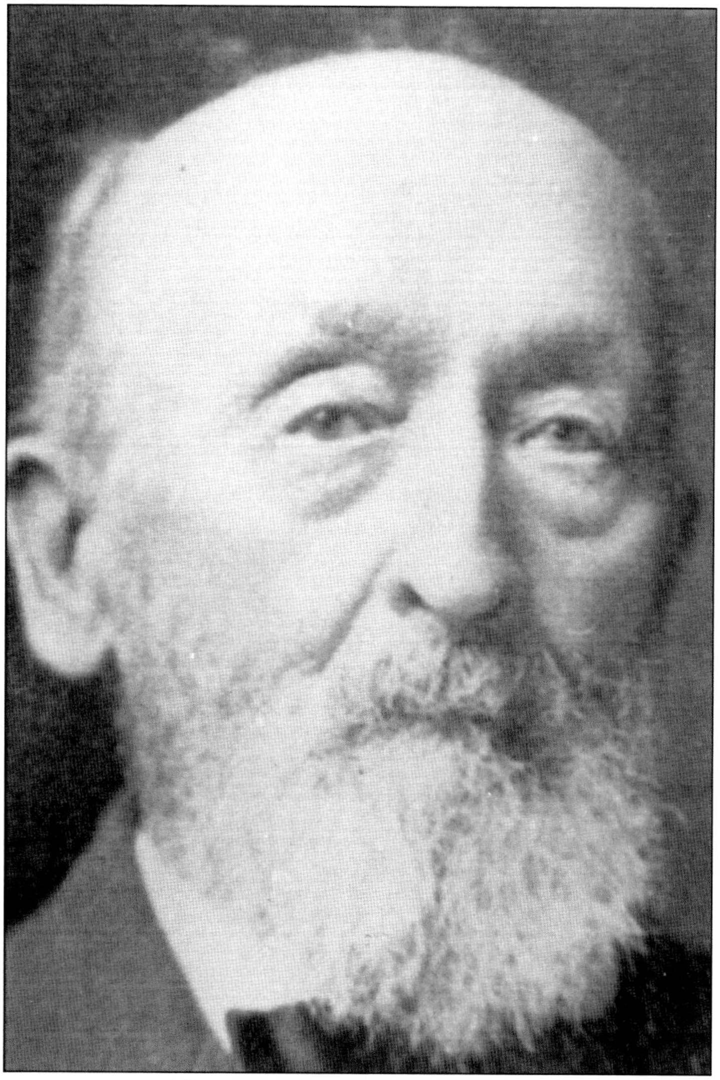

Joel Wood, Founder of the Village of Palatine. Joel Wood was neither born nor buried in Palatine, yet, in the 23 years he lived here after his arrival in 1847, he left an indelible mark on the community. He was born in Pennsylvania and died in Kansas at the age of 96.

He bought 80 acres of land at $1.25 per acre in a promising spot on the prairie. His first crop of wheat was cut with the first McCormick reaper ever used in Cook County. Wood added another 80 acres, and in 1853, he bought 80 acres along the proposed railroad line. A contract to construct 4,000 yards of embankment at 10¢ per yard created a stable financial position for him.

Wood then surveyed, platted, and recorded what became the village of Palatine. He built a depot. He donated two acres for Hillside Cemetery. He contributed the lot that became the site for the first wooden school, which was later replaced by the brick Joel Wood School. Two lots were given to the Methodist Episcopal Society for a church and parsonage. Another four lots went to the Christian Church, which was later sold to Immanuel Lutheran. Wood made other donations of land to individuals and for the construction of a gristmill.

The story is told that he offered to sell Hiram Thurston the area that became downtown Palatine for $10. Thurston laughed in his face because it was a slough filled with cattails and green water.

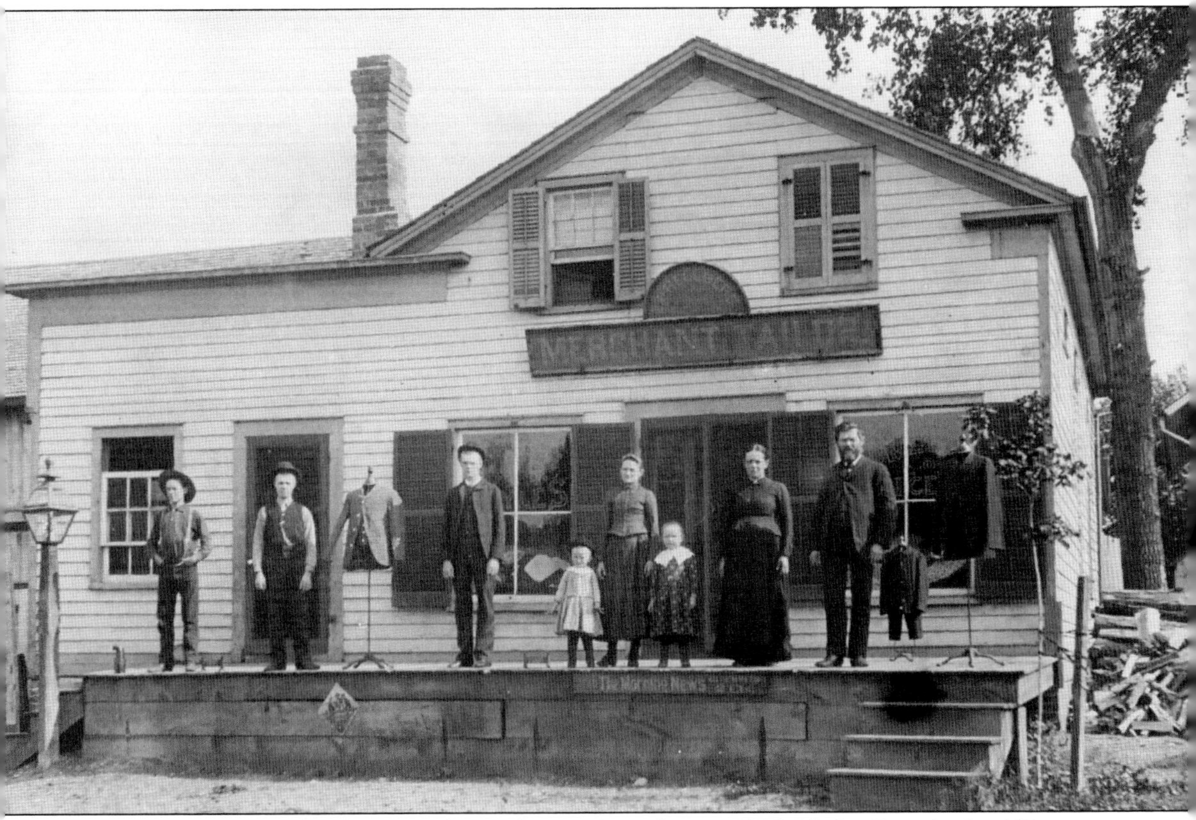

PRELLBERG FAMILY. After he arrived in Palatine Township in 1840, Elisha Pratt had a 160-acre farm at Quentin and Baldwin Roads near Clay's Crossing. He built a confectionery store that sold not only sweets but also cigars, tobacco, spices, teas, and other sundries.

When the railroad came to Palatine in 1855, Pratt moved his store to Railroad Avenue, thus becoming the first merchant in the town that was to become Palatine. Later, a house was added to the store. Pratt died in 1862. He is said to have written his accounts receivables on the beams overhead. Over the years, those records were destroyed.

For a short time, a cabinetmaker occupied the premises. Starting around 1865, Ernest Prellberg and his family of nine children lived in the building and ran a tailoring business. Sons William and Henry continued the business after their father's death in 1922. The Prellberg family occupied the premises for more than 70 years.

Unfortunately, the owner of the building in 1975 had no knowledge of its significance and had it razed.

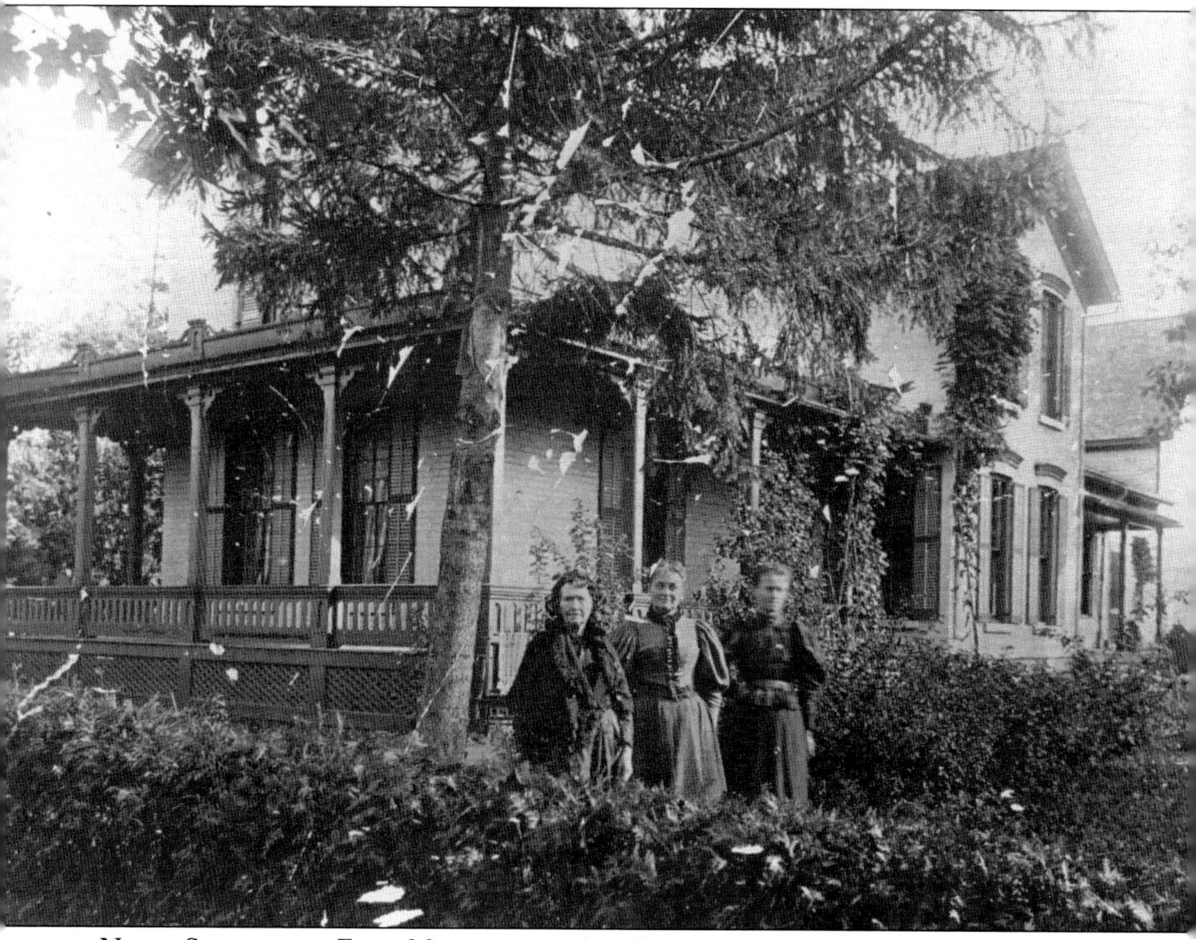

NANCY SUTHERLAND, EMMA MATTHEI, AND ANN BROCKWAY IN FRONT OF TOWN HOUSE. Nancy Boynton, the first schoolteacher in Palatine Township, began teaching children from eight families in the Cady's old cabin in 1840. She had come to Deer Grove in 1838 from New Hampshire with her parents and sister and brother-in-law. In 1843, she married Mason Sutherland.

Mason, his brothers, and their parents had arrived from Vermont in 1837. Mason had an original grant of government land and eventually owned 300 acres. The farmhouse stood approximately where the Target store in the Deer Grove Center is today. In the 1850s, the family built a brick house in town at 123 North Bothwell Street.

Mason was the first postmaster in Deer Grove and also served terms as justice of the peace and highway commissioner. During the Civil War, Mason led Company E of the 113th Illinois Volunteers as captain. He died of typhoid fever in Louisiana on January 27, 1863.

Shortly after his death, Nancy auctioned the farm property but continued to live off income from the farm. She was also awarded a widow's pension of $20 a month. However, an 1897 document states that she received $718.31 in 1864 and that was all she was due.

Five generations of Sutherlands lived in Palatine through the matriarchal line. Nancy and Mason's daughter Emma married Henry Matthei; Anna Matthei married William Brockway; Mae Brockway married George Howes; and Georgiana Howes married George Palmer.

Georgiana was an active member of the Palatine Historical Society. Before she moved to Florida in 2000, Georgiana and her mother donated to the society a wealth of papers, photographs, and artifacts, including documents from the Civil War. One artifact is a school bell, which Georgiana said had belonged to her teacher ancestor Nancy Boynton.

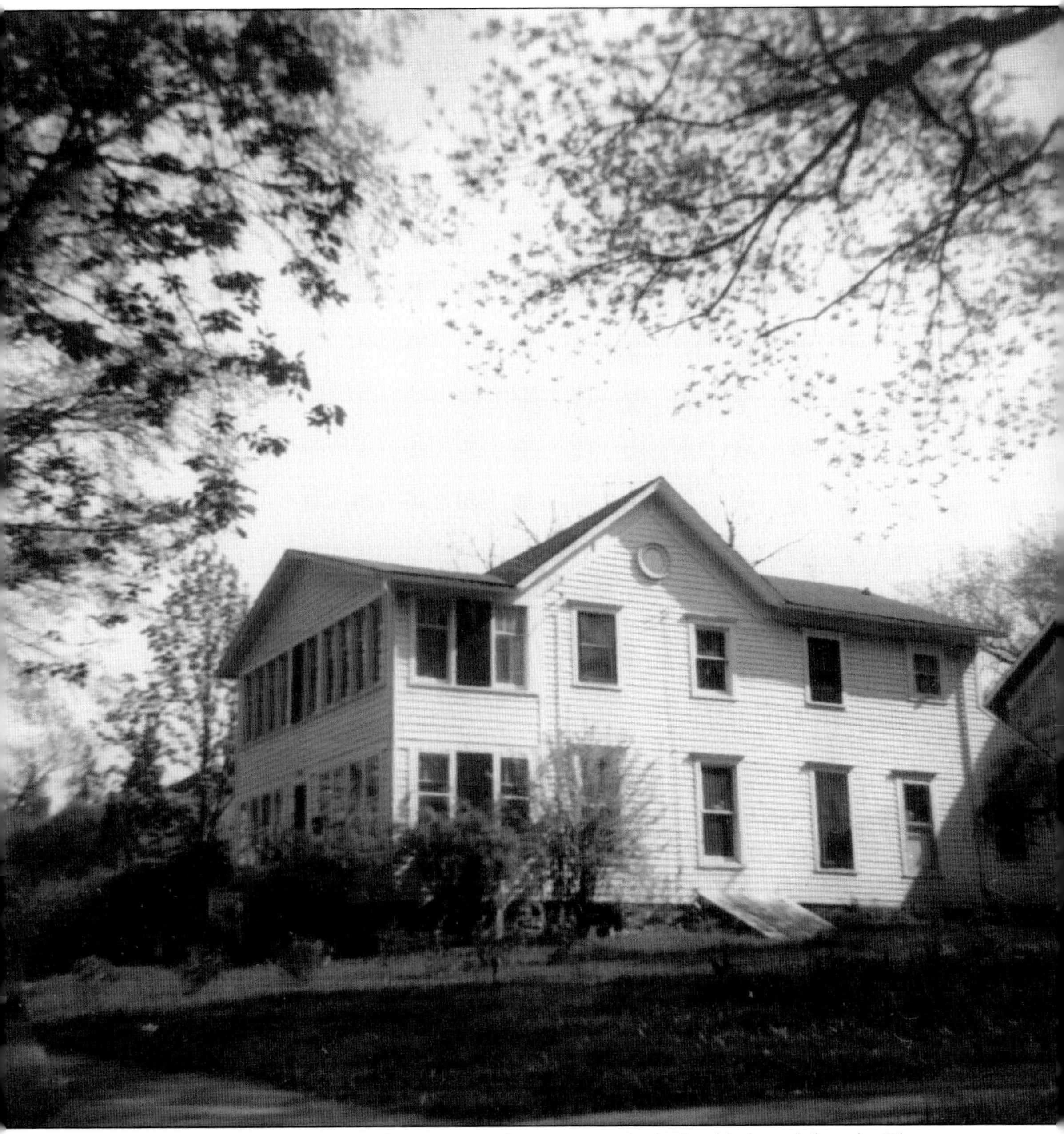

The First House in the Village. According to his memoirs, Joel Wood believed that the Thurston house was the first home to be built in the area that would become the village of Palatine. Hiram Thurston and his wife, Mary Chase, were born in Vermont and had come to Palatine in 1855.

Hiram was a carpenter and probably did most of the work on the house he built at 19 South Bothwell Street. He remained in Palatine until his sudden death in 1905 at the age of 85 and is buried in Hillside Cemetery. His sons Wallace and Julius served in the Civil War.

Other families lived in the house after Hiram's death, but eventually, it was replaced with an office building.

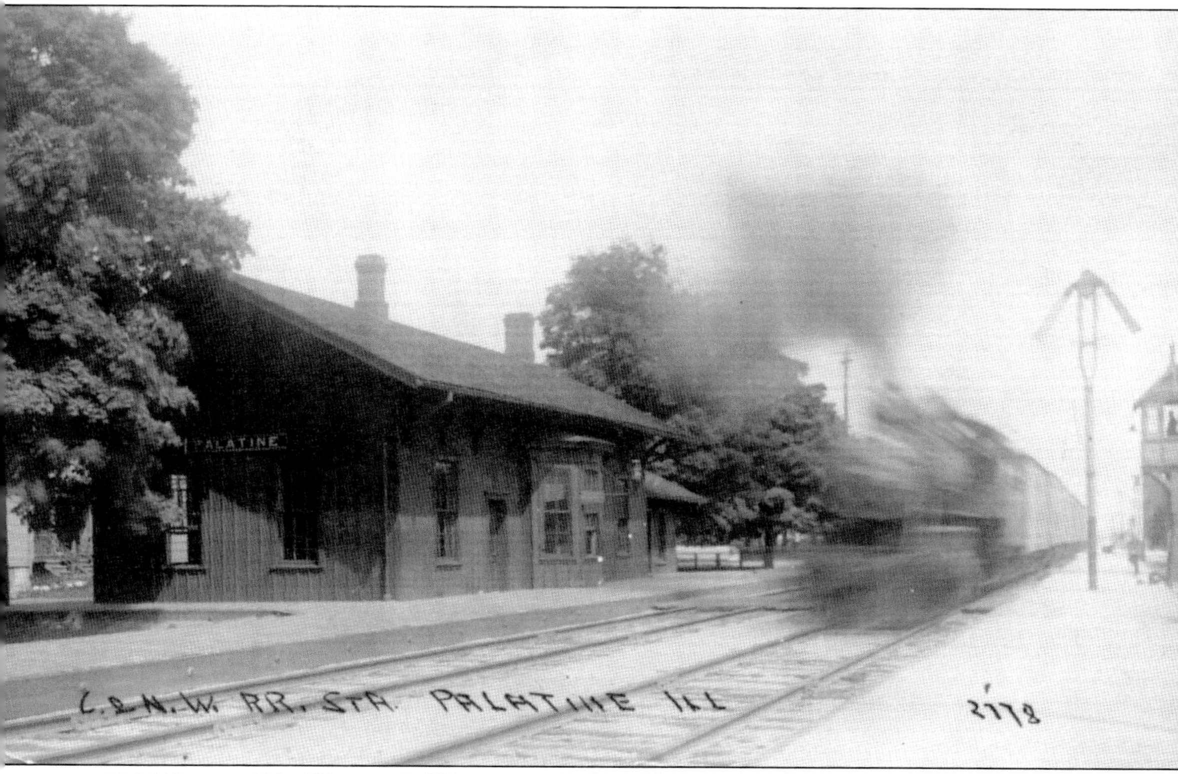

1866 DEPOT. The Illinois & Wisconsin Railroad began developing west of Dunton Station (Arlington Heights) in 1853. When Joel Wood and Mason Sutherland traveled to Chicago with an offer of $10,000 to make a stop in Palatine, they were told it was not enough. They indignantly left but were called back before they reached the street and their offer accepted.

The single-track railway service started in June 1855 with one freight train a day, which came out in the morning and returned at night. Passenger service was inaugurated in December of that year when a large crowd went to Chicago on a free excursion.

Julius Thurston was hired to attend to the freight, check bills, and turn the switch. With two other men, he filled the water tank, located west of Brockway Street, using a hand pump. For all this work, "Superintendent" Thurston was paid $15 a month.

That railroad company failed but was reorganized and became the Chicago & North Western in 1859. The North Western is unique among American railroad systems. It is left-handed. Purchase of the original engines from England may be the reason.

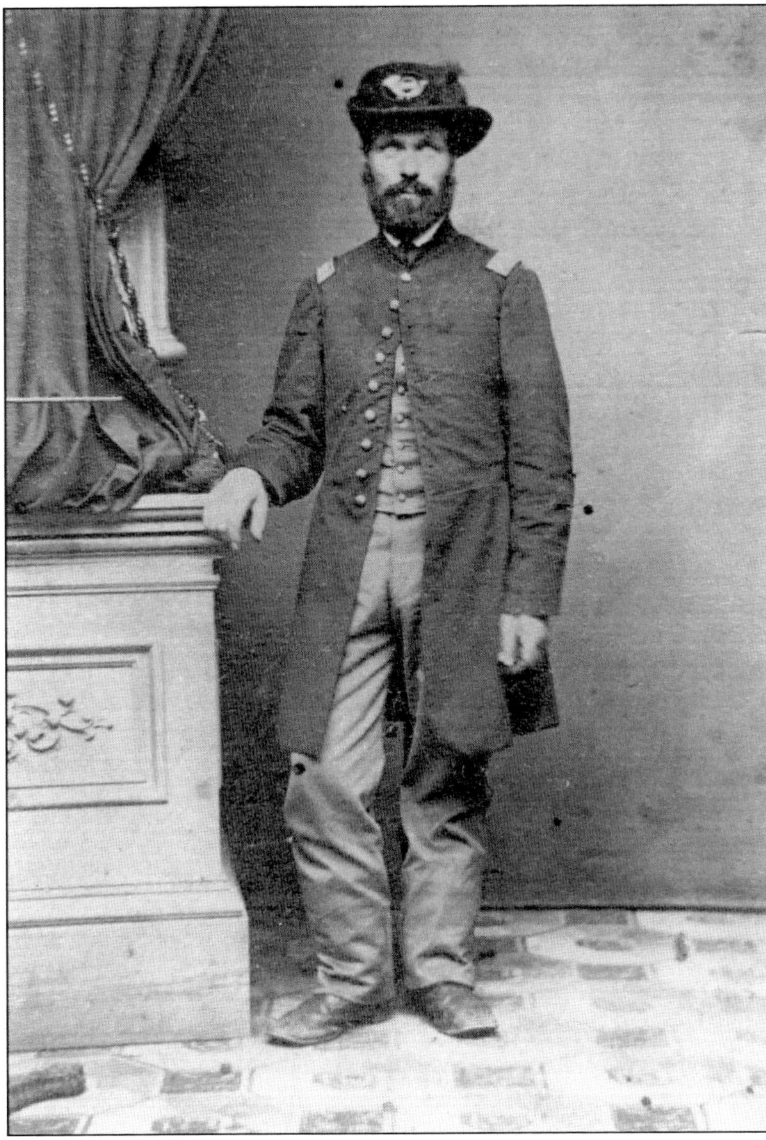

Mason Sutherland. Judge James Bradwell helped organize Company E of the 113th Regiment of the Illinois Infantry Volunteers. On August 11, 1862, at an organizational meeting in the Methodist church, 37 Palatine men volunteered. They were joined by others from Barrington, Lake Zurich, Ela, Schaumburg, and Wauconda, making a company roster of 90 men. Mason Sutherland (pictured), a 45-year-old prosperous farmer from Palatine, was appointed captain. The ladies of Palatine presented him with a sword.

The company fought at the Tallahatchie Expedition, Chickasaw Bluffs, Arkansas Post, Vicksburg, and Brices Cross Roads. After the battle of Guntown, Mississippi, in June 1864, the company spent the rest of the war in Memphis. The regiment was mustered out on June 25, 1865.

Less than half the company survived the war, most of them dying of disease. Four were captured and died in Confederate prisons. Mason Sutherland died of typhoid fever January 27, 1863, at Young's Point, Louisiana, during Gen. Ulysses S. Grant's Vicksburg Campaign. His body was shipped home for burial. There is a plaque in the Illinois Building at the Vicksburg National Cemetery that lists the names of Company E soldiers who died there.

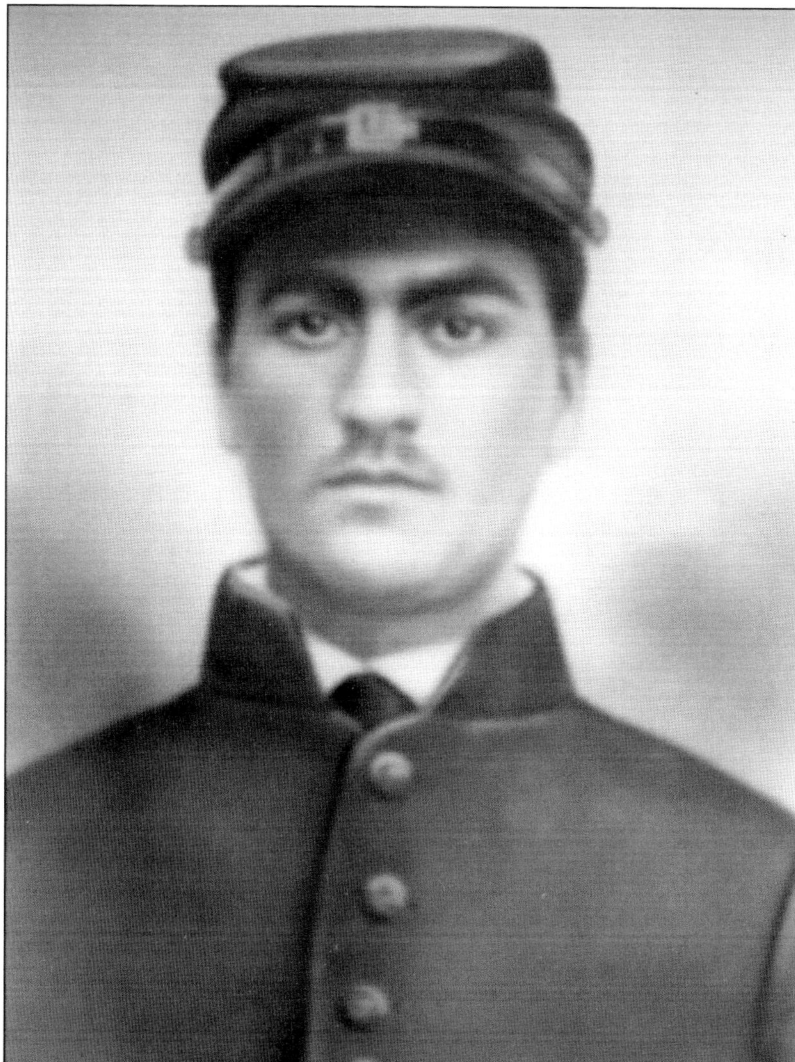

Louis Bergmann. Translated from German, the following letter was sent by Louis Bergmann on October 15, 1863:

> Dear Mother, Your letter was received 14 Oct. I see that you have many fearful thoughts about us. Dear Mom, you don't need to have such thoughts. Don't put me in the grave before I die! If I am to die here, then it is so. I am at peace about it. I trust my comrades! Forget these thoughts affecting your life. I am at peace, dear parents and siblings. Keep hope alive as I do. I have fear of death. Dear ones I thank God for His presence . . . I remain your obedient son, Louis

Louis was born in Hesse, Germany, in 1842. His parents, Jean Louis and Margaret, had immigrated to America in 1854 and settled in Palatine Township. The Bergmanns were of French Huguenot ancestry and had grown up speaking French. They had to learn German to converse with their neighbors. Louis served in Company E of the 113th Illinois Volunteers. He was captured in June 1864 at the Battle of Brices Cross Roads and sent to prison camp in Millen, Georgia. He died there in October 1865 and is buried at the Beaufort National Cemetery in Beaufort, South Carolina.

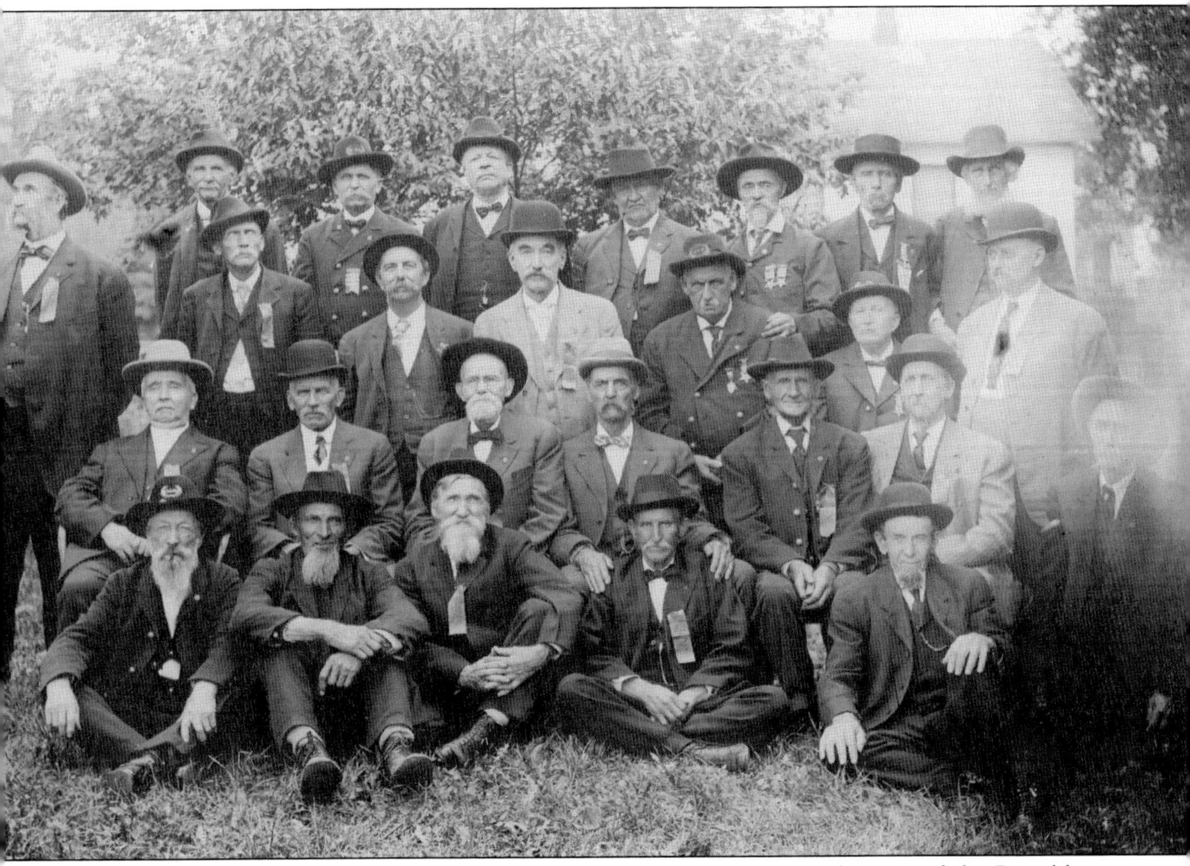

1910 GAR Reunion. Hillside Cemetery on Smith Street has a Grand Army of the Republic (GAR) plot. Two Civil War veterans and one veteran's spouse are buried there. A stirring ceremony dedicating the plot was held August 16, 2015. The Palatine Historical Society donated an engraved stone bench and Palatine Township designed a plaque to explain the historical significance of the plot.

The GAR, founded in 1866 in Decatur, Illinois, was a fraternal organization of Union veterans of the Civil War. It grew rapidly, hitting its peak in 1890 with 490,000 members. On May 5, 1868, Gen. John A. Logan, of Murphysboro, Illinois, the commander-in-chief of the GAR, declared May 30 to be Memorial Day, which established that tradition.

Annual encampments were held yearly from 1866 to 1949. There were three reunions of the 113th Regiment that were held in Palatine, one being the 10th in 1894. The 19th reunion held in 1903 was attended by 50 surviving veterans and Nancy Sutherland, widow of Capt. Mason Sutherland. She had to be carried in a chair because of feeble health. At the 26th reunion in 1910, there were nine Company E veterans.

The GAR was dissolved in 1956 when its last member, Albert Woolson of Duluth, Minnesota, died at the age of 106. It was succeeded by the Sons of Union Veterans of the Civil War, which still exists.

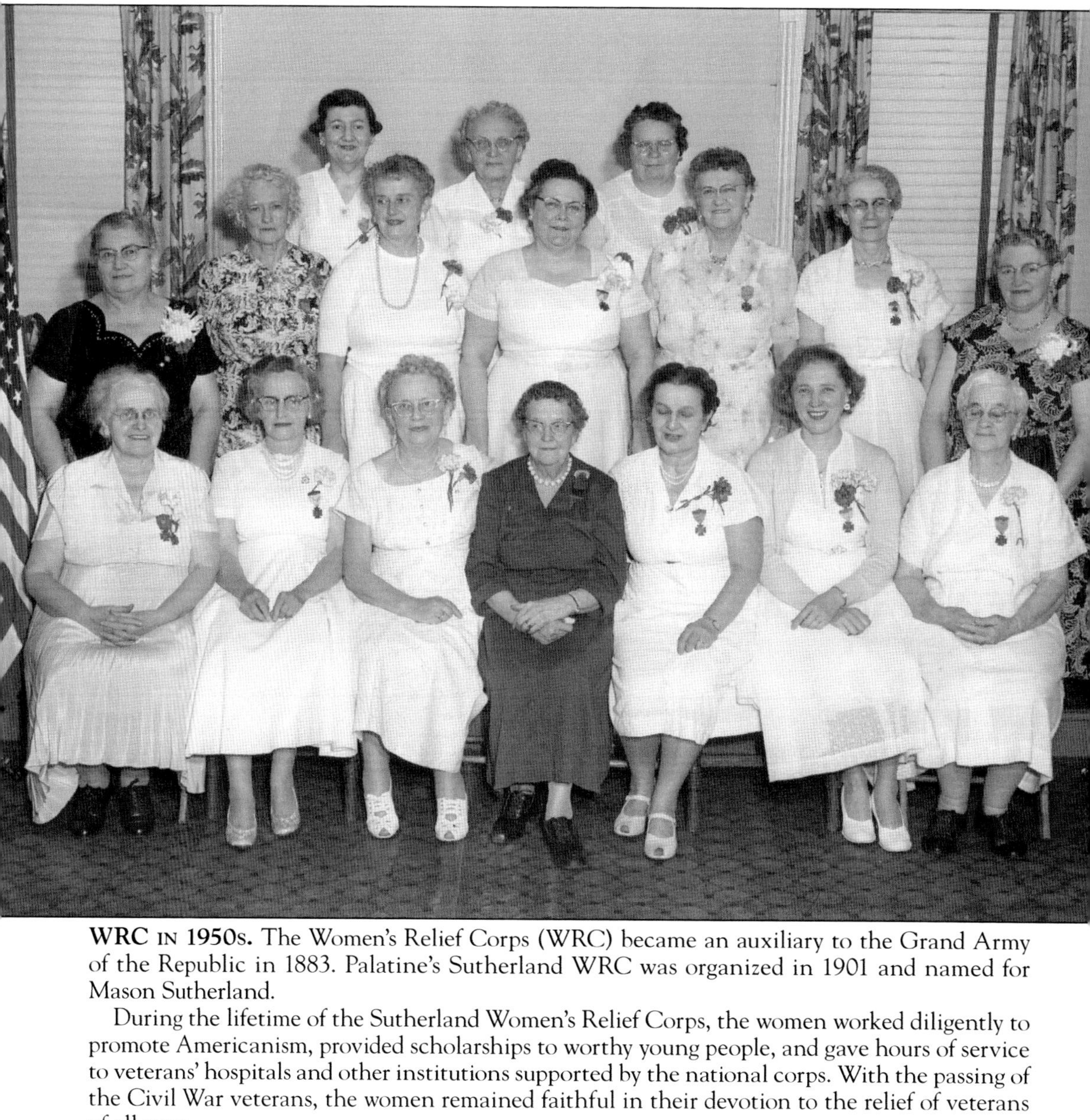

WRC IN 1950s. The Women's Relief Corps (WRC) became an auxiliary to the Grand Army of the Republic in 1883. Palatine's Sutherland WRC was organized in 1901 and named for Mason Sutherland.

During the lifetime of the Sutherland Women's Relief Corps, the women worked diligently to promote Americanism, provided scholarships to worthy young people, and gave hours of service to veterans' hospitals and other institutions supported by the national corps. With the passing of the Civil War veterans, the women remained faithful in their devotion to the relief of veterans of all wars.

Members had to be descended from Civil War soldiers. Three of those whose ancestors were Palatine soldiers were Marie Titcomb, Cora Comfort, and Mae Howes, who was a direct descendant of Mason Sutherland.

The highlight of the year for members was to march in Palatine's Memorial Day Parade wearing white dresses tied with red-white-and-blue sashes and carrying flags. In later years, they reluctantly had to ride in cars but still wore their colors.

Two

Developing the Village

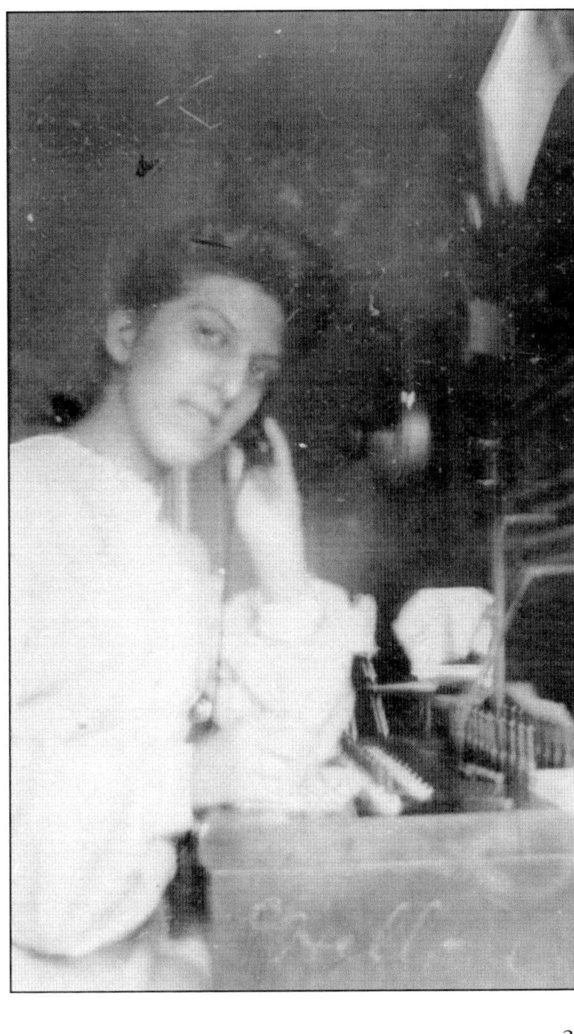

Henrietta Torgler. The first simple telephone switchboard was placed in the back room of Mosser Drugs on the corner of Slade and Bothwell Streets about 1898. The phone was answered by anyone who was around, but only during business hours. There were not many subscribers. The doctors were the first to install phones, which were single-party lines for $4 per month.

In 1902, the switchboard was moved to the dining room of Henrietta Torgler, a widow who lived at 55 North Plum Grove Road, and it remained there until 1919. Henrietta was the operator. The house was always full of young people, including her daughter Betsy and her friends, and they all knew how to operate the switchboard and had great fun making nuisance calls, especially to boys. Betsy's friend Margaret Godknecht was hired as a part-time operator in 1906.

With the installation of many party lines, a second switchboard was required and the telephone was moved to another location. Zelda Bennett was the first regularly employed operator. Illinois Bell erected a building to house dial equipment at the corner of Brockway and Johnson Streets in 1957.

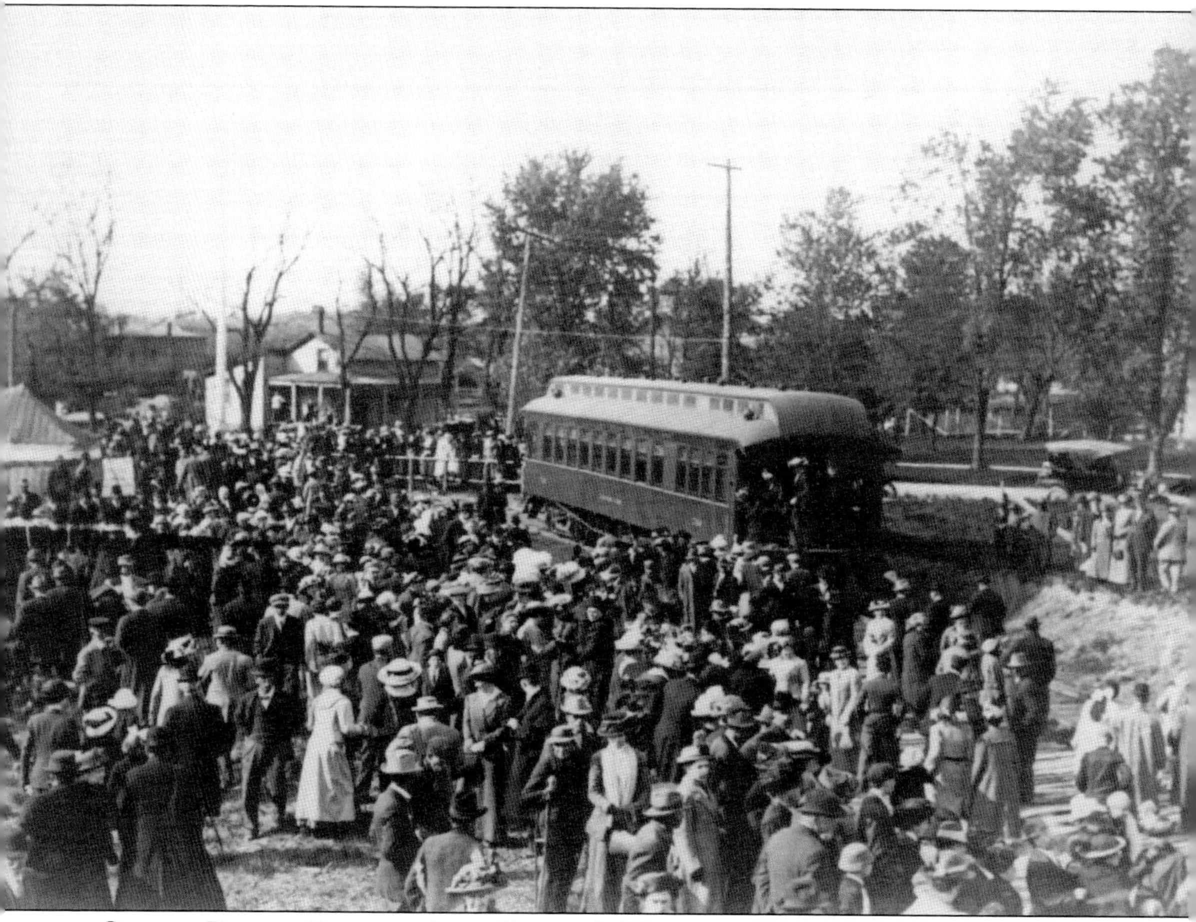

Opening Day for Palatine, Lake Zurich & Wauconda Railroad. Summer visitors from Chicago to Lake Zurich, Wauconda, and Deer Grove increased in the early 1900s, and local interest arose to provide train transportation from Palatine. People had been transported from Palatine by a horse-drawn "buss."

Money was raised, right-of-ways were donated, and farmers and workforces started grading and leveling the roadbed from Wauconda through Lake Zurich and Deer Grove to Palatine. Much of the work was volunteer.

With 36 hours left to go before the grand opening on September 16, 1911, the roadbed was unfinished and there was neither an engine nor cars. The Chicago & North Western sold the Palatine, Lake Zurich & Wauconda (PLZ&W) Railroad an engine and rented the newer rail line a car. The engine was christened *Maud* after a popular comic strip. The rails did not reach Wauconda until May 14, 1913.

Cars and trucks cut into the service almost as soon as it was built. In 1918, the 15 miles of track were in receivership. Three engines and five cars were put up for auction. Two different owners operated the line until 1925, when a government mail contract was lost because they were unreliable. The PLZ&W helped its own demise by carrying supplies for the paving of Old Rand Road in the early 1920s. All who put money into the PLZ&W lost their shirts.

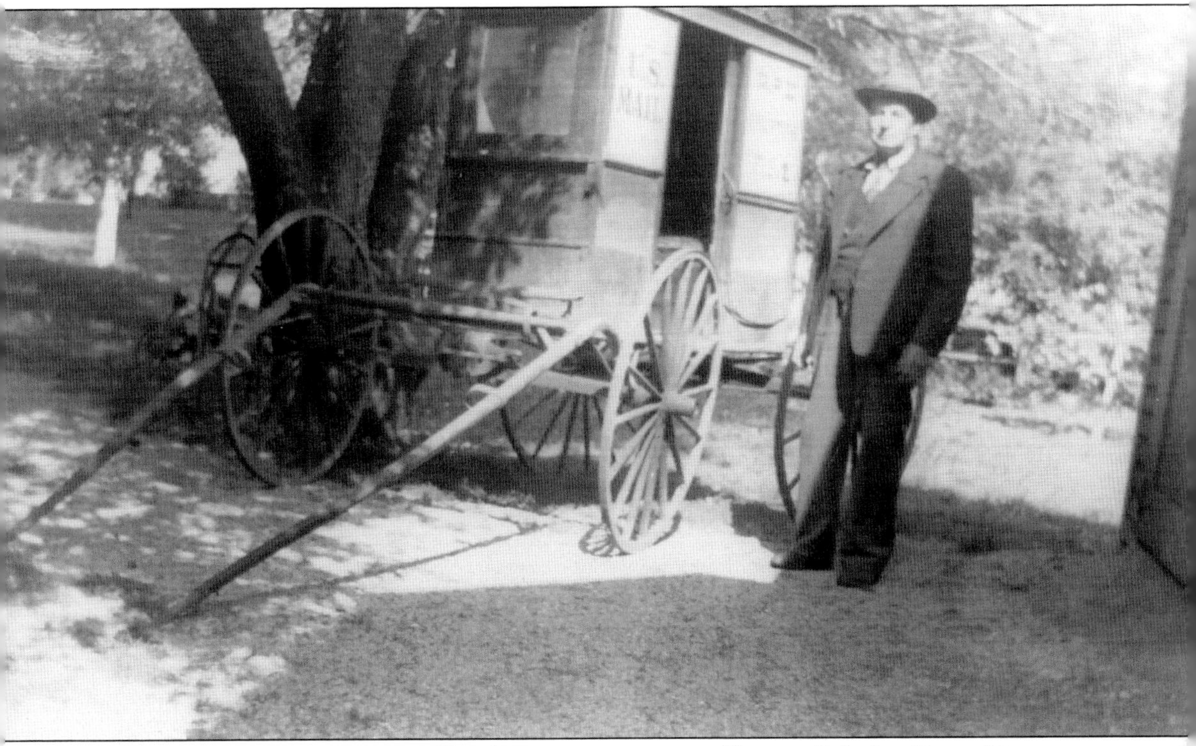

A Rural Mail Carrier. Originally, there were two post offices in Palatine Township—one in the north and one in the south. With the coming of the railroad in 1855, a single office was located in the D.B. Woods Store in town. The post office rented space in several different stores and buildings until 1946, when postmasters William Kehe and Louis Miller moved it to one of the new stores they had built on West Slade Street. Kehe had been the postmaster of Palatine from 1933 to 1946. Eventually, a post office building was erected on South Brockway Street. In 1971, the last move was to West Colfax Street, where it remains today. The Brockway building has been incorporated into World Wide Liquors.

Rural delivery began in 1904. Clark Keyes delivered Route No. 1, and Henry Wildehagen had Route No. 2. City delivery began about 1945.

Kehe said the following about his tenure as postmaster: "There were 635 boxes and you had to remember every box. We had about 100 families in general delivery, so we had to remember all of that. There was no bank (from 1932 to 1944), so Mrs. Weseman and I wrote as high as 150 money orders a day. Our rural carriers went through Schaumburg, up to Quentin Road and east on Dundee to Arlington Heights Road."

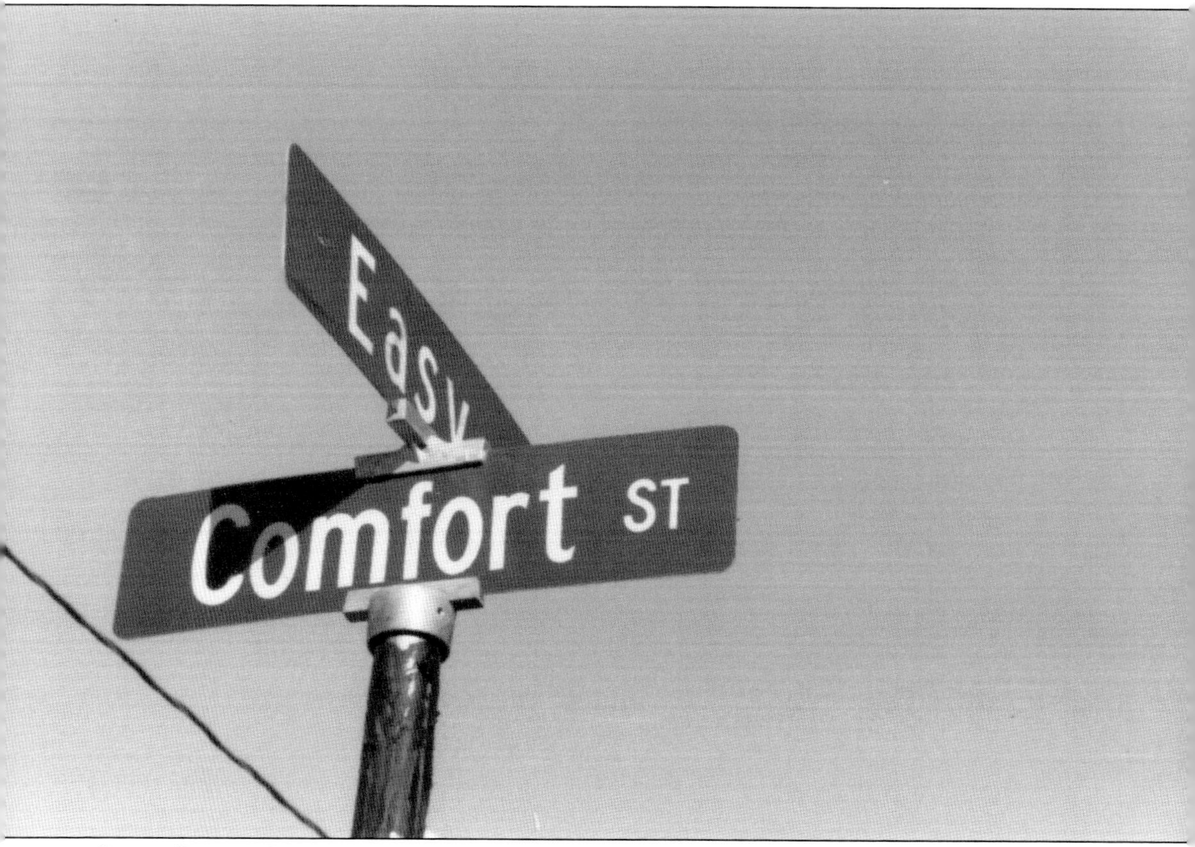

Local Street Names. Many streets in the older part of the village and in Winston Park Unit No. 1 are named for early settlers. Palatine founder Joel Wood originally named streets (both now present-day Wood Street) after his son Thomas Benton, Benton Street, and his daughter Miriam Wood Hale, Hale Street. Hiram Thurston built the first house in Palatine, thus Thurston Drive.

Cady Street, Slade Street, and Ela Road were named for families who came early to Deer Grove. Israel Smith purchased a farm across from Hillside Cemetery, so Cemetery Road became Smith Street. Paddock Drive was named for Stuart Paddock, publisher of the *Daily Enterprise*.

Several roads acquired names because of location. The Quentin brothers occupied three businesses at Quentin Corners (Rand and Quentin Roads). The Baldwin family owned farms on both sides of Baldwin Road (part of which is now Northwest Highway). Plum Grove Road went south into the Plum Grove area, and Hicks Road began farther south at the Hicks farm.

Lincoln Street got its name from Benjamin B. Lincoln, an early settler. Richmond Road is named after Matthew and Cuthbert Richmond, who operated creameries in Palatine.

Fremont and Sherman Streets were named for Civil War generals. Streets in one unit of Winston Park bear the names of early astronauts. Comfort Street was located on property owned by Wesley Comfort. He called the one block north-south "Street Easy" because "it was so easy to sell the lots."

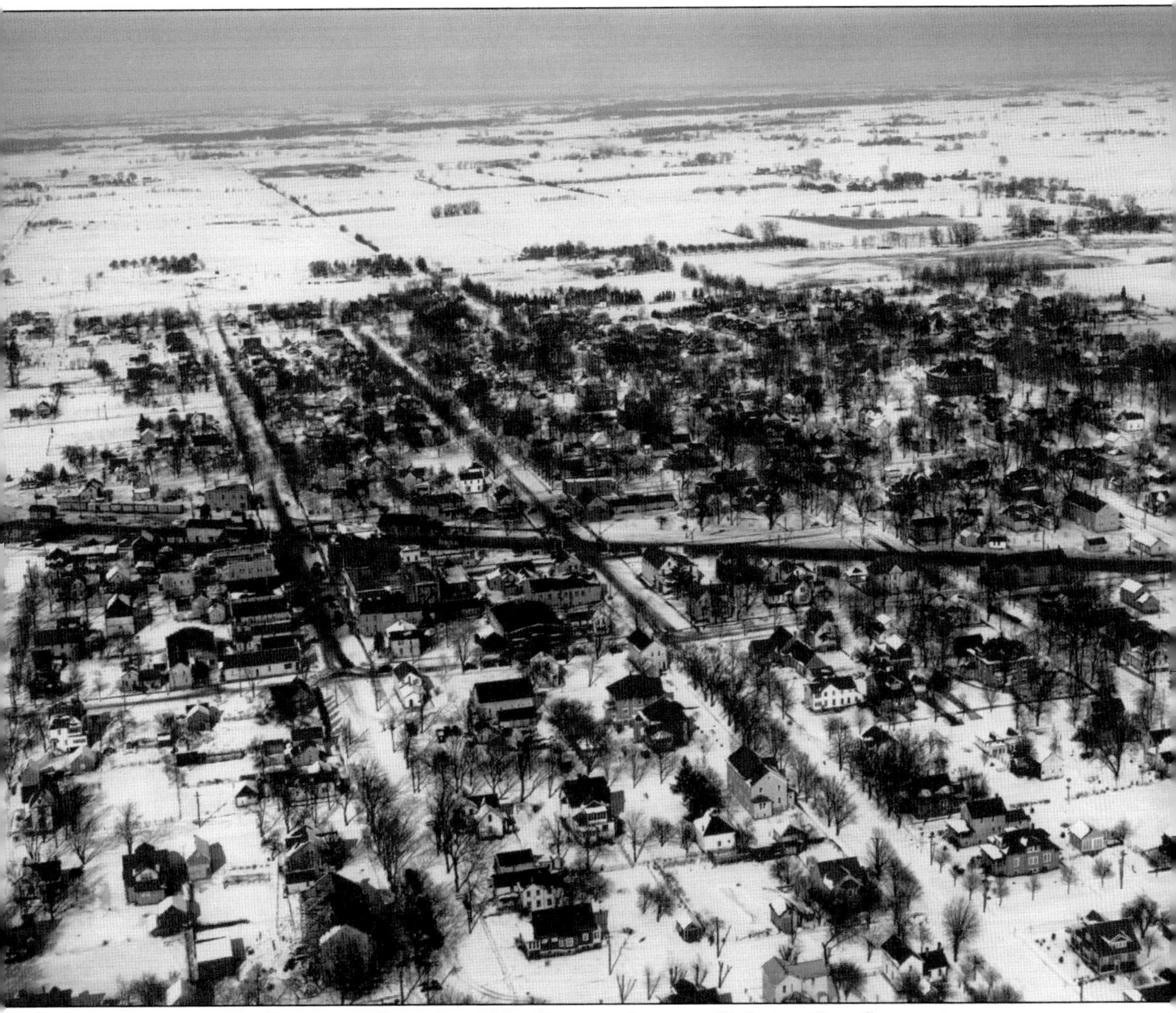

Chicago Avenue (Palatine Road), 1929. Chicago Avenue (Palatine Road), running east-west in the center of this image, was the main drag through the village of Palatine. Originally, Palatine Road was a patchwork of little roads. West of town, it was known as Kitson Road and ended in a swamp near Quentin Road. East of town, it was called Palatine Road. Until the construction of Northwest Highway in the 1920s, it was the direct route east to Milwaukee Road and then to Chicago.

It was a gravel road with potholes and dust, which the village occasionally oiled, until Cook County paved it to Roselle Road in the 1920s and on to Algonquin in 1930. Cave-ins at the Quentin Road Bridge over Salt Creek were so frequent that the county moved the creek. The Illinois State Highway Department installed the first traffic lights at the Northwest Highway intersection in 1949.

Cook County changed Palatine Road into a "junior expressway" in 1959. Residents successfully objected to running four lanes through the village, so the widened road stopped at Hicks Road (Northwest Highway). In 1967, the system of local and express lanes was described as a "nightmare" at two "death corners," Schoenbeck and Buffalo Grove Roads.

The name of the Chicago Avenue portion of the road was changed to Palatine Road in 1966.

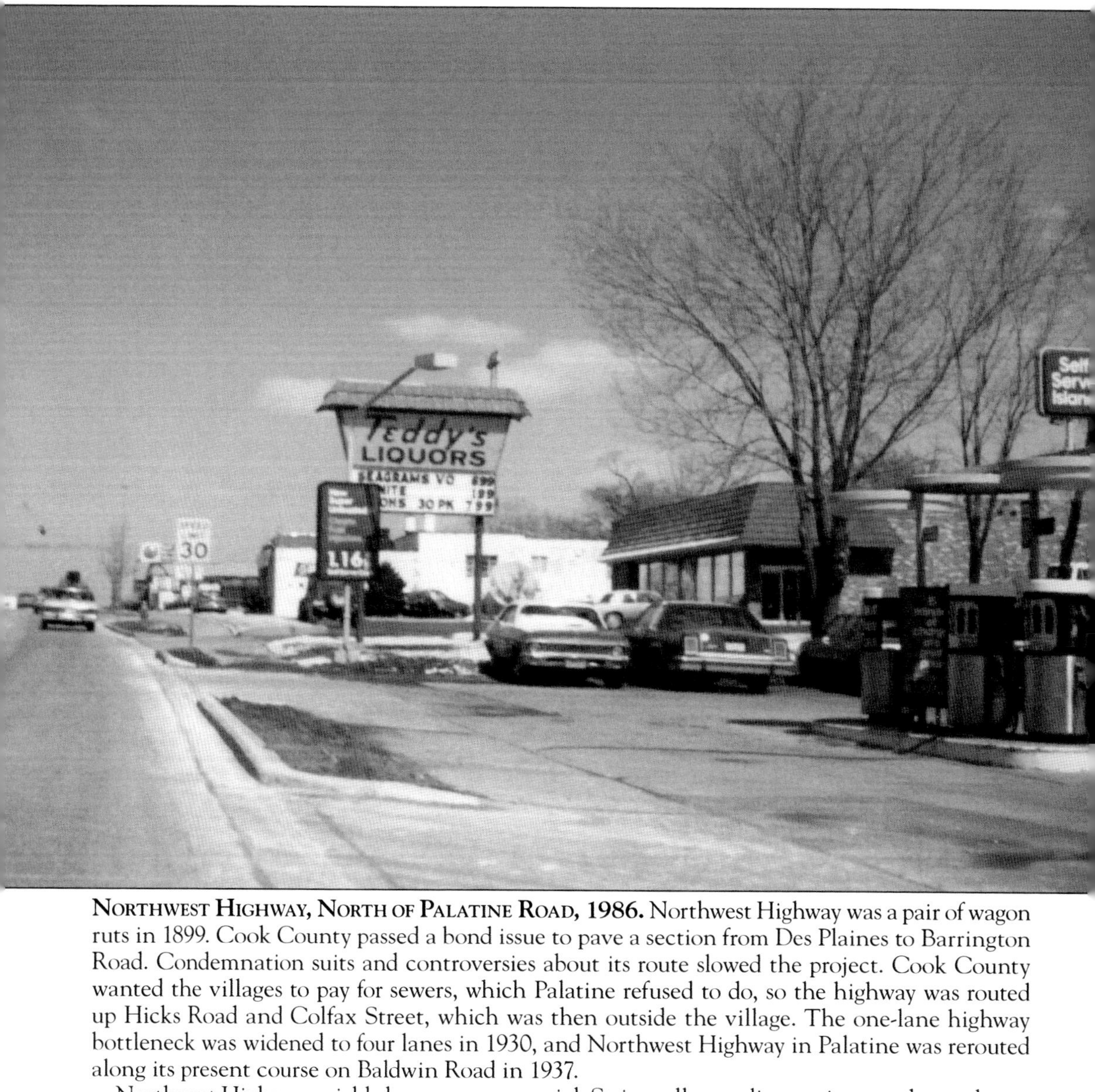

NORTHWEST HIGHWAY, NORTH OF PALATINE ROAD, 1986. Northwest Highway was a pair of wagon ruts in 1899. Cook County passed a bond issue to pave a section from Des Plaines to Barrington Road. Condemnation suits and controversies about its route slowed the project. Cook County wanted the villages to pay for sewers, which Palatine refused to do, so the highway was routed up Hicks Road and Colfax Street, which was then outside the village. The one-lane highway bottleneck was widened to four lanes in 1930, and Northwest Highway in Palatine was rerouted along its present course on Baldwin Road in 1937.

Northwest Highway quickly became commercial. Strip malls, gasoline stations, and some larger stores sprang up from the eastern to western boundaries of the village. The largest shopping center within village limits was the 30-store Palatine Plaza at the junction of Hicks and Baldwin Roads, opened in June 1961. S.S. Kresge, National Tea, Kroger's, and Pankau Drugs were among the original tenants. Today, the plaza is still a viable mall.

A major controversy arose when the US Postal Service wanted to build a processing and distribution center on Northwest Highway east of Highway 53. The village considered that area the "gateway" to Palatine, and the effort to prevent it involved a costly lawsuit. The village lost. The center was opened in 1992.

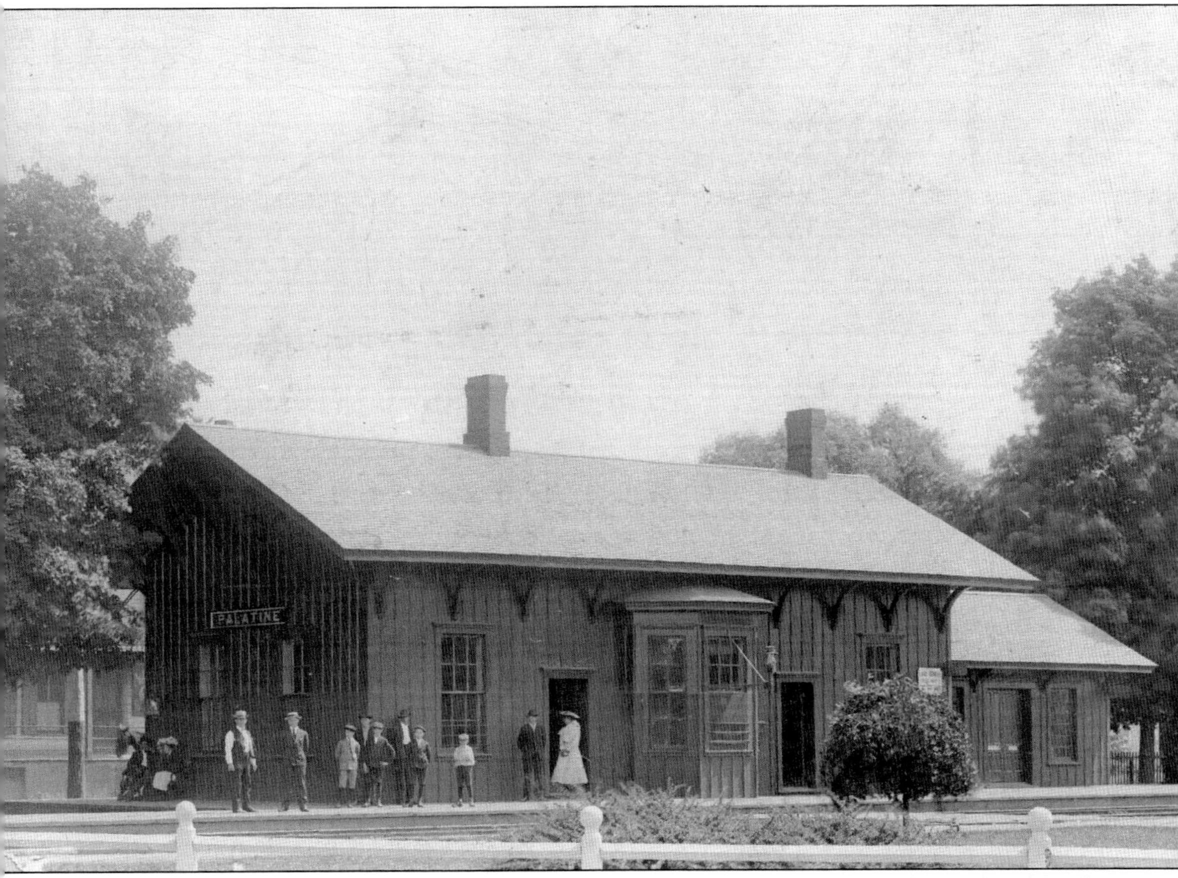

1866 DEPOT. The first railroad depot in 1855 was built by Hiram Thurston, with wood and land donated by Joel Wood, although some old-timers claim the first depot was only a freight car.

The second station, built on the north side of the tracks in 1866, remained in use for 83 years. In 1948, an etching of the building hung in the Smithsonian Institution in Washington as an example of an early American depot. There were separate waiting rooms for men and women. The building was lit by oil lamps and heated with wood-burning stoves.

The "modern" depot, the third one constructed, was dedicated February 19, 1949. It had fluorescent lights and the latest bathroom facilities. The crossing at Bothwell Street had been eliminated and became the site of the new building. Automatic gates were installed at the Palatine Road, Plum Grove Road, and Brockway Street crossings.

Opened in September 1971, the Palatine Transportation Center was north of the tracks and west of Smith Street with parking for more than 800 cars. The building had space for nine stores. It lasted 20 years and was never successful. Today, the Palatine Station Townhouses occupy the south side, and on the north side are a multilevel garage and a strip mall, which includes Durty Nellie's.

The present Palatine Train Station was dedicated June 22, 2001. It sits on the north side of the tracks at Wood Street, east of Smith Street. A coffee shop is on the premises. The building is in a style reminiscent of the 1866 depot. Found on the dedication program, the station's motto is the following: "Remembering Our Past . . . Embracing Our Future."

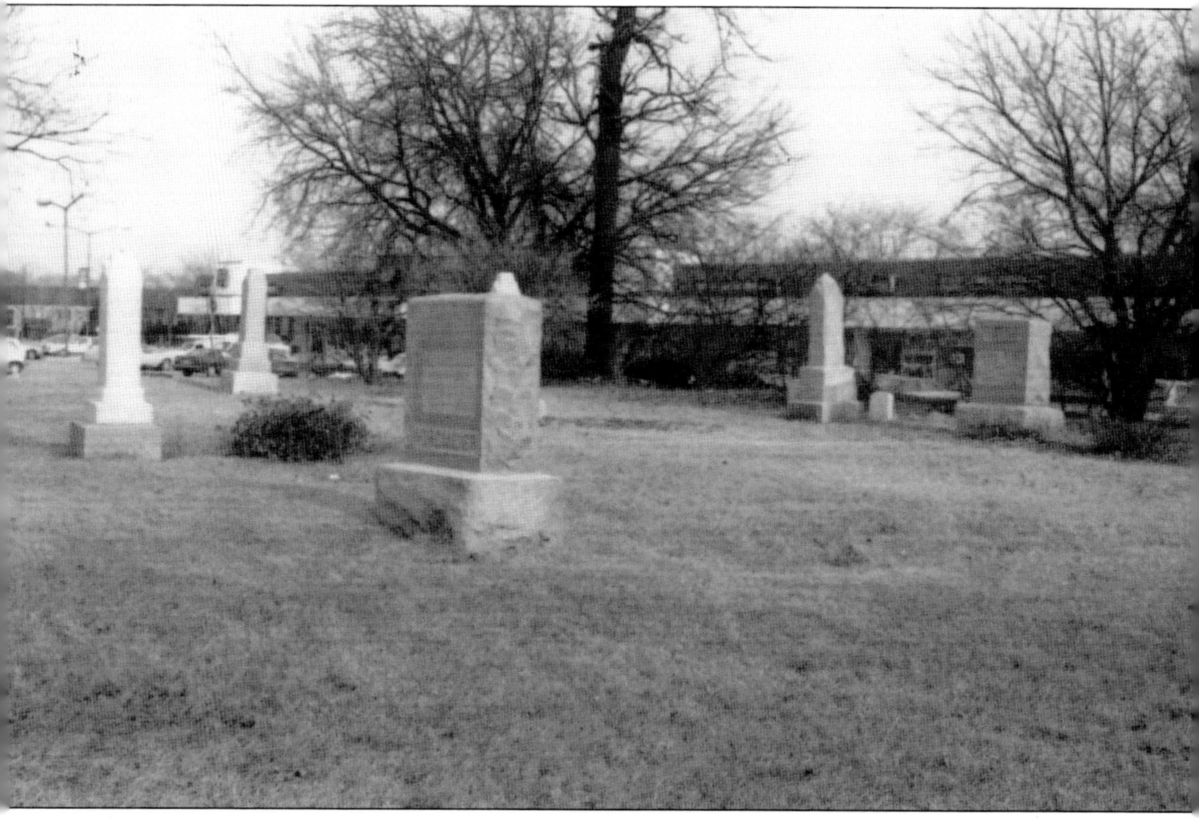

SALEM CEMETERY. Palatine Township has stewardship of five early Palatine cemeteries.

Joel Wood deeded two acres for Hillside Cemetery on Smith Street north of Colfax in 1855. His wife, Hannah, was one of the first burials in 1857. Frank G. Robinson donated the Filbert addition in 1881, and Albert Olms donated the Greendale Section in 1908. Palatine Township assumed responsibility for the cemetery in 1996.

There are 18 plots dedicated as a potter's field, an area for indigents. In the GAR plot, two Civil War veterans and a spouse are buried. A ceremony was held August 16, 2015, to dedicate an engraved stone bench donated by the Palatine Historical Society and a descriptive plaque from Palatine Township explaining the historical significance of the GAR plot.

Cady Cemetery is located west of Ela Road, about a quarter mile south of Dundee behind what was once the Cady farm. The earliest burial there was seven-year-old Wilbert Cady in 1841. The property was deeded to Palatine Township in 1856.

Salem Cemetery originated as the Frederick and Dorothy Theis family cemetery in the 1850s and was deeded to Salem Evangelical Church in 1922. It was placed in the custody of Palatine Township in 1974. It is uniquely located on the corner of Plum Grove and Kirchoff Roads in front of a strip mall.

Sutherland Cemetery in the north on Old Hick Road was on the farm of Silas and Lucinda Sutherland. Silas Sutherland's father, also Silas, was buried there in July 1840 and burials continued until 1957. It was deeded to Cook County in 1863, and Palatine Township took over in 2002. Farmer Silas is not buried in his cemetery. He died during the Civil War at the Battle of Kennesaw Mountain in 1864 and is buried in Marietta National Cemetery.

Wolfrum Cemetery was formerly known as the "Lost Cemetery" because it was forgotten for many years. It was deeded to Cook County in 1856, and when restoration efforts began, Palatine Township took over in 1994. The county named it for Avery Wolfrum, a local historian who had spent many years researching cemeteries. It is at 5281 Old Plum Grove Road.

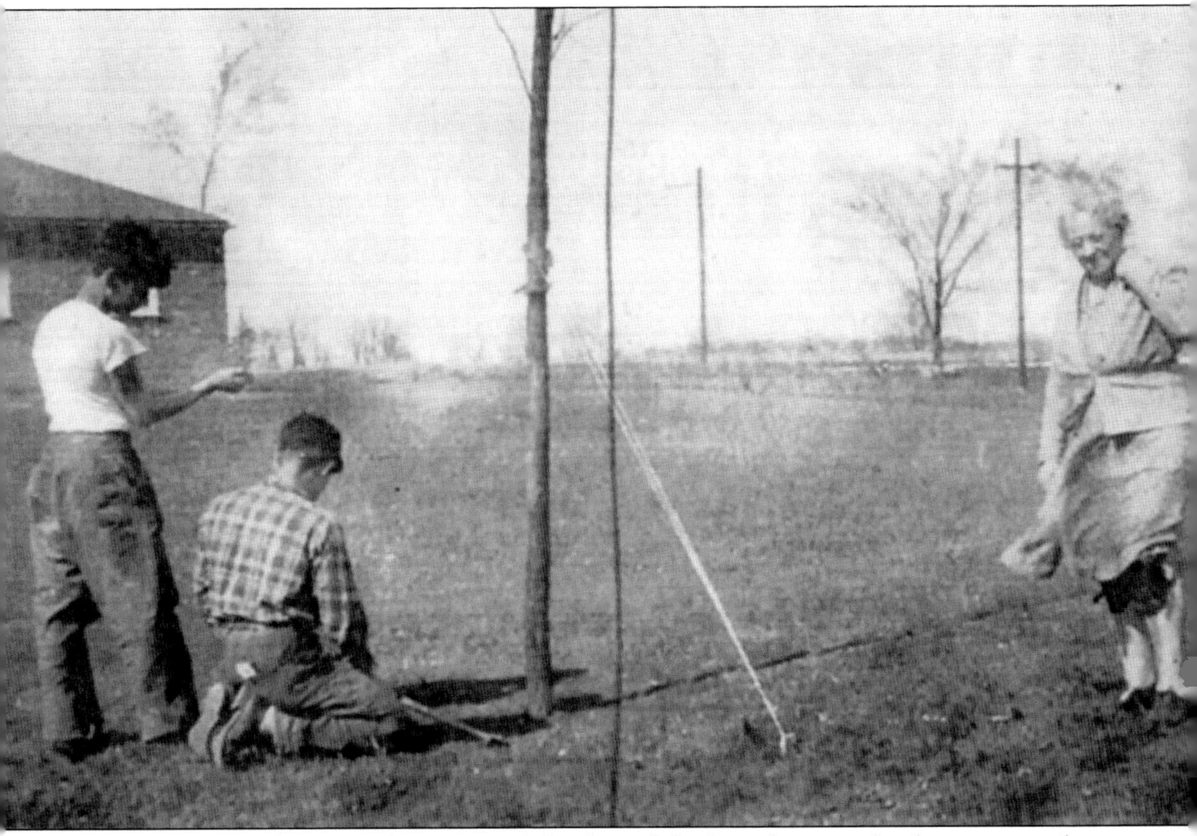

PALANOIS PARK. Palanois Park was one of the first of the large housing developments in the northwest suburbs after World War II. Arthur C. McIntosh (developer of Inverness) had acquired the land bounded by Rohlwing Road on the east, Northwest Highway on the south and west, and Lincoln Street on the north. The economy during the Depression had prevented him from building earlier.

Many returning servicemen came home to find a lack of housing in Chicago, so they ventured out to the "boonies," later known as the "suburbs." Palatine was an established community with train transportation available to the city where the jobs were.

Palanois Park offered brick four-to-five-room houses for prices of $10,000 or less. For a few hundred extra dollars, a full basement and attached garage were included. It was also possible to buy an adjacent lot for $1,000. A minimal down payment, along with the GI Bill offering four percent mortgages, made it within the veterans' means. For instance, one family who occupied a home in 1946 had a monthly mortgage payment of $35 and an $80 annual tax bill.

In the beginning, there was no mail service, no paved roads, and no sewers (septic tanks were necessary). Active community groups rose to address these problems. The neighborhood continues to be desirable, and many of the homes have been remodeled, modernized, and expanded.

Here, Bob Green (kneeling) plants an elm tree by this new house in 1947. His brother Edgar and mother, Josephine, are also pictured.

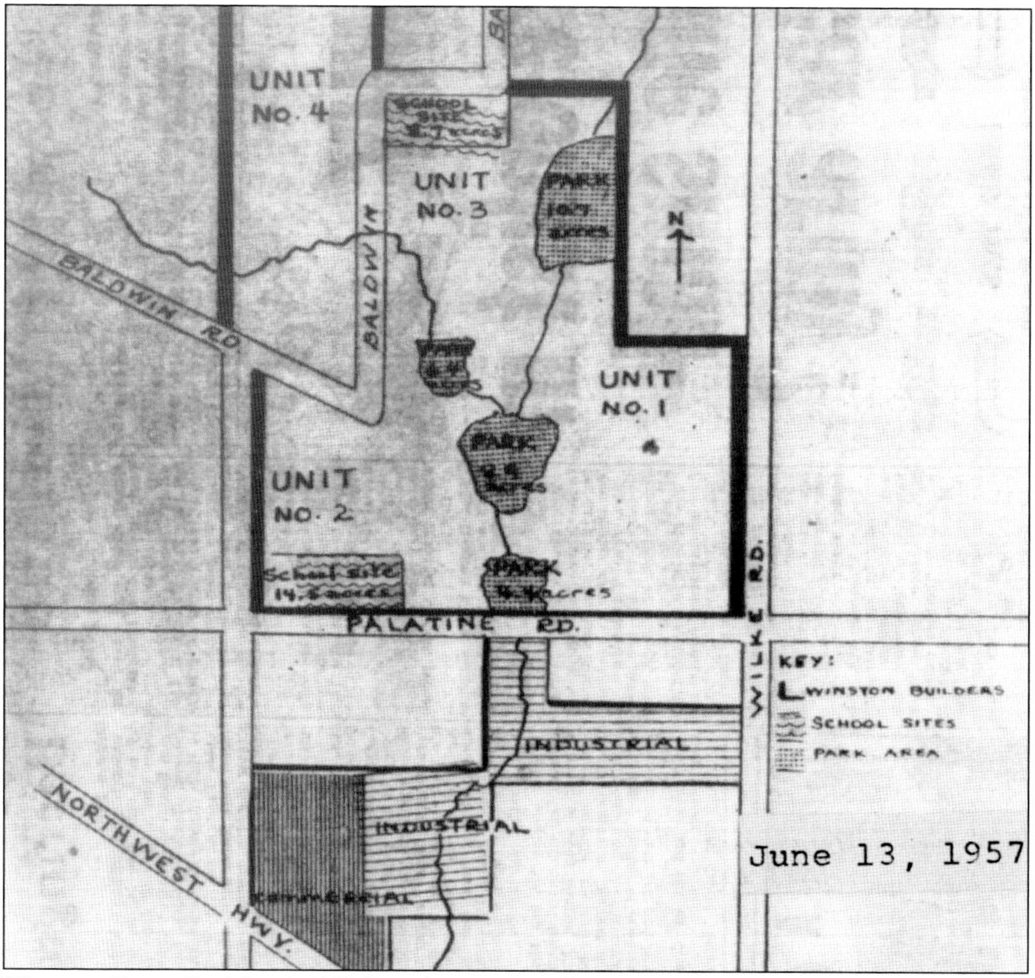

WINSTON PARK. On May 6, 1957, David Muss, president of Winston Park Northwest, asked the Village of Palatine to pre-annex 755 acres he wished to develop, a proposal that would almost double the population of Palatine.

The area stretched from Wilke to Rohlwing Roads (east to west), on both sides of Palatine Road. It called for 2,000 single-family homes plus park, school, and church sites on the north side of Palatine Road. The shopping center and industrial area proposed for the south side of Palatine Road did not materialize and more houses were built there.

Winston Park was a planned community. All electric and public utility cables were installed underground, and streets were paved. A waterworks and sanitary sewer system were installed.

The models changed in the different units. Some were retained, some were dropped, and new models were introduced. The houses were roomy three-and-four-bedroom ranches, trilevels, raised ranches, and two-stories, all with attached garages. They were well priced, and the financing was good. Winston Park today is a well-maintained community of homes, parks, schools, and churches.

Three

Government Institutions

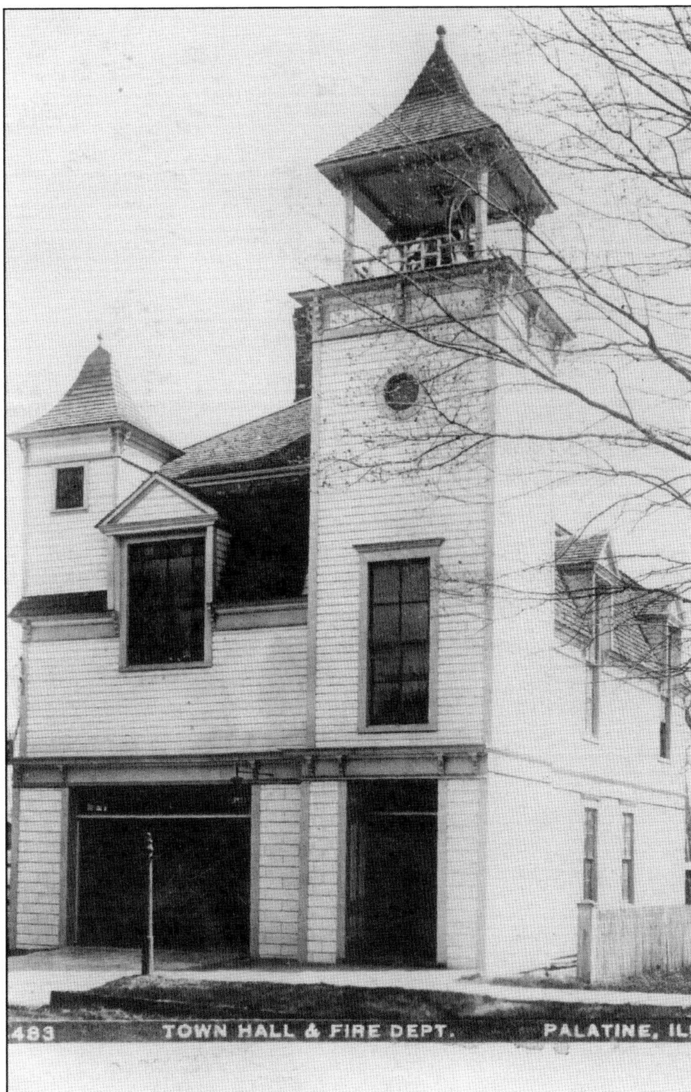

The Village of Palatine. Palatine Village began in 1855 when the railroad stopped there and Joel Wood laid out streets around the station. Township voters approved the incorporation of the village—73 for, 20 against. A week later, five trustees and a police magistrate were elected. The legislature approved the incorporation on March 5, 1869.

The trustees of 1870 exempted themselves of the toll tax, and in 1873 voted themselves $15 a year and a limit of 10-minute speeches. The six saloons that were allowed paid for costly licenses.

Robertson and Patten subdivisions were the first annexations in 1894. The big population boom followed World War II. The present population is more than 70,000.

The village hall on Slade Street opened in 1889. The lower floor housed a fire engine and fire equipment. A tower held the fire bell. The building was razed in 1939.

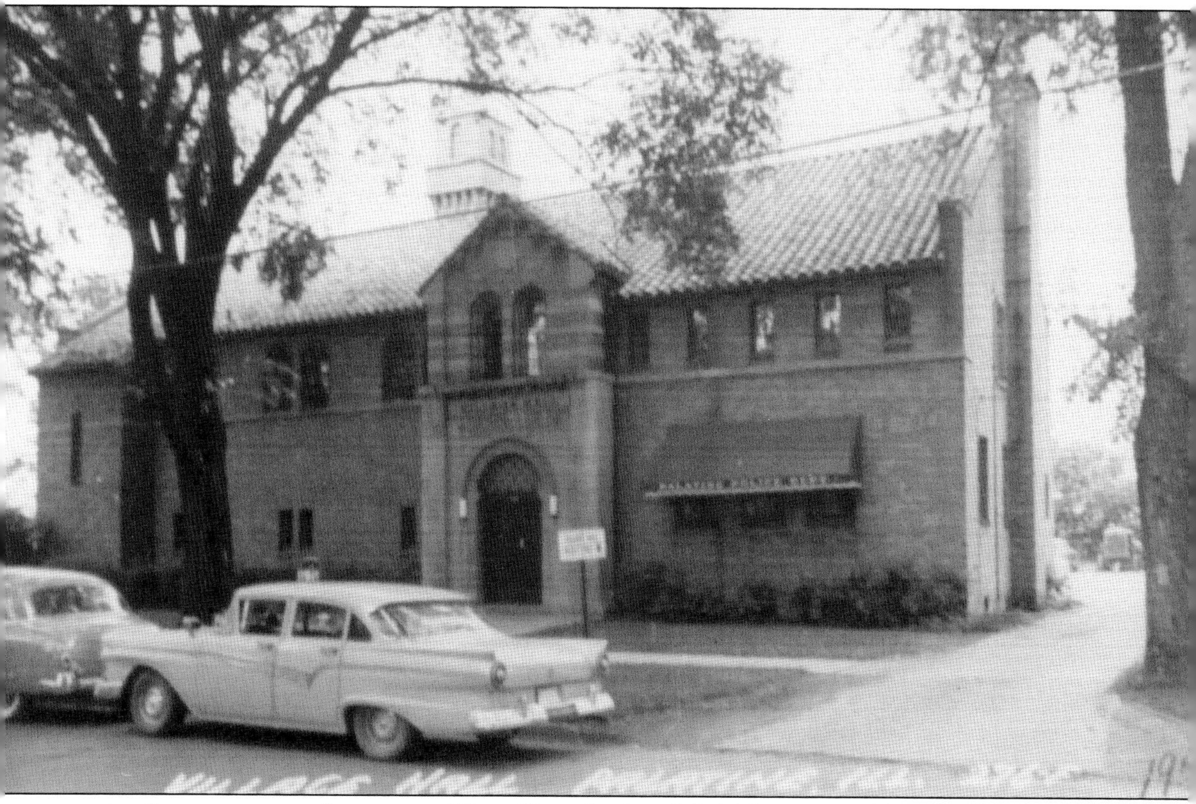

An Inconvenient Jailbreak. The village built a $43,000 municipal building in 1929 that housed all the village offices, garage space for two fire engines, and a jail. It was located on South Brockway Street, replacing a water reservoir.

A dedication ceremony was planned for a Tuesday. Mayor W.S. Dollinger had moved his staff to the new quarters on Monday. So, police chief George Henning decided he should also have the jail occupied.

The police force went out Monday night and captured a Chicago man to be a prisoner. He was locked behind the new special-composition, nonmalleable, inescapable bars on the windows. But when Tuesday morning arrived, the prisoner was gone and the jail window was a wreck. So, the dedication was postponed until the jail could be repaired.

A new police facility was added on Washington Street behind the municipal building in 1964. This hall was used until 1978, when the village and park district moved to their new quarters (formerly Palatine High School) on Wood Street. The hall was sold for $400,000 in 1985, torn down, and replaced with Tamack Retirement Residences.

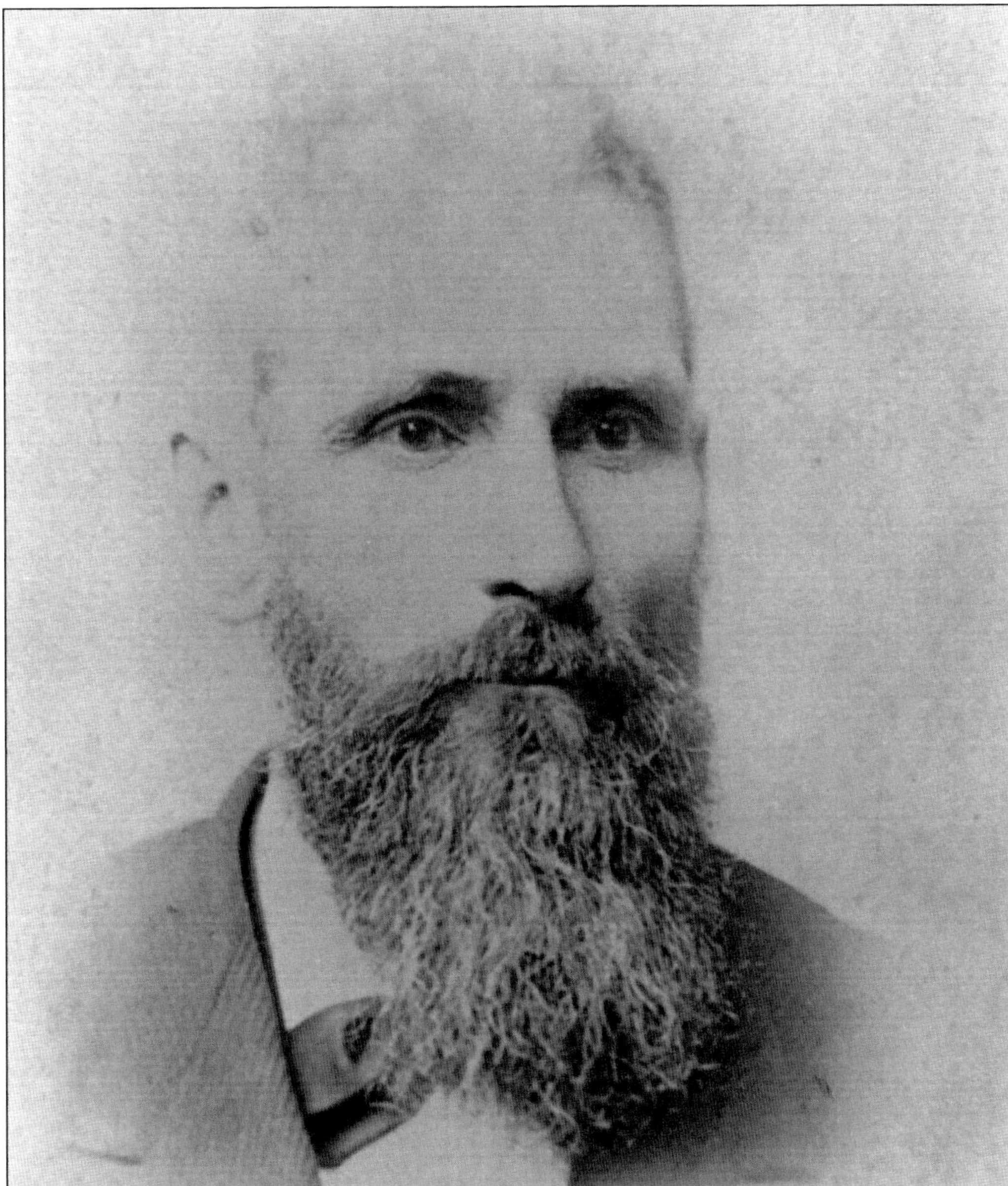

Myron Lytle, First Mayor. Myron Lytle was elected mayor of the new Village of Palatine at the first meeting of the trustees on April 10, 1866. He held the office for only one year, which was not unusual as most mayors served only one to two years until the 1950s.

As a 12-year-old, he came to Chicago from New York State via the Great Lakes. His family had a tavern in Chicago on Milwaukee Street. Myron came to Palatine in his twenties and married Ann Bradwell, whose father was a justice of the peace and a prosperous farmer.

Myron and Charles Pierce started a grocery store in 1856, and he was a lumber dealer in 1870 and ran a grain elevator. At the time of his death in 1889, Myron had a poultry farm. His obituary notes he was "a good citizen, an affectionate husband, a kind father and an honest man."

His only daughter, Annie, was a schoolteacher and married another schoolteacher, Charles Cutting, who became principal of the Palatine School and founder of the first Palatine High School.

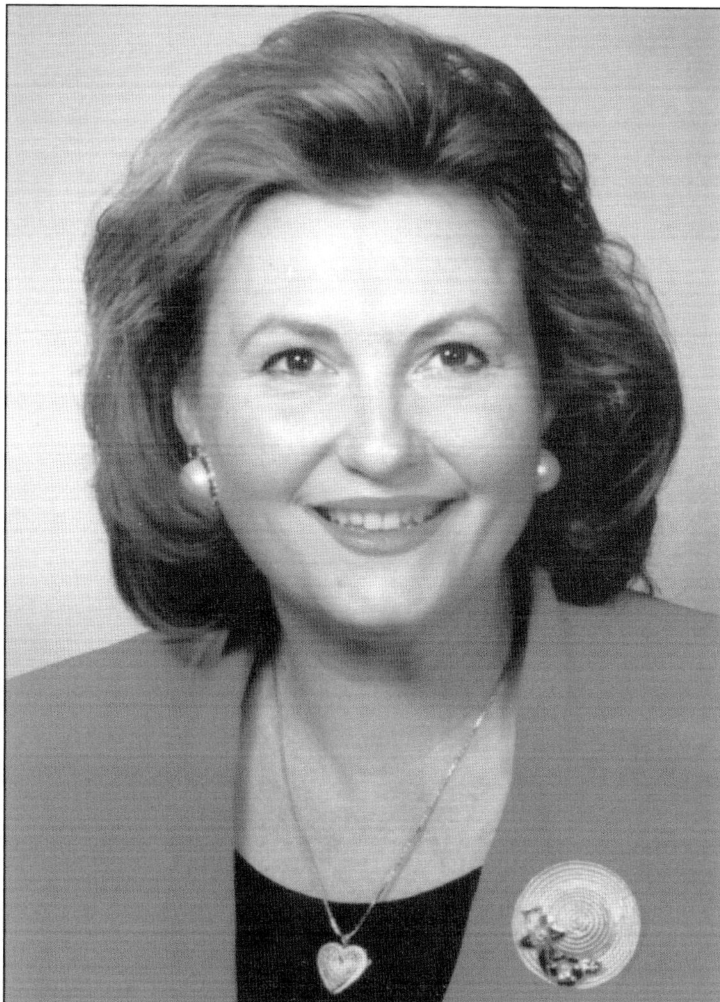

MAYOR RITA MULLINS. After 123 years, Palatine elected Rita Mullins, the first female mayor, in 1989. She served for 20 years. Her goal was to make Palatine a beautiful place to live, work, and play, so all its citizens would be proud to call Palatine "a Real Hometown."

She created the beautification commission, which was responsible for many visual landscapes and projects. She formed the economic and downtown redevelopment committees to promote downtown reconstruction as a support base for businesses in the area.

She sought state money to buy the property and appointed a design committee to create Towne Square, which was then deeded to the park district.

Funds ($4.7 million) from Cook County Housing and Urban Development (HUD) Authority bought the property and built affordable senior housing at Hicks and Baldwin Roads.

Mullins persuaded Target to anchor a shopping center on Dundee Road and brought in Walmart, Arlington Toyota, Home Depot, Walgreens, and many other businesses, increasing sales tax revenue for the village.

Under her tenure, four new fire stations were constructed, property was secured for a new police station, and a $10,000,000 five-year flood-control project addressed a major flooding problem.

Under Mayor Mullins, the village of Palatine doubled in area, population, and services for fire, police, water, sewer, and roads.

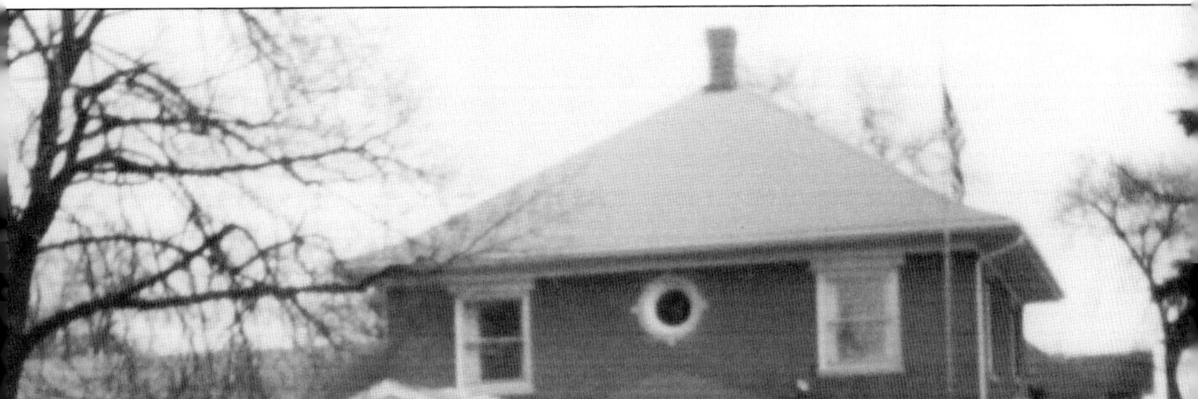

PALATINE TOWNSHIP. The Illinois Legislature passed an act in 1850 creating townships within each county. The men of Township No. 42 met and chose the name "Palatine." There are differing reasons for that choice. On April 2, they elected a supervisor, a town clerk, a collector, an overseer of the poor, three commissioners of highways, two constables, and two justices of the peace.

For more than 100 years, Palatine Township had no home. Township records were kept in the supervisor's home and highway records were kept in the highway commissioner's home. Regular meetings were held in homes and businesses. Town meetings were held in the railroad depot, the 1869 Masonic Hall, a room adjoining a tavern where rent was free due to the "drinking business" that resulted, and in other halls in town.

The township finally rented an office in 1957 at 12 West Chicago Avenue, which was not adequate for its needs. So, when the Schultz home at 37 North Plum Grove Road became available after Sophie's death, the township purchased it for $30,000. At a cost of more than $80,000, the exterior was refinished in gray brick, a 30-by-60-foot addition with a basement was added, and the interior was remodeled. The county offices moved into the building in December 1960 and remained until the move to their present location at 721 South Quentin Road. On that property, the township also operates the Bridge Youth and Family Services Center.

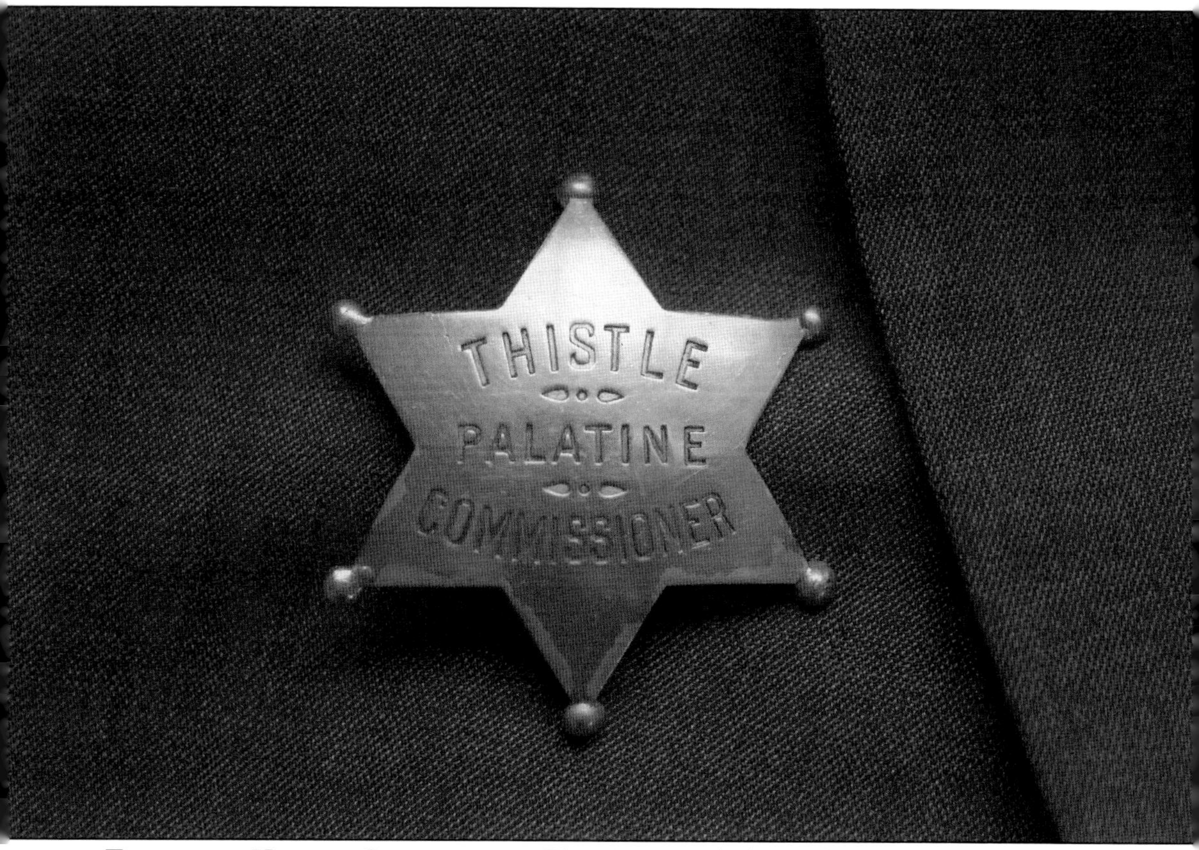

Thistle and Highway Commissioners. Plum Grove and Ela Roads were among the first roads laid out by the township. There were more petitions for roads in those days than there are roads today. The commissioners did not always accept a road petition. Laying out of new roads was the major activity of the highway commissioners.

The township was divided into 25 road districts. The care and maintenance of roads fell upon road overseers. Adult males were supposed to report to work on the roads to pay out their poll tax or pay for some other person to do the work. The road overseers were supposed to file a report with the three highway commissioners of all work done on roads in their territory and make an accounting of the funds collected.

Vernon Frost states that the township had a thistle and weed commissioner whose job was to inspect property for thistles and write a citation and levy a fine if violations were found. As a youth, Vernon spent his summers trying to chop the weeds at the family farm.

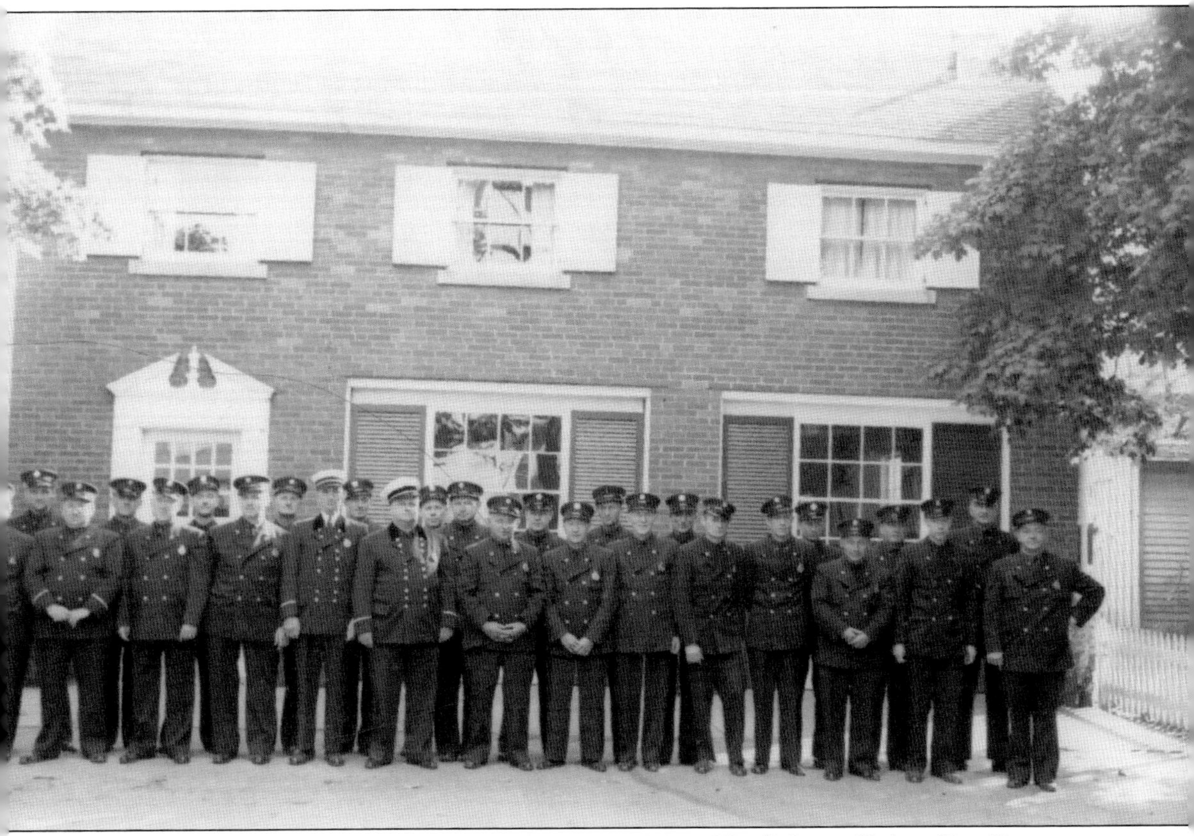

Palatine Firefighters at Slade Street Station, 1940s. The Palatine Deluge Fire Company was formed in the summer of 1877. Frank G. Robinson was appointed the first fire marshal by the village board, and 45 men volunteered. A horse- or hand-drawn fire pumper, along with a hose cart and hose, was purchased in 1887 for $1,000. At the same time, a fire alarm bell cost $280.05. The equipment was housed in the village hall on Slade Street, which was built with a tower to hold the fire bell.

The fire company was reorganized in 1892 and again in 1895, with fewer members. Firemen were paid 60¢ per month (later $1) and were fined 50¢ if they failed to attend a drill.

The volunteer firemen raised money to purchase other equipment. The first automotive fire engine was acquired in 1932. The 1929 municipal building on South Brockway Street had room for only two fire engines. Needing more space, the firemen were allowed to tear down the old village hall on Slade Street and erect a fire station, for which they raised money and provided labor. In 1953, they purchased an adjoining lot and erected an addition, which cost $40,000, and provided an upstairs hall for community use. It was closed and sold in 1981.

In 1972, Palatine was one of the first villages in Illinois to acquire an ambulance and begin training paramedics. Palatine hired its first full-time firefighters in 1971, and the last of the volunteers were retired in 1984.

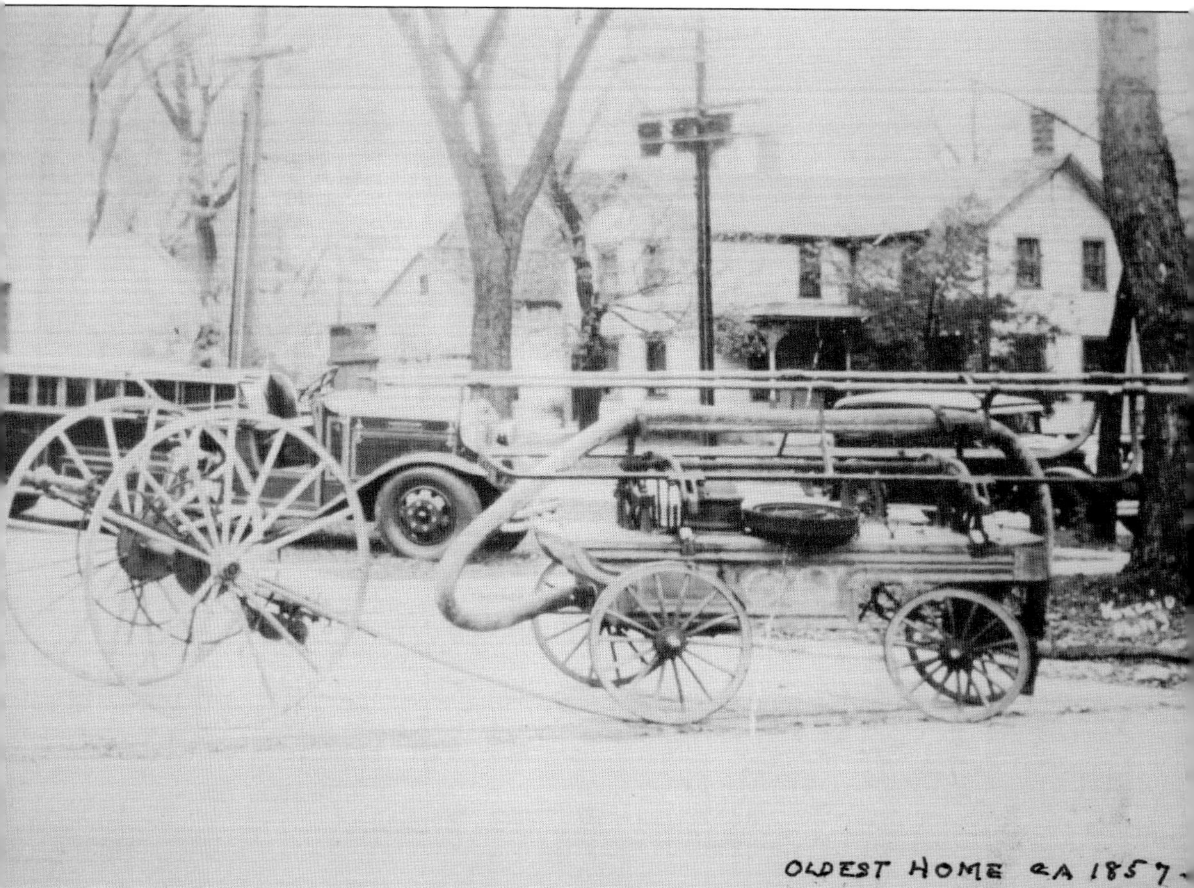

HISTORY OF THE FIRST FIRE PUMPER. The 1887 hand-pumper fire engine was purchased in 1887 after fires had burned down a flax mill on Johnson Street and the Meyer Hotel on Plum Grove Road. At the same time, a brick cistern was built to hold rainwater from the Schoppe Store and the Kunze Saloon at the corner of Brockway and Slade Streets. Smaller cisterns were built in other parts of town.

At the sound of the fire bell at the town hall, men with carts and horses came on the run; the first team to arrive received $5 for hauling the engine to the fire. If no horses were available, the pumper was pulled by a rope and about 20 men.

That pumper was used for about 50 years before modern equipment made it obsolete. It was purchased by Schaumburg Township, used for years, and then sold at auction. It was purchased by a Mr. C. Zepp of Chicago, who began restoring it. In 1956, he returned it to the Palatine Fire Department for its historic value. The fire department presented it to the Palatine Historical Society, where it is displayed in the Deluge Fire Company & Museum–Carriage House and has been restored.

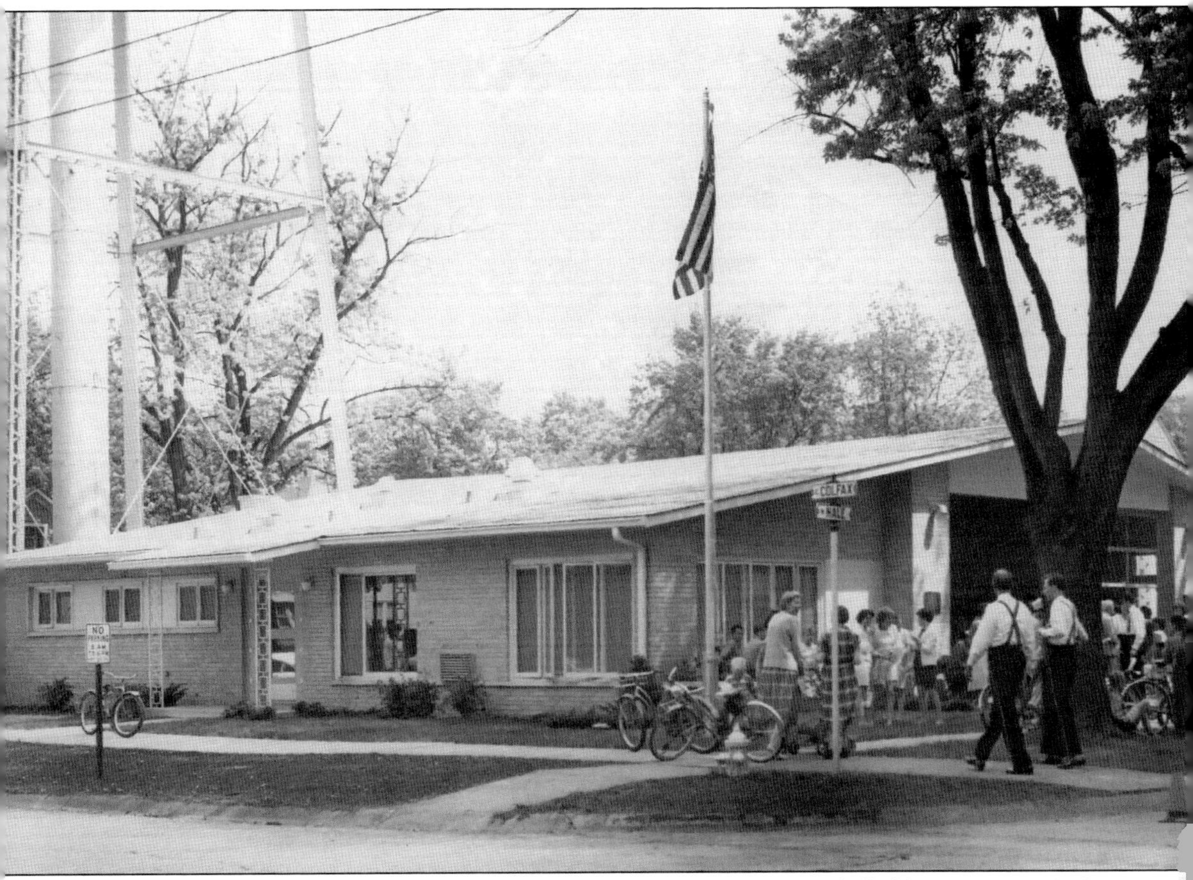

OPENING DAY AT ORVILLE HELMS FIRE STATION. After two firemen were killed by a train in 1946 while answering a fire call, a fire station north of the tracks was needed. In May 1960, a new station opened at Colfax and Hale Streets on property that formerly held the standpipe.

The station was named after fire marshal Orville Helms, who had served 42 years with the Palatine Fire Department. He joined as a volunteer in 1937 when the department had 22 volunteers and three pieces of equipment. In 1953, fire department officers elected him chief. He was named full-time chief and the only paid full-time fireman in 1960.

Helms was appointed fire marshal in 1976. To honor him on his retirement in 1979, the village board decreed that no other person would ever be given the title of fire marshal.

The Colfax Street firehouse is the central station out of five current firehouses, with two in the south and two in the north. It is the administrative and headquarters station of the Palatine Fire Department.

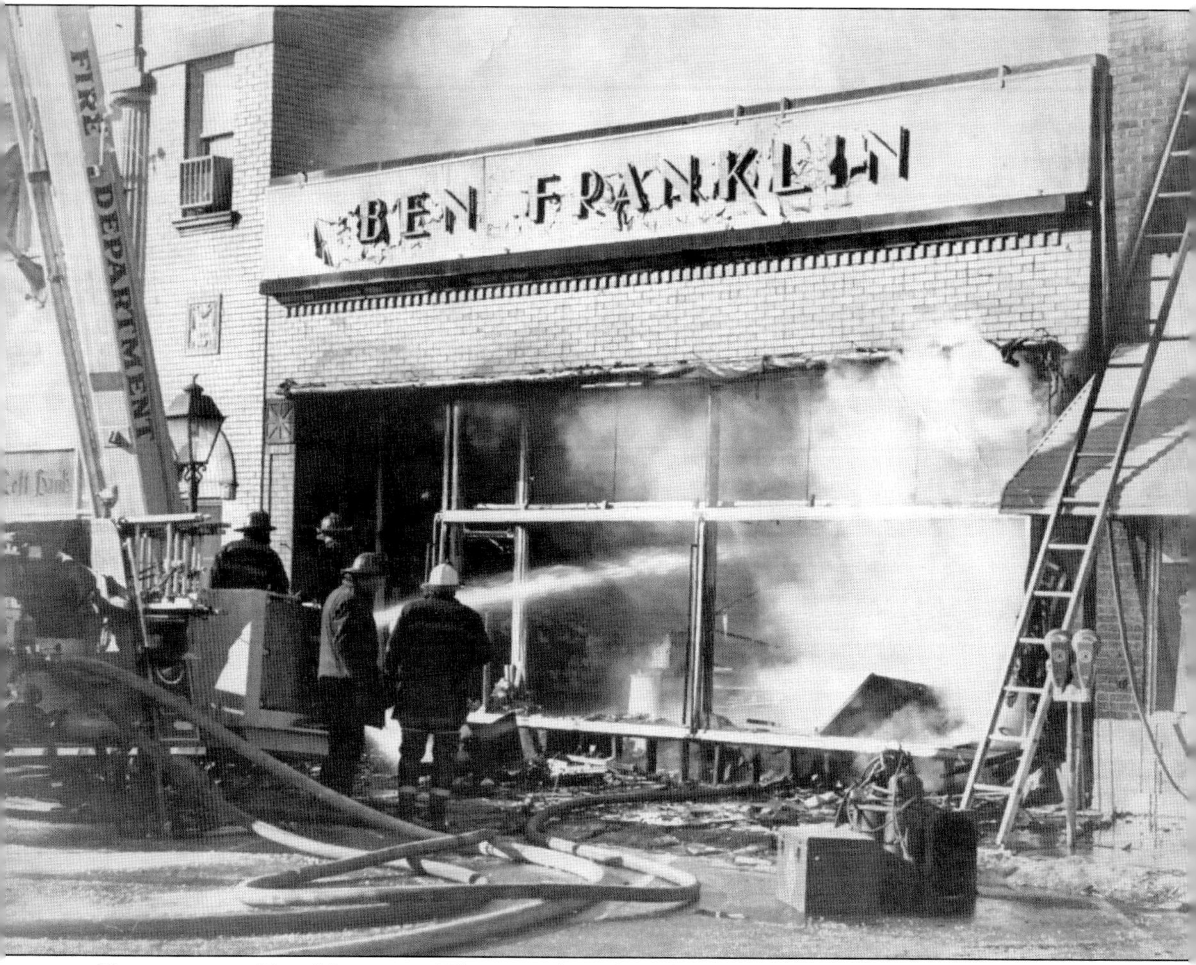

Fires and the Fire Memorial. There are three fires that many Palatine residents still remember. The restaurant on Northwest Highway at Quentin Road, called La Romana at the time it burned down in 1981, was more fondly known as Uncle Andy's Cow Palace. A very large cow statue sat in front of the building. The restaurant was originally built as the Radio Club during World War II.

The 26 North Mod Shop on the southwest corner of Brockway and Slade Streets was the Schoppe Store from the 1890s until 1967. It was truly a landmark building when it burned down in November 1970. It has been replaced by a new brick structure.

The Ben Franklin variety store fire on Brockway Street (pictured) was a tragedy that occurred on February 23, 1973. Three volunteer firemen—John Wilson (also the store owner), Warren Ahlgrim, and Richard Freeman—died fighting the fire.

The village has erected a memorial in the triangle formed by Brockway and Slade Streets and the railroad tracks to honor these three firefighters as well as Wesley Comfort Jr. and Leonard Nebel, who were hit by a train while crossing the tracks in October 1946. This was the site of the three-story Batterman Building and, later, the Bank of Palatine.

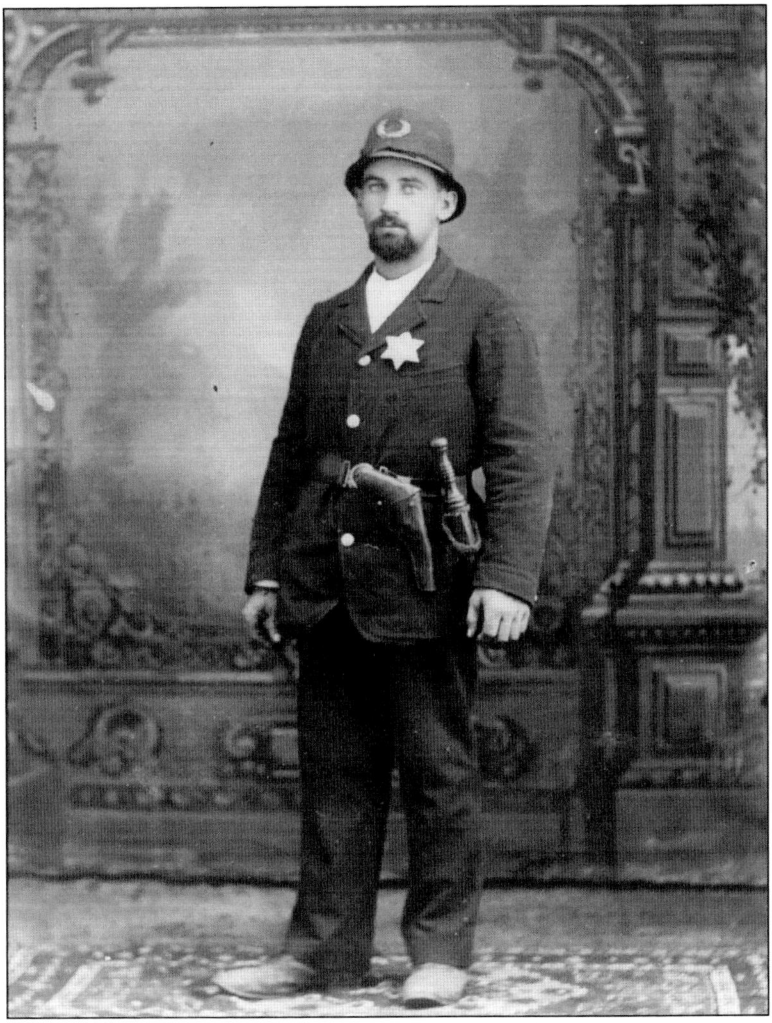

POLICEMAN HERMAN SCHRADER. The appointment of constables began shortly after the village was incorporated. They worked primarily at night, and duties included serving as poundmaster for horses, dogs, pigs, and sheep; carrying out ordinances; collecting licenses from "peddlers and showmen"; and collecting fines from saloon operators. They received no salary other than a portion of the fees and fines or special compensation when performing out-of-the-ordinary duties.

Henry Law was hired as a night watchman and lamplighter at $40 per month in 1896. Herman Schrader was appointed a special night watchman without pay in 1895 and allowed $5 a month in 1897. On May 5, 1913, the board voted to hire two police for $55 per month "who must be in regulation uniform when on duty." Henry Law and Herman Schrader became the first uniformed police officers.

The police force had two policemen until 1942, when there were three. By 1951, the department consisted of four officers and six patrolmen. The motorized age began in 1925 when the first motorcycle was purchased for $275. In 1928, the village board was paying officers $15 a month to use their own cars. The first police car was a two-door Buick, which cost $813 in 1938.

According to its current website, the Palatine Police Department now has 112 sworn officers and 44 civilian personnel. Police duties today are far beyond anything that could have been imagined in 1866. The department is housed in the attractive, efficient building on Hicks Road that was built in 2013.

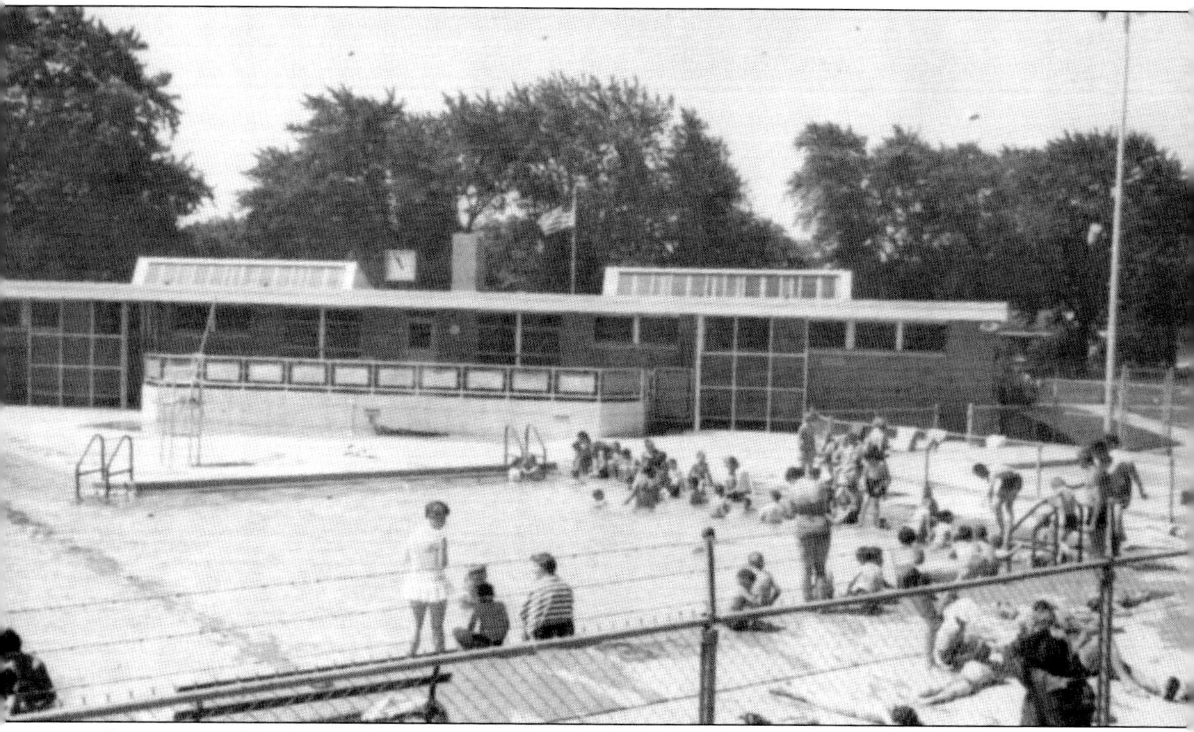

Community Pool, c. 1949. When Palatine residents voted to establish a park district on July 31, 1945, the population of the village was 3,000 and the war was still being fought in Japan. A special election in May 1947 approved a $75,000 bond issue to buy 18 acres owned by Arthur T. McIntosh. The newly formed Consolidated School District No. 15 received six acres, the site of Sanborn School, and the park district obtained 12 acres, which became Community Park. Using bond-issue proceeds and private donations, the park was developed and additional land was purchased to front on Palatine Road.

Dick Welty was hired in 1949 as part-time director. A $190,000 bond issue approved in the fall of 1954 built the first community park pool, which opened in July 1955. Bill Milne was hired as full-time director in 1962.

Major additions to the park district have been made over the past 71 years. The Palatine Park District now manages 39 parks, three reservoirs and three swimming pools. It offers classes in fitness, sports, arts and crafts, and general interest for preschoolers through seniors. It has facilities for parties and for a variety of sports and activities.

Palatine Golf Course was developed in the late 1960s. In 1978, the park district acquired the east end of the old Palatine High School as a community center, which included a gym, Ost Field, and Cutting Hall Performing Arts Center. Palatine Stables, purchased in 1989, has become a popular facility. The Palatine Trail for pedestrians and bicycles was developed in the 1970s. Part of the trail follows the old PLZ&W railroad tracks. The Clayson House Museum is another part of the park district.

Four

Schools and Libraries

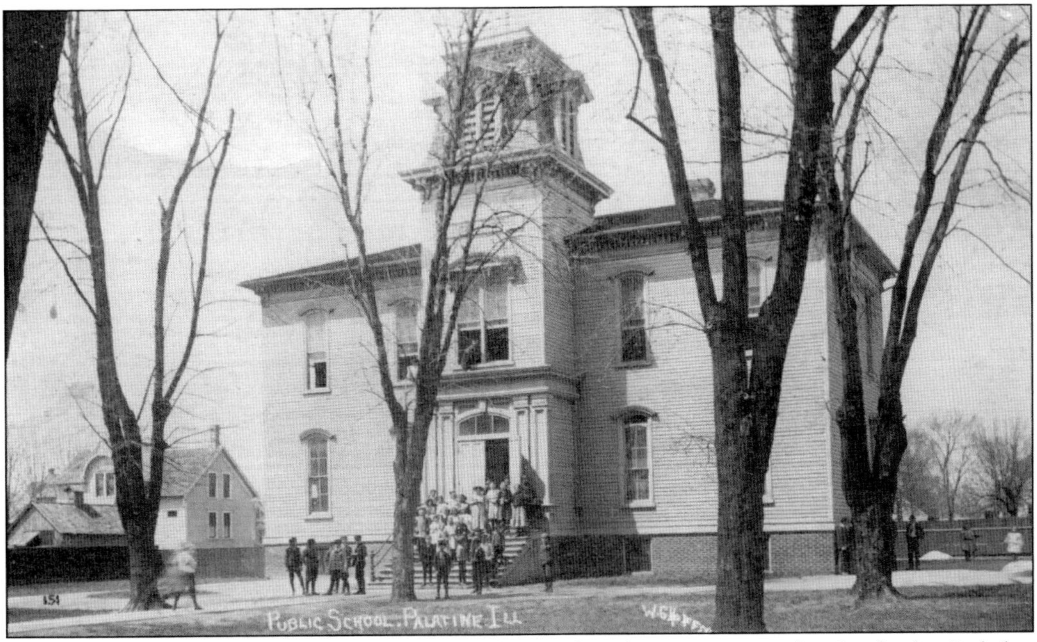

Wood Street Wooden School, 1860. Legend has it that there were six early schools: the Cady log cabin in Deer Grove, a log cabin in Plum Grove, the Hasse house on Chicago Avenue, a building just outside town, an 1860 building on Wood Street, and the Masonic hall (now Lamplighter).

A two-story, four-room wooden school was built on Wood Street at Benton in 1860. Two rooms were added to the back in 1888. This building served grades one through eight and, after 1875, the high school—until 1913, when it was replaced with a modern large brick building on the site. Under a Cook County mandate in 1901, this became School District No. 15.

A separate Palatine Township High School District No. 211 was formed in 1914 and occupied the brick building until 1928, when it moved into its own building farther east on Wood Street.

The first kindergarten was established through efforts of parents and a Depression-era program that paid for a teacher.

The brick school was formally named the Joel Wood School, but no one ever called it that. Newspapers referred to it as the "Palatine School," and doorway lintels also read "Palatine School." It was commonly known as "the Wood Street School."

The building was used until 1979, razed in 1983, and replaced by Victorian-style houses.

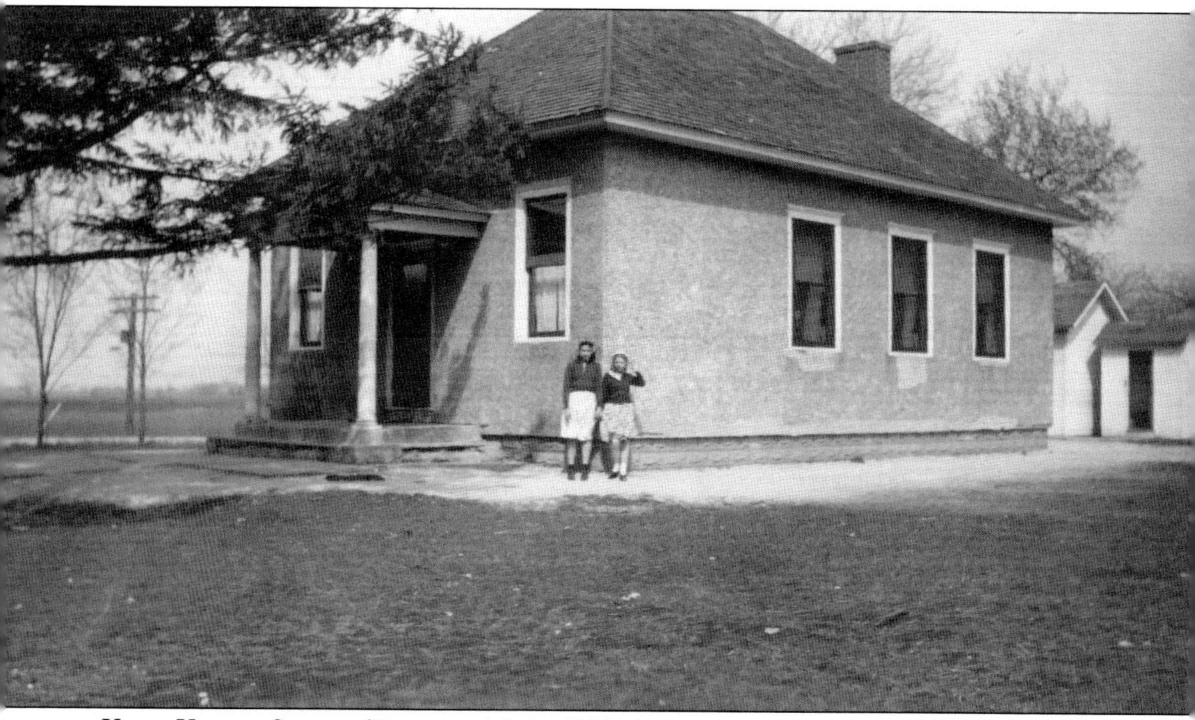

KITTY KORNER SCHOOL (DISTRICT 14). In 1946, there were seven one-room schools in Palatine Township. Four of them had been replaced on-site by newer buildings. Three had been improved in the 1930s.

The Bradwell School of 1921 (District No. 17) at Ela and Bradwell Roads was modern but with chemical toilets. The 1923 Wittenberg School (District No. 13) also had chemical toilets. This was the third site for the school on Quentin Road, north of Baldwin Road (Northwest Highway).

Deer Grove School (District No. 12) at Ela Road north of Northwest Highway, built in 1926, was modern; it had running water. The small Wente School (District No. 16), south of what became Fremd's football field, was replaced by the two-room Hillside School farther north on Quentin Road in the 1930s; it also had running water.

Plum Grove School (District No. 18) on south Rohlwing Road was probably on the site of the original log cabin building. It was improved in 1932. This school became the richest one-room school in the township after 1927 because it received revenue from the newly built Arlington Park Racetrack.

Kitty Korner School (District No. 14) at Dundee and Rand Roads was a small stucco building, which had replaced a wooden school in 1911. It was later modernized. Highland Grove School (District No. 16), which, according to newspaper accounts, was built in 1849 on Ela Road south of Algonquin, was modernized in the 1930s.

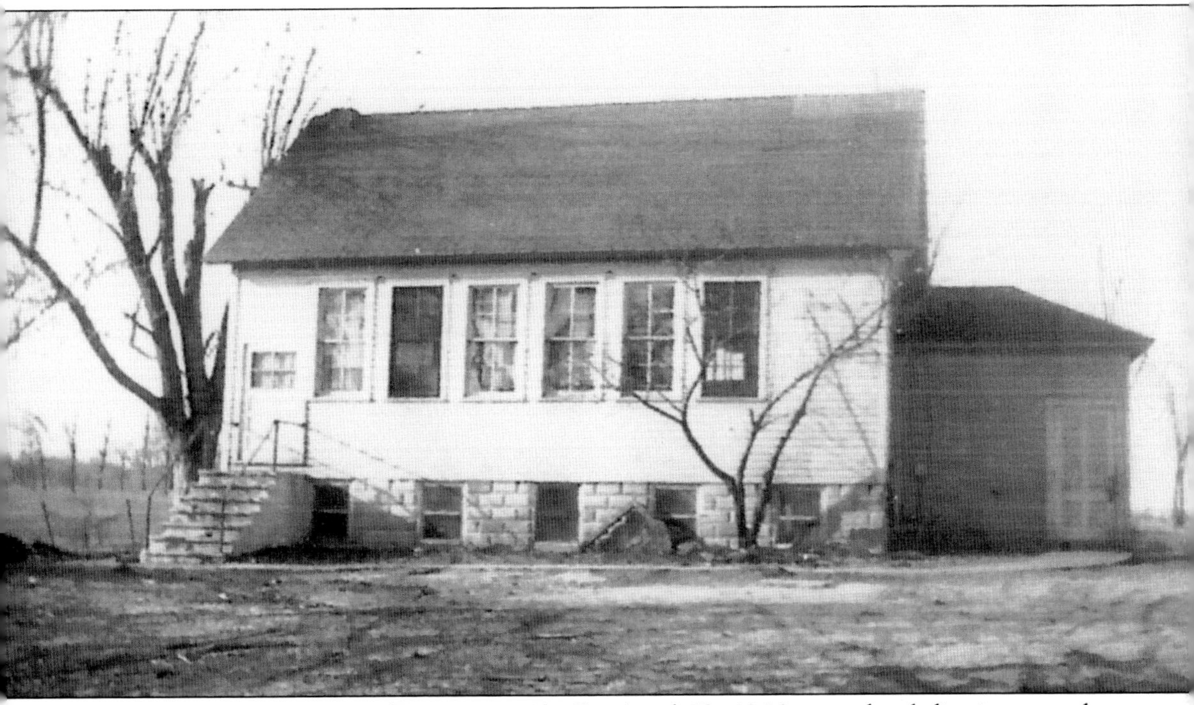

Highland Grove School (District 18). On April 13, 1946, six school districts voted overwhelmingly to consolidate into District No. 15 (the Palatine Township School).

Plum Grove School (District No. 18) and Kitty Korner School (District No. 14) were sold in February 1949 for $5,295 and were moved to other locations to be used as houses.

Three of the schools were kept in use for several years. Wittenberg School (District No. 13) and Bradwell School (District No. 17) were sold in 1954. Both were converted into homes and still stand at the same sites. Hillside School, a two-room building (District No. 16), was used for a longer period and was finally razed in 1964. From 1965 to 1992, this became the site of the District No. 15 administration building, which is now the Palatine Township Senior Center.

Deer Grove School (District No. 12) opted out of the referendum because it intended to join the Barrington School District. Barrington later sold the building, which is now a house.

Highland Grove School (District No. 18) also opted out. It was run by a board of three farmers who had been educated in one-room schools and thought that was good enough and did not want to pay Palatine taxes. However, an influx of city people who did not want to send their children to a one-room school and were paying to send them to Palatine finally forced the district to consolidate in 1958.

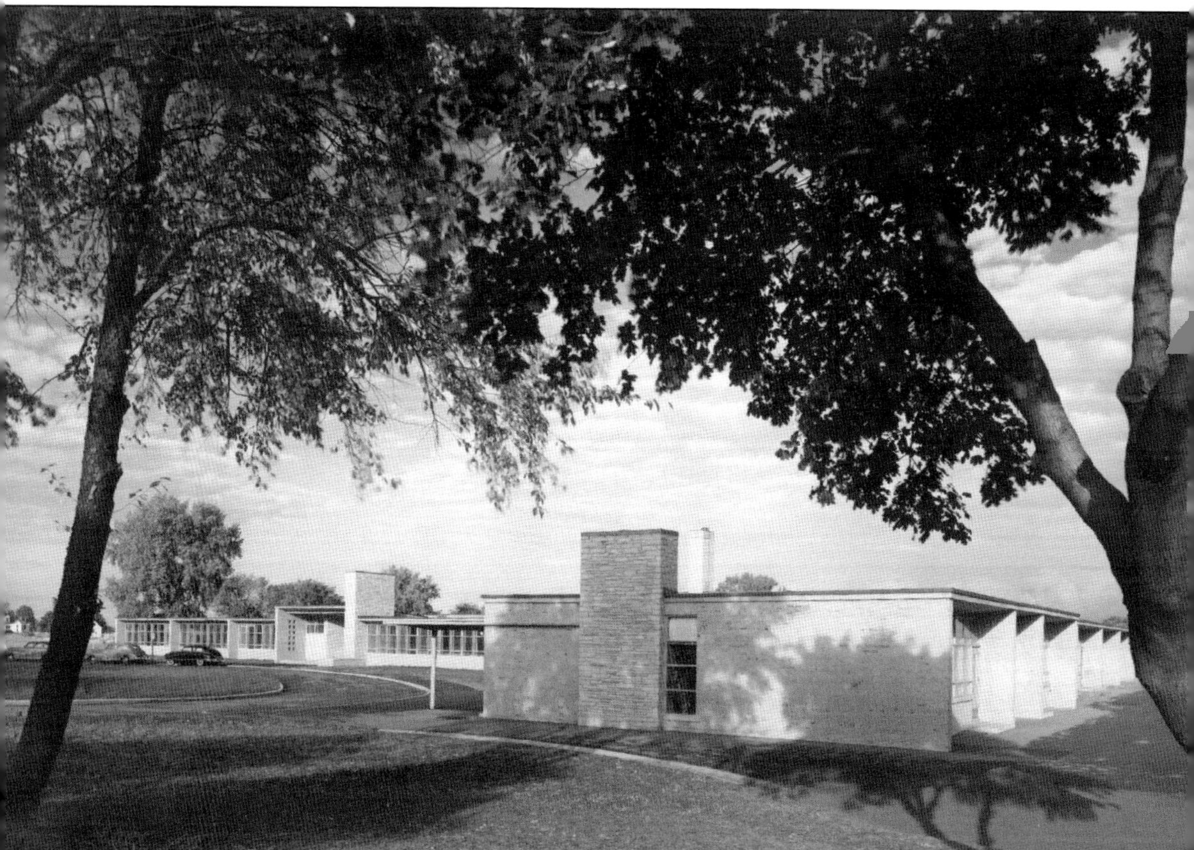

Sanborn School. Immediately after consolidation of District No. 15 in 1946, it was evident that additional classrooms were needed. In September 1948, the Oak Street School was opened at Wood and Oak Streets. It was later renamed in honor of Gray M. Sanborn.

The rapid influx of new homes created conditions that forced the district to build 20 more elementary and junior high schools between 1954 and 1989. Of the district's 22 schools, 13 were in Palatine, 7 in Rolling Meadows, and 2 in Hoffman Estates.

Three schools were later abandoned. Wood Street School was closed in 1979 and torn down in 1983. Jonas Salk (Rolling Meadows) closed in 1981 and was leased and then sold to the Rolling Meadows Park District. Cardinal Drive School (Rolling Meadows) was closed in 1975 and later sold to the Church of Christ.

Two schools were razed and rebuilt on the same sites. They were Kimball Hill in 1990–1992 and Central Road in 1995–1996, both in Rolling Meadows. Sixteen of the schools were renovated between 1989 and 1996, with an additional eight rooms built onto Sanborn in 2001.

Only the last school built, Whitely in Hoffman Estates, was not renovated.

The district bought Sacred Heart School in Rolling Meadows in 1995. It became the John G. Conyers Learning Academy, which was renovated in 2004.

Administration offices are on North First Bank Drive. District No. 15 is now the third-largest elementary school district in Illinois.

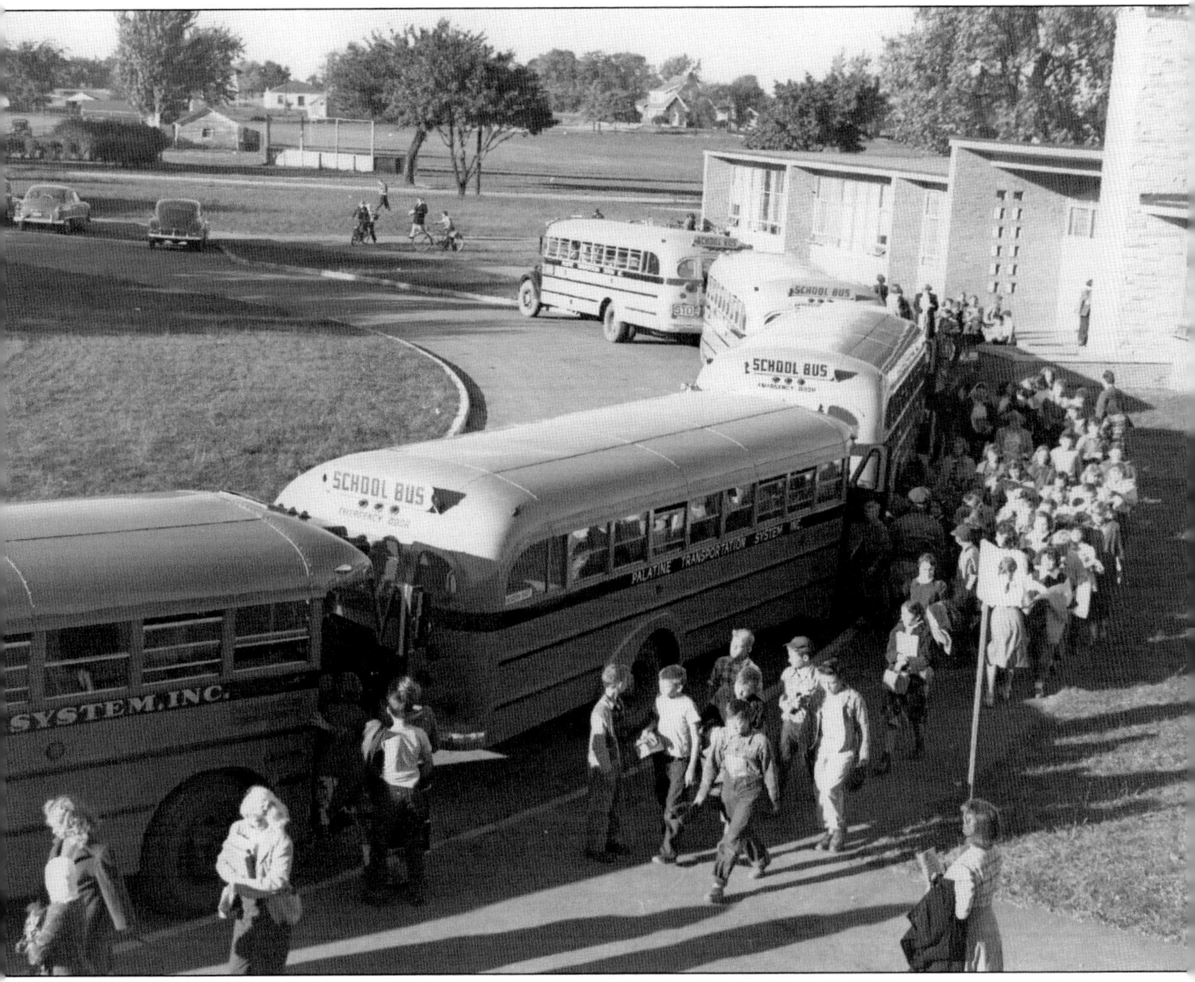

District 15 Buses in 1950s. The first bus service provided for students in District No. 15 was in 1943. Parents were to pay one-fourth the cost, and the state would pay the rest.

Marvin Plate determined in the early 1950s that the large area now covered by the district with its exploding population would require a much larger bus fleet. So, he started the District No. 15 Transportation System.

He decided on the type of equipment that would give the greatest safety and comfort to students. A lot behind the local Sinclair Station was used to house the buses. He erected a Butler Building in which to do maintenance work. This was a metal building that could be put up quickly and with few workers.

After Sundling Junior High was built on North Smith, the buses were stored there and the basement was used for maintenance. A maintenance/warehouse facility was obtained in 1997.

District No. 15 has a fleet of 162 buses that transport 10,500 public and parochial schoolchildren. In 2003, it was selected as winner of the top transportation award in the nation, presented by the National Association for Pupil Transportation.

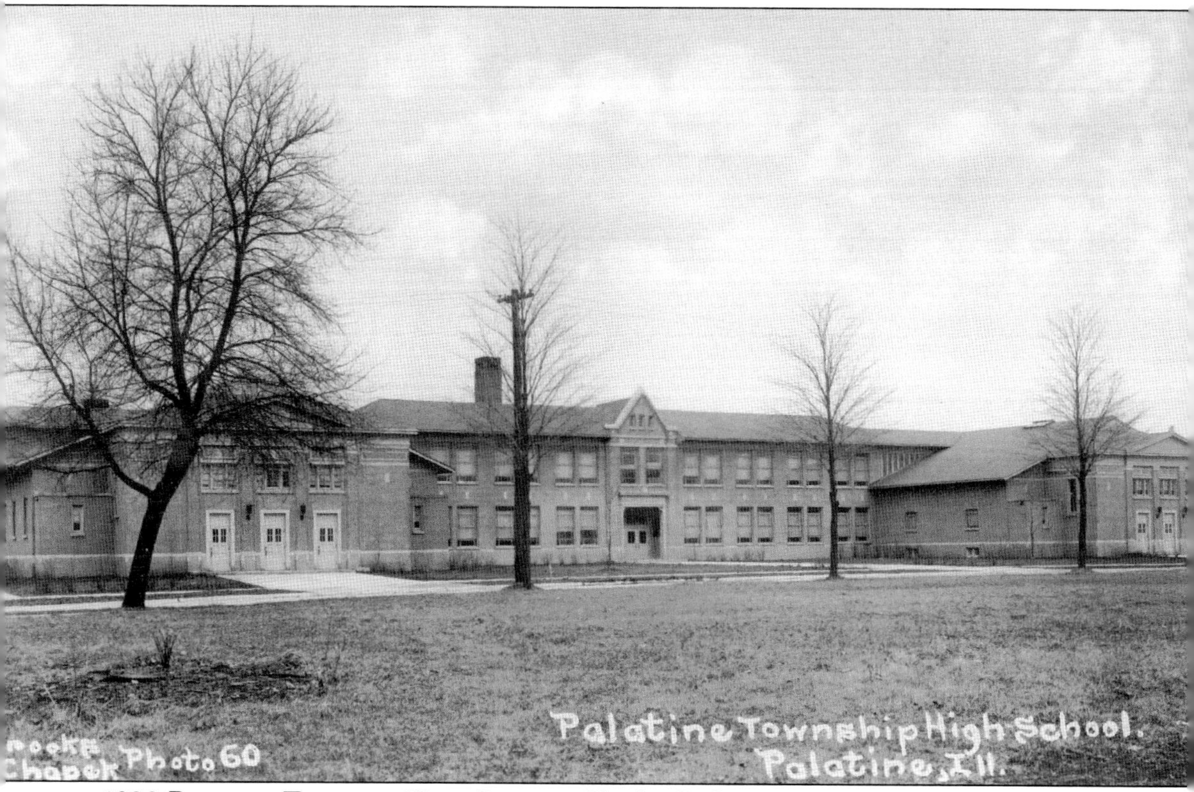

1928 PALATINE TOWNSHIP HIGH SCHOOL. Charles S. Cutting was principal of the Palatine School (later District No. 15) in 1875 when he started a two-year study program beyond eighth grade. Palatine High School was one of four suburban high schools and the first in the northwest suburbs. Classes were held on the top floor of the old Wood Street School.

Palatine Township High School District No. 211 was formed in 1914, renting space in the 1914 brick Wood Street School. The high school moved into its own new building at 150 Wood Street in 1928. The U-shaped structure had a cafeteria, a theater on the west side, and a gymnasium on the east side and could accommodate 300 students.

The growth in population after World War II necessitated a large addition in 1952–1953 to house 1,000 students and a larger gym. (Interestingly, Glenbrook North High School in Northbrook had lost its elementary school facility and had not yet completed its building on Shermer Road. Two hundred fifty Glenbrook North students and teachers were bused to those new empty classrooms in Palatine for the year 1952–1953).

Additions to the front and rear of the 1952 building in 1967 created a capacity for 1,800 students. By 1976, it was deemed that the building had insufficient land to expand, and the cost of needed repairs was impractical. The building closed in June 1977, one year after Palatine High School celebrated 100 years of existence.

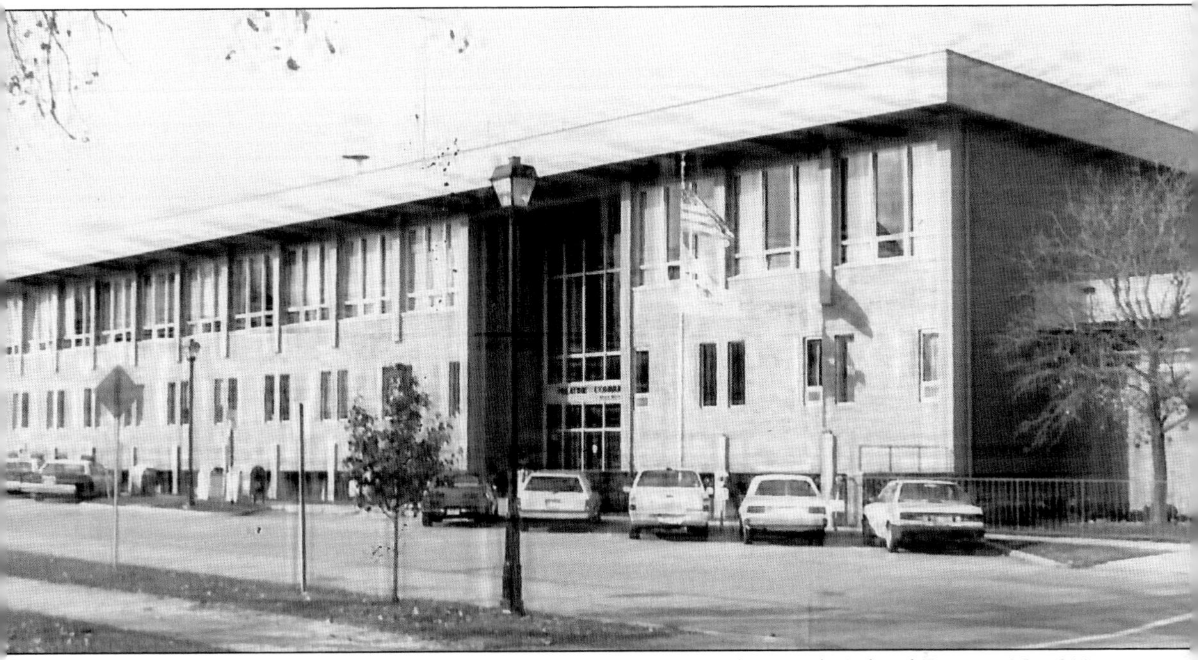

New Village Hall on Wood Street. When Palatine Township High School District No. 211 vacated its building on Wood Street in 1977 and moved into the new school on North Rohlwing Road, the Village of Palatine and the park district purchased the property.

In June 1977, voters, by an overwhelming margin, authorized the village to issue bonds in the amount of $660,000 to purchase and renovate the facility. They also approved issuing bonds not to exceed $1.2 million to finance renovation. The village's share was 60 percent, while the park district would assume the balance.

The original 1928 building (except for Cutting Hall) was razed and used as a parking lot. The park district took over the east end of the 1952/1967 building, which held the gym, and built a new lobby for the now freestanding Cutting Hall. Some renovations were made on the second floor of the village facility.

Now more than 60 years old, the building underwent a $12.7 million transformation. Beginning in December 2014, the structure was gutted. A year later, the exterior was refurbished. The building was occupied in 2016. Design plans allowed for more light into the interior of the building, enlarged council chambers, and two meeting rooms to hold 25 and 120 people.

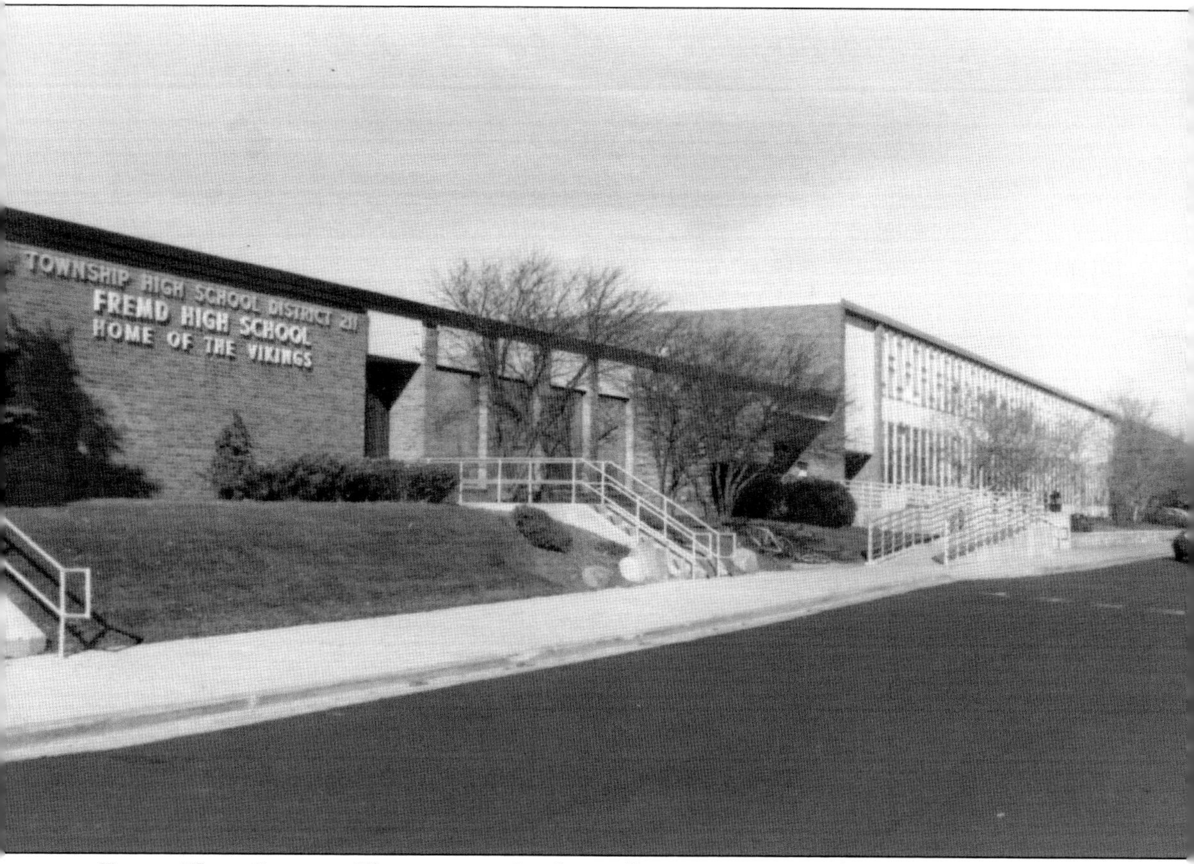

FREMD HIGH SCHOOL. Elementary school enrollments in 1959 indicated there would be an increase in high school students beyond the capacity of Palatine High School. A 40-acre site at the intersection of Quentin and Illinois Roads had been purchased when Palatine High was expanded. Voters in the district now approved a bond issue to build a new school on that site.

The new high school opened in 1961 and was named for William Fremd, a graduate of Palatine High School, a District No. 211 board member for more than 30 years, and an area school board member for 45 years.

From 1961 to 1967, freshmen and sophomores attended Fremd High School while juniors and seniors attended Palatine High. Then Fremd became a four-year school.

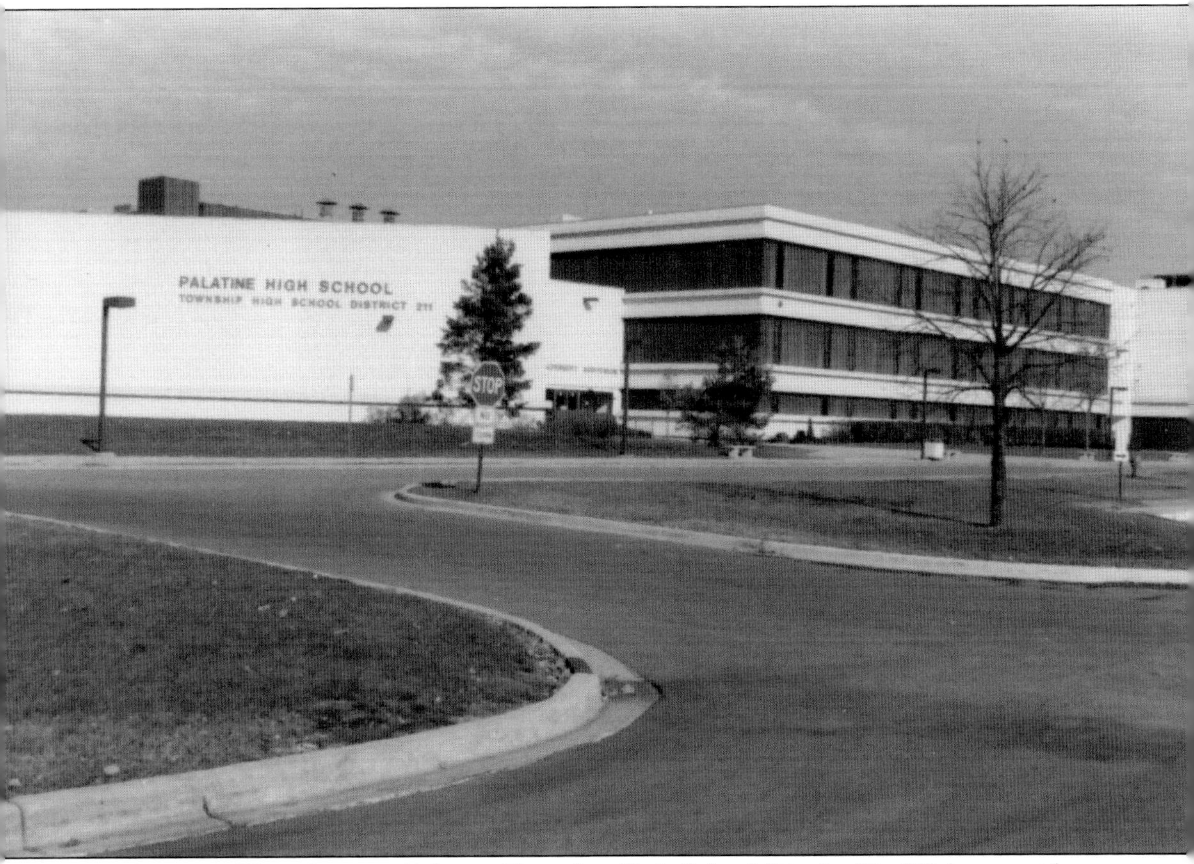

1977 PALATINE HIGH SCHOOL. Palatine Township High School District No. 211 began with a single Palatine High School in 1875 and expanded to two buildings in Palatine Township with the building of Fremd. In 1954, Schaumburg Township joined District No. 211.

Schaumburg Township also saw rapid growth. The large Hoffman Estates development (and village) brought about the erection of District No. 211's third school in 1964, named after the educator James B. Conant. It was the first in Schaumburg Township.

An administration center was built on Roselle Road in 1967 and named after Gerald A. McElroy, who had served District No. 211 for 38 years as a teacher, coach, principal, and superintendent.

Two other schools were built in Schaumburg Township. Schaumburg High School opened in 1970 on Schaumburg Road, and Hoffman Estates High School opened in 1973 on Higgins Road.

The sixth school approved in 1974 became the new Palatine High School on Rohlwing Road in 1977, replacing the 1928/1952/1967 building. Additions and improvements have been made to all the schools from 1967 through 2015.

The district also operates two therapeutic special education schools that serve approximately 150 students. District No. 211 Academy North is located in Palatine, and the Higgins Education Center is in Hoffman Estates.

High School District No. 211 is the largest high school district in Illinois.

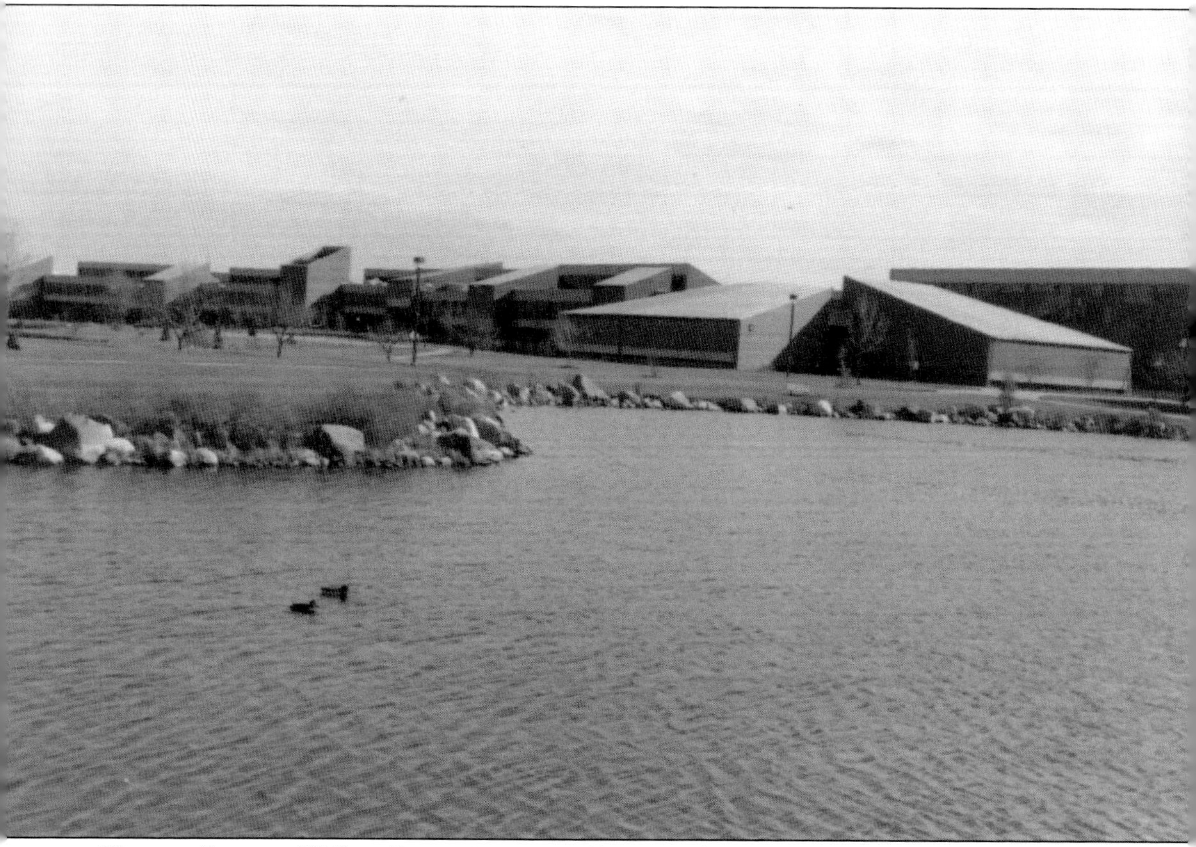

Harper College. William Rainey Harper College in Palatine serves 40,000 students a year from 23 northwest suburban communities.

Discussions began as early as 1959 about the concept of a community college, and by 1961, an active committee was working on the project. In March 1965, a referendum established a community college and elected a board that proceeded to hire the first president, select architectural firms to design the campus, and hire a consulting firm to aid in curriculum planning and growth projection.

A $7.375 million bond issue referendum passed in June 1966 to finance the 200-acre farmland site at Algonquin and Roselle Roads. The first building was opened in 1969, and the campus facilities have grown and are still growing.

The first faculty of 38 began teaching 1,725 students in January 1967. The young teachers were forced to make up the school's curriculum with a combination of their limited experience, a lot of long hours, and a little bit of guesswork. Classes were held from 4:00 p.m. to 10:00 p.m. in Elk Grove High School. The administrative offices and a Quonset building for faculty were on the back side of the parking lot and "without facilities."

Today, Harper College offers associate degrees, certification programs, advanced career programs, workforce training, professional development, continuing education classes, accelerated degree options for adults, and developmental education programs.

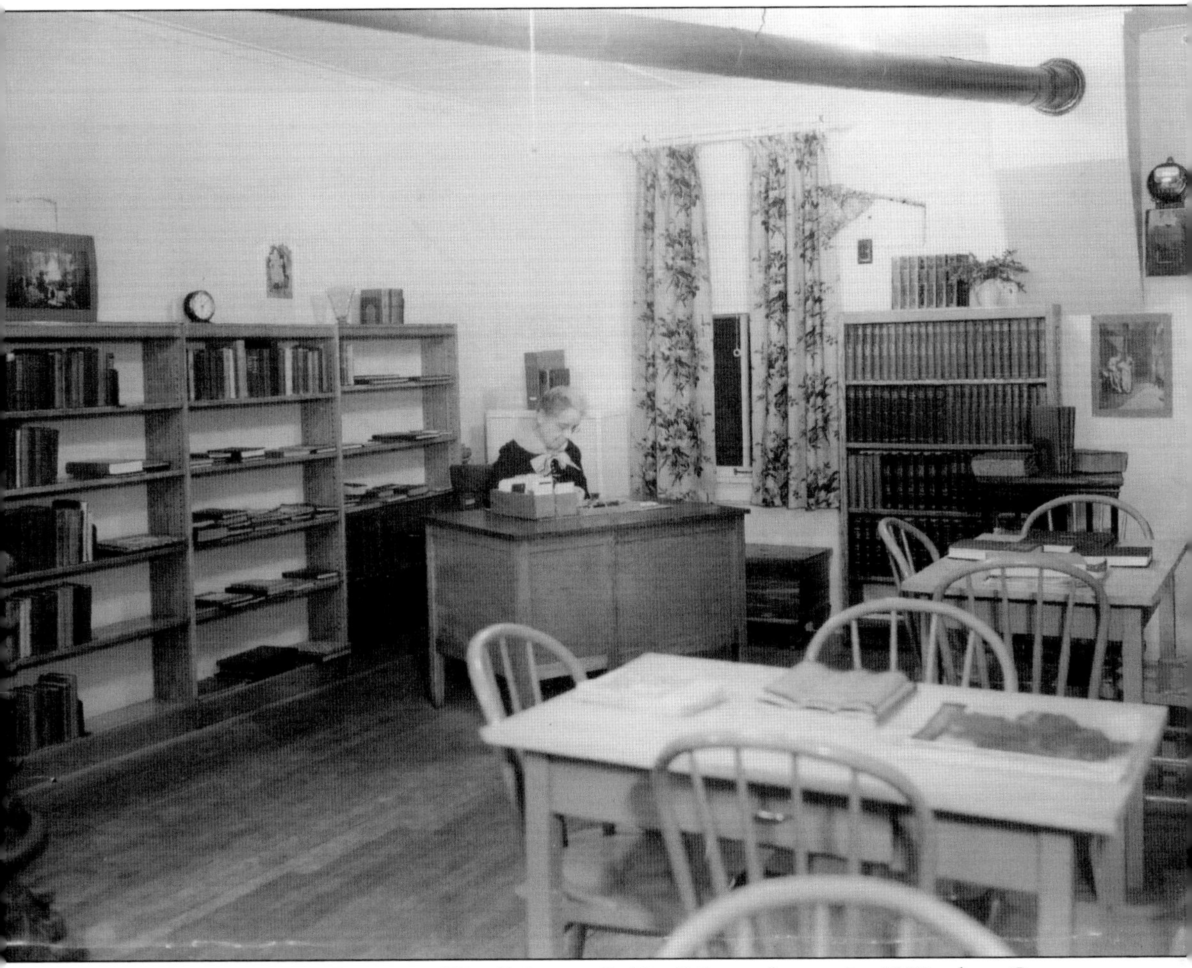

Lottie Hart in 1923 Library. The Palatine Public Library began in 1920 when George Minneberger, Scoutmaster of Boy Scout Troop No. 1, conceived of a project for his boys to collect books. They were stored in the Wood Street School for three years and were not always available at convenient hours.

A citizens' committee raised enough money to rent a small store at 11 North Bothwell Street behind the Matthei Building on Railroad Avenue. The decor of the room was planned by Bertha Torgler Thompson and Grace Van Horne Greener. Lottie Hart, a retired teacher, became the librarian, a post she held for more than 25 years.

The library opened in September 1923 with 64 borrowers registered. Margaret Schering was the first to check out a book, *Our National Parks*. A referendum to create a Palatine Public Library carried by a small majority on May 5, 1924. The first library trustees were elected that year.

A fire in 1934 closed the library for a month with minimum damage to the books. The inside was refinished and repainted, new lights were installed, and the furniture was refinished. The library remained at that location until 1947.

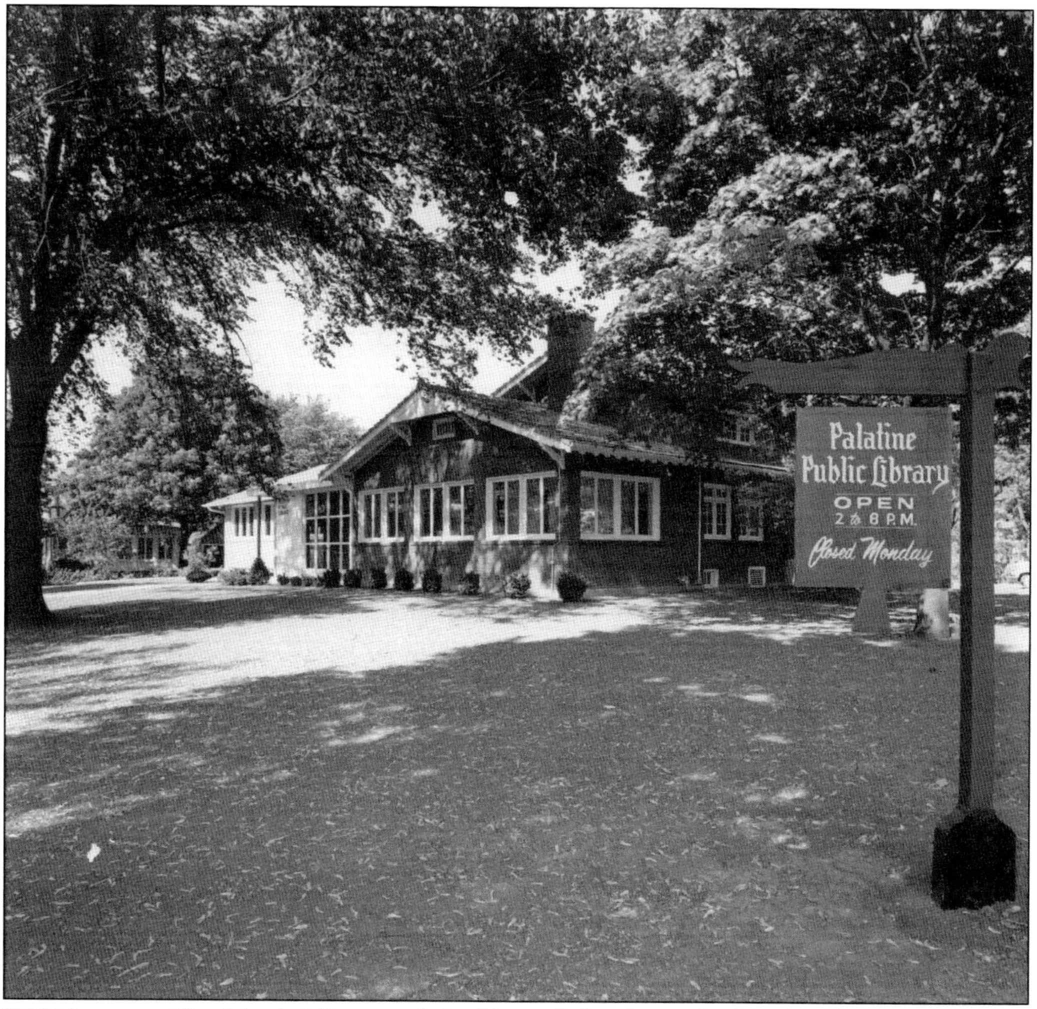

1958 LIBRARY. The Matthei Store and the library behind it at Railroad and Bothwell Streets were torn down in 1947 to build the Pepper Block. The library moved to the first floor of the Plate Building at 55 West Wood Street.

In March 1950, the library board purchased two lots on Oak Street for $1,700. Buying the lots did not immediately result in building plans, but the enthusiasm it incurred resulted in the creation of Friends of the Library. The library moved to the ground floor of the Masonic Building at Plum Grove and Palatine Roads in 1951 until an opportunity arose to purchase the William G. Ost home at Wood and Brockway Streets.

A $125,000 referendum on February 16, 1957, was approved by voters to buy the Ost property, make alterations to the house, add a 40-by-60-foot addition with a basement, and make a parking lot. On June 8, 1958, the library opened with a home of its own. The Oak Street lots were sold. The basement was finished and furnished in 1962 to create a children's library. When the North Suburban Interlibrary system came into being in 1966, Palatine was one of the initial 22 libraries participating.

The library with 8,000 square feet of space became overcrowded as new subdivisions were built. The library board was planning for a new library to be built by 1969. It took until 1975 to make that happen.

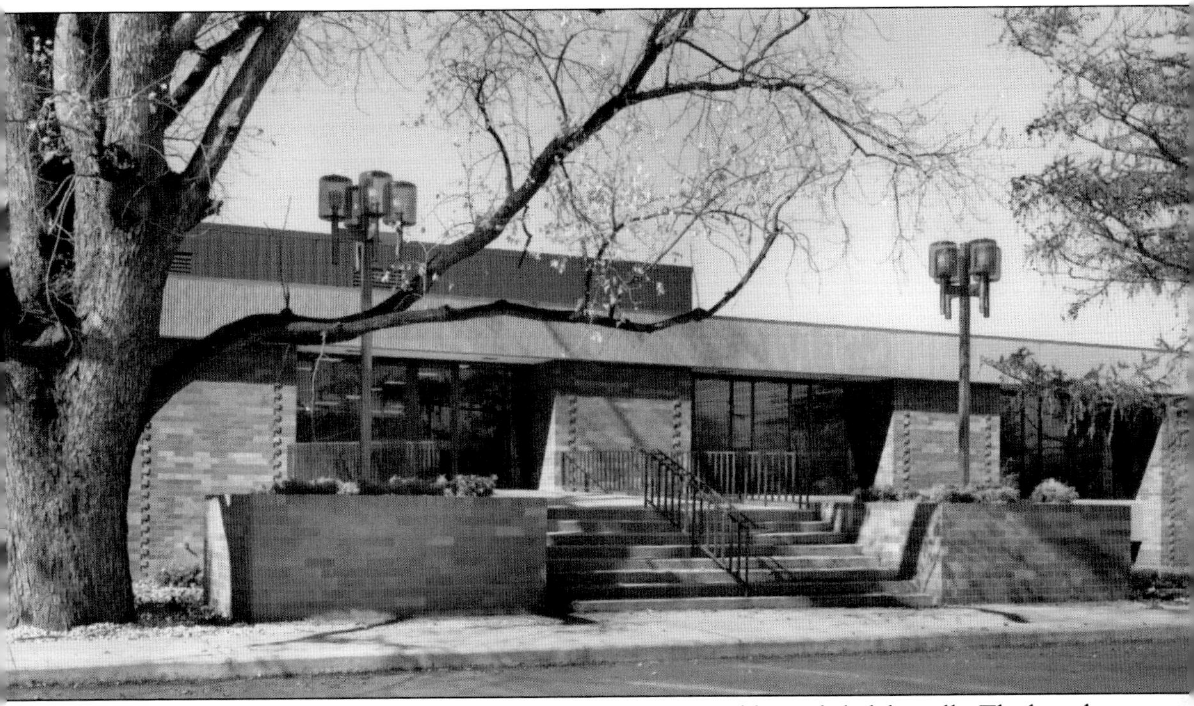

1975 Library. The first attempt at a referendum to build a new library failed dismally. The board wanted $2,200,000 for a library to be somewhere downtown, but it did not have a site chosen or purchased. A second referendum, proposing less money, also failed.

The library bought a site at the southwest corner of Benton and Northwest Highway and received approval from the village board to build a library. In 1973, voters passed a $1,300,000 referendum to erect and furnish the building. A grant of $208,000 was also received from the state.

Before the Benton Street library was completed, a referendum was held in September 1974 to create a public library district, so the Palatine Village Library became the Palatine Public Library District.

The new library was dedicated November 23, 1975. The meeting room was named for the late Walter Rennack, longtime president of the library board. This building is now the Quest Academy.

An auction was held to sell the Brockway Street library's furnishings, including shelves and chairs; everything but the fire extinguisher was put up for sale. The property was sold to the Unitarian Church for $136,000. The Unitarians have since moved, but the building currently still houses a church.

The Palatine Library District today serves 90,000 residents in a 96,000-square-foot main building at 700 North Court and in two branches, one in Hoffman Estates and one on North Rand Road. The main building was occupied in December 1993. The upstairs was renovated in 2009 and the downstairs in 2013. The programs at the library have been greatly expanded, and a digital media center has been opened.

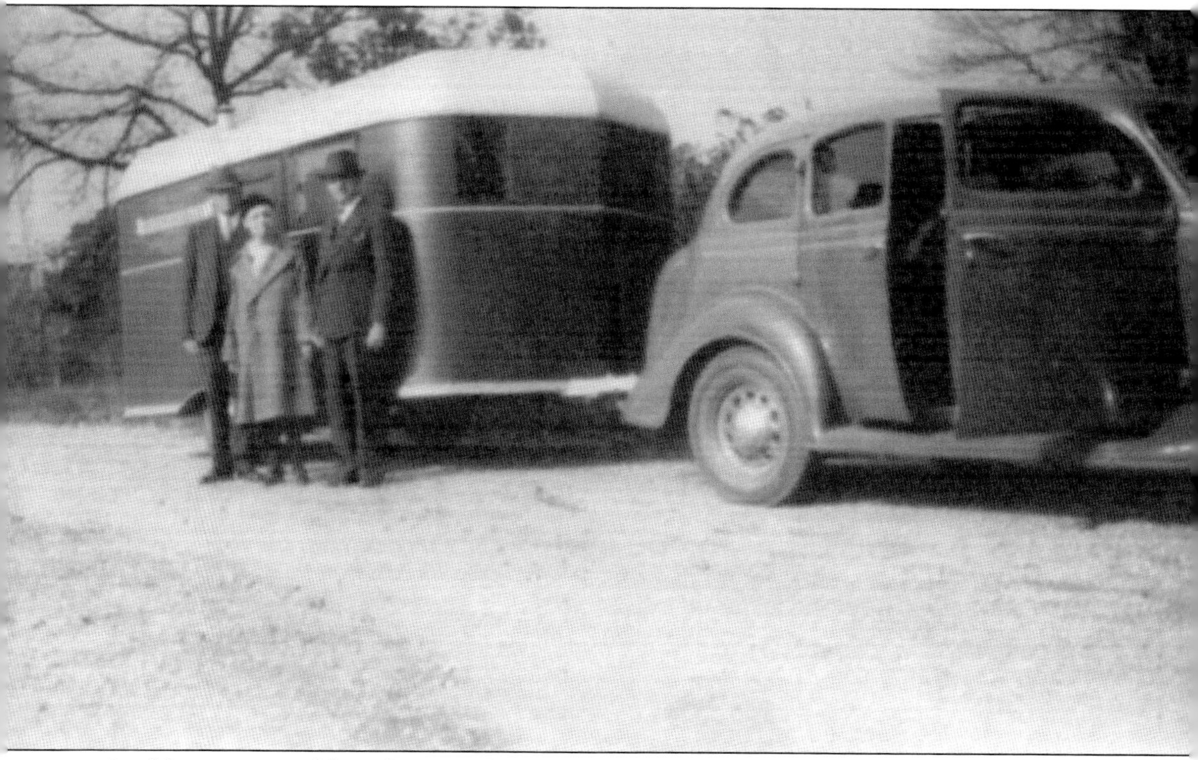

AN UNIDENTIFIED MAN, LOTTIE HART, AND NOBLE PUFFER. The first bookmobile in Cook County started in Palatine in 1936. Nobel Puffer was county superintendent of schools and a Palatine resident. He had found that children in rural schools did not read as well as those in city schools because they lacked books.

Having spent the summer pulling a trailer through the northwest, he conceived the idea of creating a library in a trailer. He received help from Lottie Hart, the Palatine librarian, and she accompanied him on his first trip to the 22 schools who had contributed $10 each to support the bookmobile.

Puffer pulled the trailer with his own car and, eventually, traveled to 61 one-room schools. The interior of the trailer was fitted with shelves of books, a small desk, and a charcoal stove for warmth. The program was discontinued in 1941 when gas rationing during World War II created problems.

Five

COMMERCIAL PALATINE

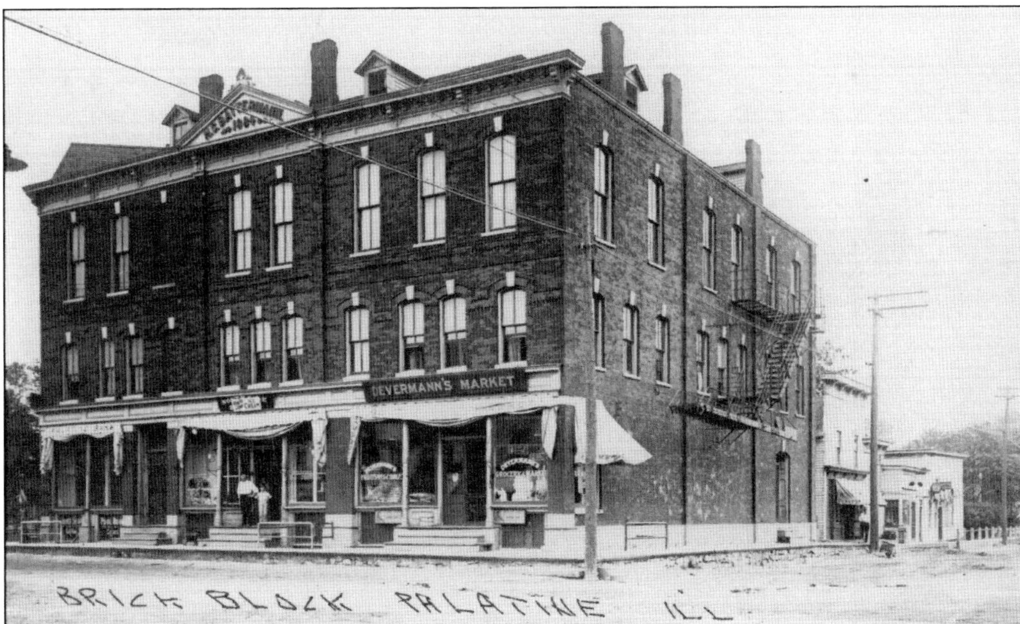

THE BATTERMAN BRICK BLOCK. In Palatine, the name Batterman meant the "Brick Block," a three-story building erected by Henry C. Batterman in 1894; it was the tallest building in the area. Batterman had come to Palatine in 1866 and began a grain and lumber business with John Slade. Later, with his son-in-law August Abelman and retired Lake County farmer Charles Ost, the firm operated grist, flax, and planing mills and a lumberyard on property south of Palatine Road and west of Greeley. When the mills burned down in 1892, the company moved next to the tracks, west of the Comfort and Sons lumber mill and grain elevator.

The Batterman Brick Block was situated on the triangle formed by Slade and Brockway Streets and the railroad tracks. The street level held retail stores and Charles Patten's Bank of Palatine. Offices and apartments were located on the second floor. On the third floor was the opera house, with a stage and dressing rooms. After a dinner in the old town hall, Palatine High School alumni would march in all their finery to the Batterman Building to enjoy the dance hall.

When Batterman died in 1902, his grandsons Drs. Henry and William Abelman inherited the property. A skating rink was opened in 1908 with 100 pairs of rental skates available for 25¢, and spectators paid 10¢. However, the building slowly deteriorated. It was razed in 1938. The triangle remained empty except for a temporary World War II Roll of Honor Roll board until 1962, when the First State Bank and Trust Company of Illinois opened its doors. The Palatine Firefighters Memorial now occupies the site.

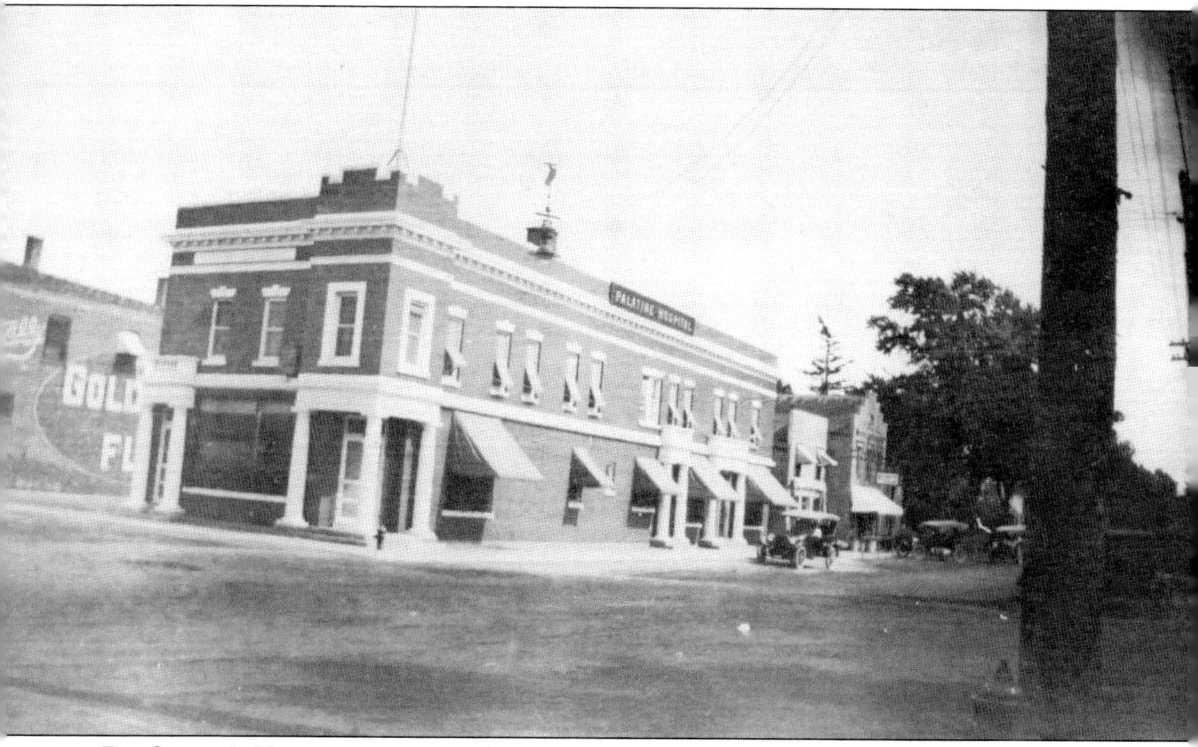

Dr. Starck's Hospital. C.A. Starck served as Palatine's doctor for more than 50 years. The son of a Long Grove minister, he had ridden his bike 14 miles every day in order to attend Palatine High School, graduating in 1900. A job driving a local doctor around and assisting him, led Starck to the College of Physicians and Surgeons of the University of Illinois.

After graduation in 1904 and a year spent practicing with another physician, Dr. Starck opened his own office in Palatine. He rented rooms, which he shared with a dentist, on the second floor of Mosser Drugs, making for a crowded office. Starck purchased the wooden Kunze Saloon building on the southeast corner of Slade and Brockway Streets in 1916.

After extensive remodeling, which included bricking the building and finishing a second floor, Dr. Starck's Palatine Community Hospital opened on January 1, 1919. The first floor was occupied by the State Bank of Palatine, the Chicago Telephone Co., and the post office.

A private entrance led to the hospital upstairs. The facility had a sun parlor, 10 beds with private closets, a kitchen, and a single-line telephone. The operating room had natural and artificial light, a sterilizer, an X-ray machine, and a laboratory with drugs. Dr. Starck also conducted a training school for nurses.

The hospital closed in 1950 because of a lack of nurses. The building has had many tenants since then.

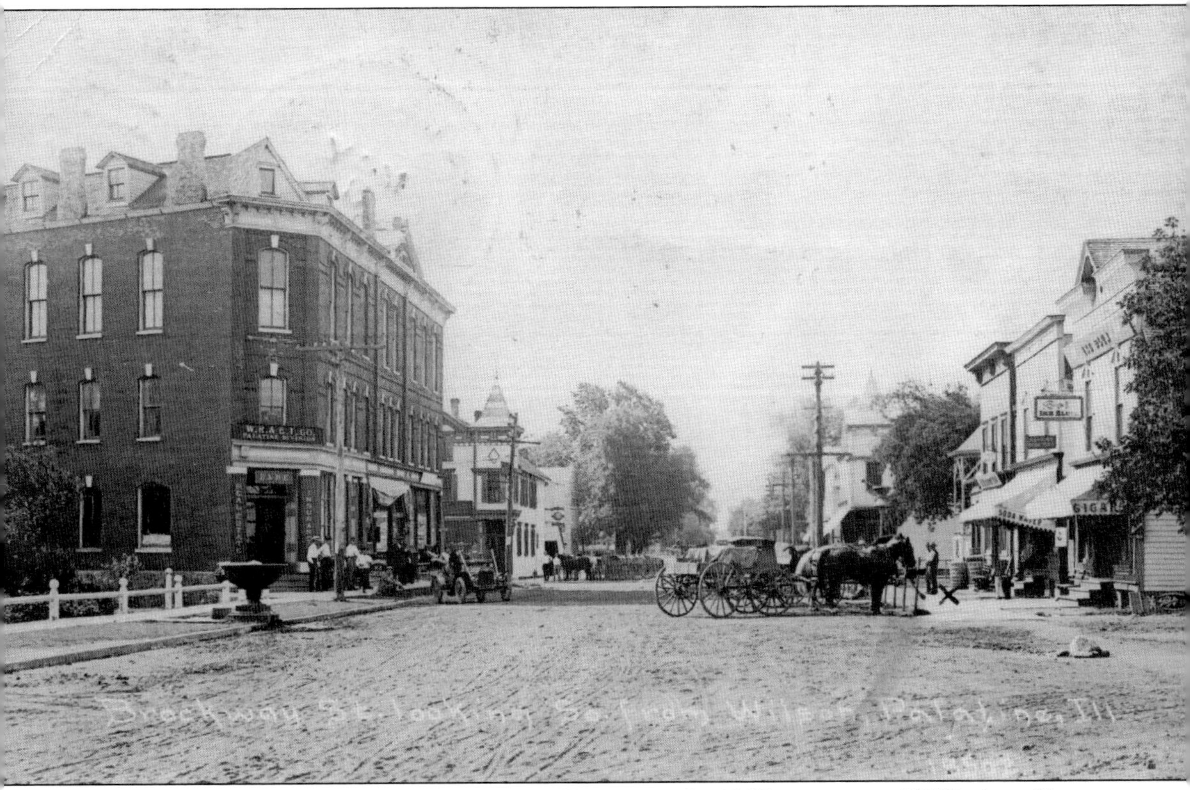

FOUNTAIN ON LEFT IN FRONT OF BATTERMAN BUILDING. In 1907, at a cost of $175, the village installed a public water fountain on Brockway Street just west of Railroad Park near the Batterman Building.

It stood four feet, three inches high, allowing horses to drink without unhitching. The main bowl was four feet, seven inches across and 17 inches deep.

A small bowl on the side accommodated children and pedestrians; this meant that their drinking cups would never have contact with the main bowl. A dog bowl was near the base.

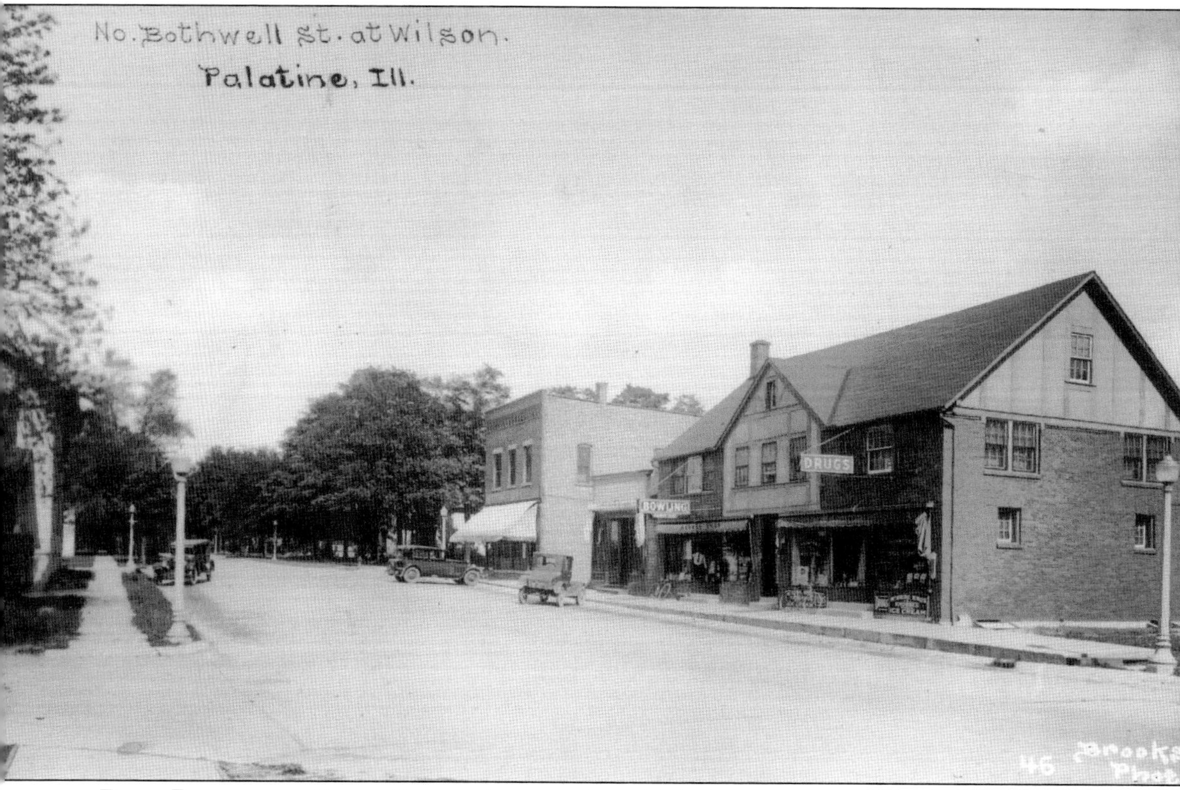

DINSE BUILDING ON RIGHT FRONT. A generation of Palatine young people have memories of the old Durty Nellie's on North Bothwell Street, which was replaced by the Providence Condominiums in 2006. But there is a much longer history to the building.

Ira Fry moved his livery stable to the site in 1901. His son Fred took over when Ira died in 1906, but there are no records of a business there from 1910 to 1924.

Charles Dinse had a barbershop and poolroom in 1916 in the basement of the three-story Batterman Block. In 1924, he converted the Fry stable into a structure that would remain until 2006. The building held Dinse's barbershop and pool hall, a confectionery and ice-cream parlor, and a bowling alley to the rear. Upstairs, his family lived in a seven-room apartment.

Dinse retired in 1945 and sold the building to Ed Brockman, who operated it as the Palatine Recreation Center before selling it to Jack Wilcox in 1947. Wilcox added a cocktail lounge, a restaurant, and a liquor store. He closed the ice-cream parlor and barbershop and later, the bowling alley, and his family lived upstairs until the early 1970s, when it became Durty Nellie's Irish Pub.

In November 1948, Wilcox had opened a bookie station above the lounge, which was raided the day it officially opened. He abandoned that idea.

A lot of boozers came to Jack's. One night a big, tough construction worker started a fight, and a couple of cops tried to arrest him. He took their guns away and threw them out on the tracks.

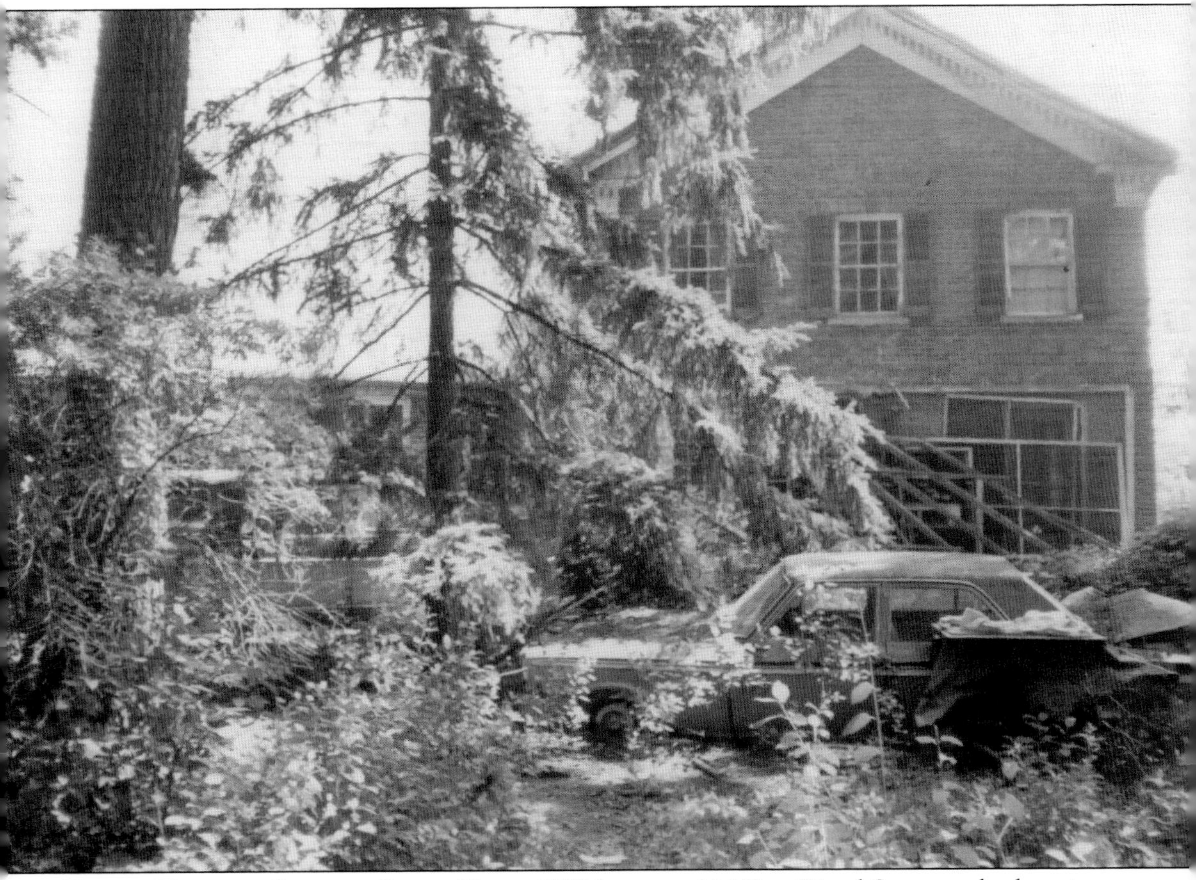

KITSON HOME ON QUENTIN ROAD. The c. 1870 house at 104 East Wood Street and others in Palatine are made of the soft, unusual-colored Kitson bricks, which were manufactured locally.

John and Ann Kitson came to the United States from England and, in the late 1840s, settled on a farm in Palatine with their nine children. John Kitson had learned the pottery trade in England, and with his sons' help, he ran a brickyard on the west side of Quentin Road, north of Palatine Road. He also owned 160 acres southwest of Palatine and Quentin Roads and 80 acres southeast of the same corner.

The family lived in a tent until they were able to produce the bricks to build their own house at 32 North Quentin Road in 1851, and family members lived in the house until 1927.

As a boy, Avery Wolfrum came to live in the house with his parents and remained there until his death in 1990. The house was torn down years ago, but Wolfrum described in detail the character, color, and size of the bricks, the house itself, the location of the Kitsons' properties, and the buildings. There is a Kitson brick in the archival files of the Palatine Historical Society.

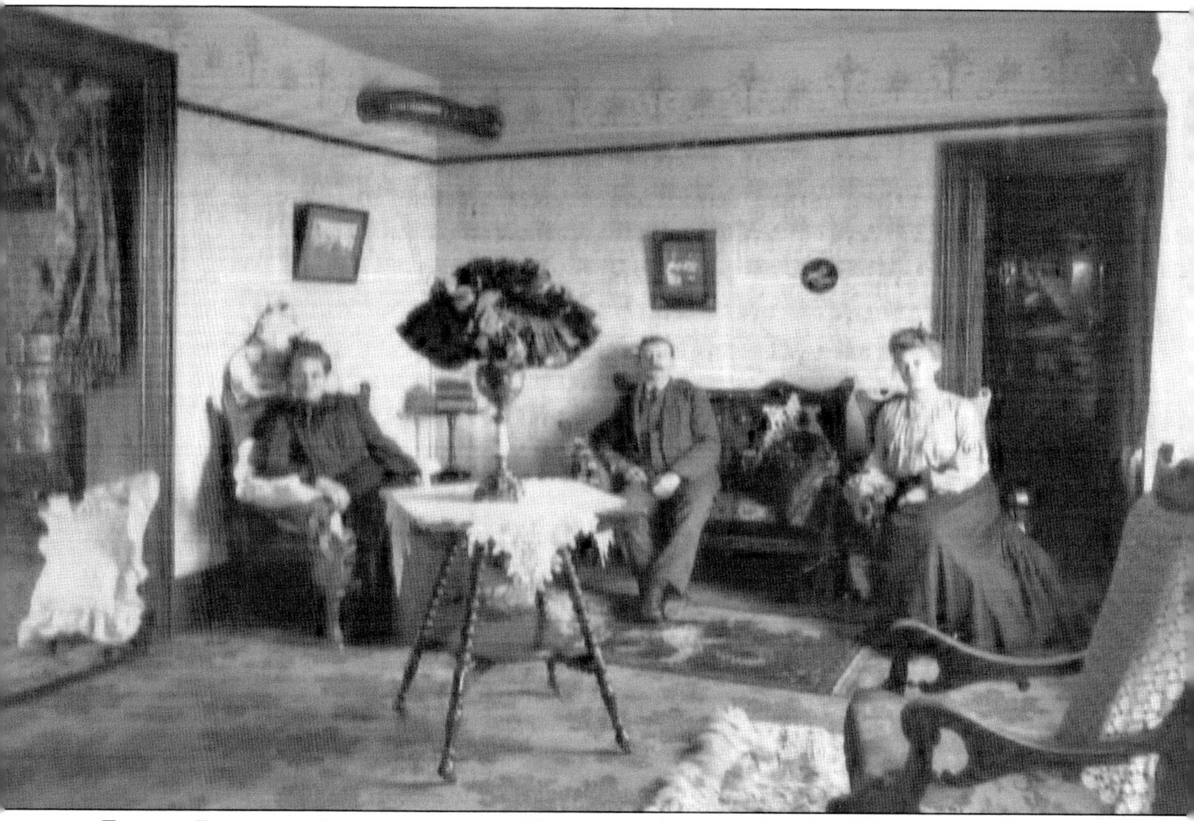

Zimmer Family in Apartment over Hardware Store. The oldest continuous business in Palatine, Zimmer Hardware, was founded in 1883 by Albert Zimmer at the corner of Bothwell and Slade Streets and moved a little later to its present location at 18 North Brockway Street. Albert Zimmer was born in Wheeling in 1856 and apprenticed as a tinsmith. The Zimmer family lived in the apartment above the store.

After his death, the hardware store was operated by his stepdaughter Lydia Wienecke and her nephew Howard Freeman until Lydia's death in 1958. The Freemans continued to live above the store and run the business until it was sold to Mike Lemonidis and Dick Brumm in 1972.

Nancy Martino purchased the store in 1996, even though it was a new type of venture for her. The building has been remodeled and enlarged over the years, but it still retains some of its old-time features such as a wooden elevator and squeaky wood floors. In October 2000, Zimmer Hardware was honored as one of the "Retailers of the 20th Century" by the Illinois Retail Merchants Association.

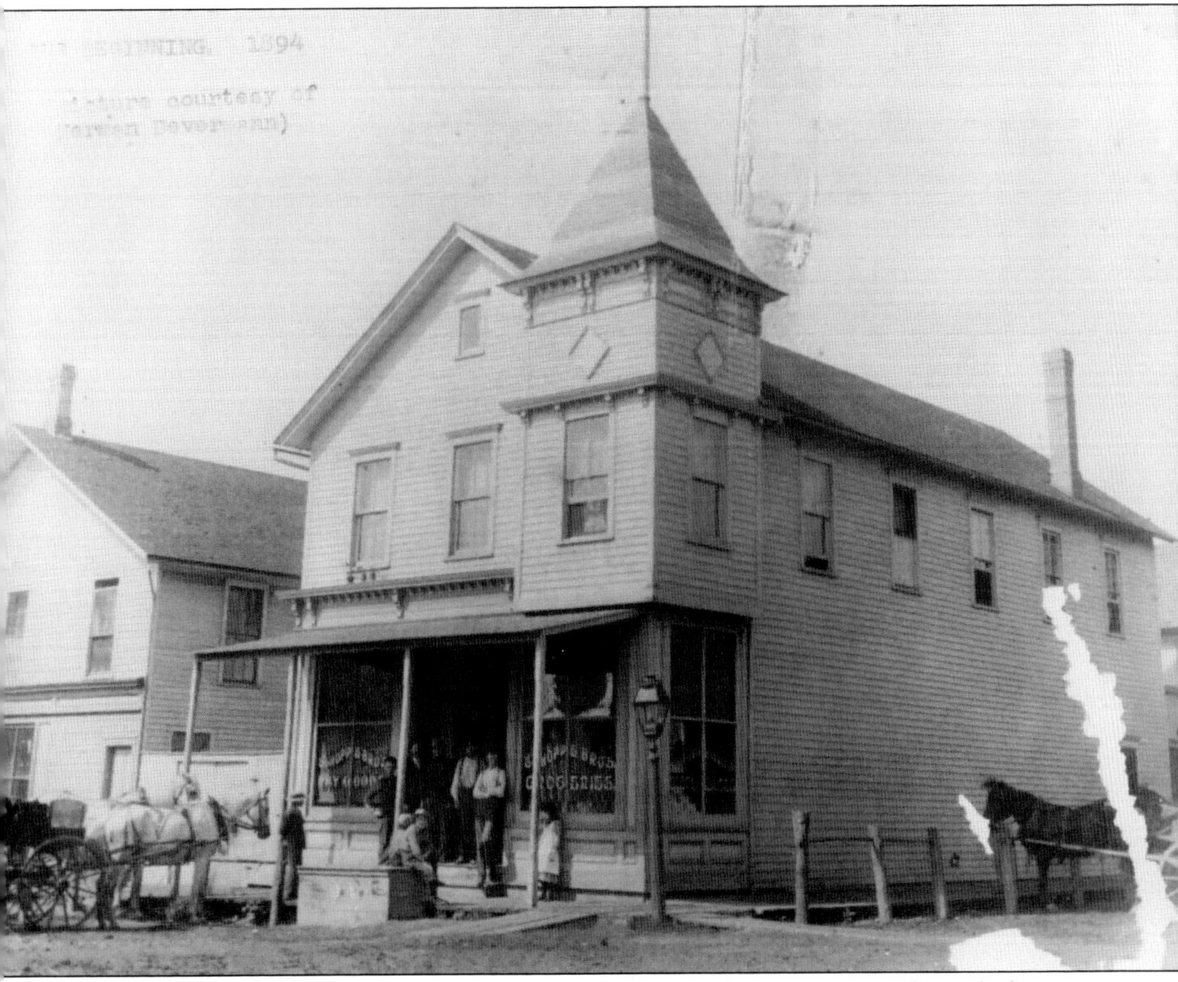

SCHOPPE BROTHERS BEFORE 1901. When Harry Schoppe died in 1966, it was the end of an era of old-timers gathering around a potbellied stove and dipping into the tobacco container to light their pipes.

Brothers Louis and Harry Schoppe opened their store in 1892, catering to farmers seven days a week. The wooden building on the southwest corner of Brockway and Slade Streets carried a variety of goods, even farm equipment. Groceries were part of the inventory until 1944. A two-story addition with basement was added to the south in 1901. Also, a gas plant with 33 gas jets to light the store at night was installed.

Louis died in 1944, but Harry ran the store until his death, and his daughter Helen operated it for one more year before closing in 1967.

Harry was a volunteer fireman and a trombone player in the Palatine Military Band. Robert Paddock of Paddock Publications recalls Harry and Louis Schoppe handing out ice-cream cones at the band concerts. Both the fire chief and police chief at the time of Harry's death recalled as kids "old man Schoppe" giving them candy. Harry's business card read, "Harry Schoppe, old-timer, no business, no money, lots of time, lots of friends."

When it burned to the ground in 1970, the building housed 26 North Mod Shop. It has been replaced by a brick structure.

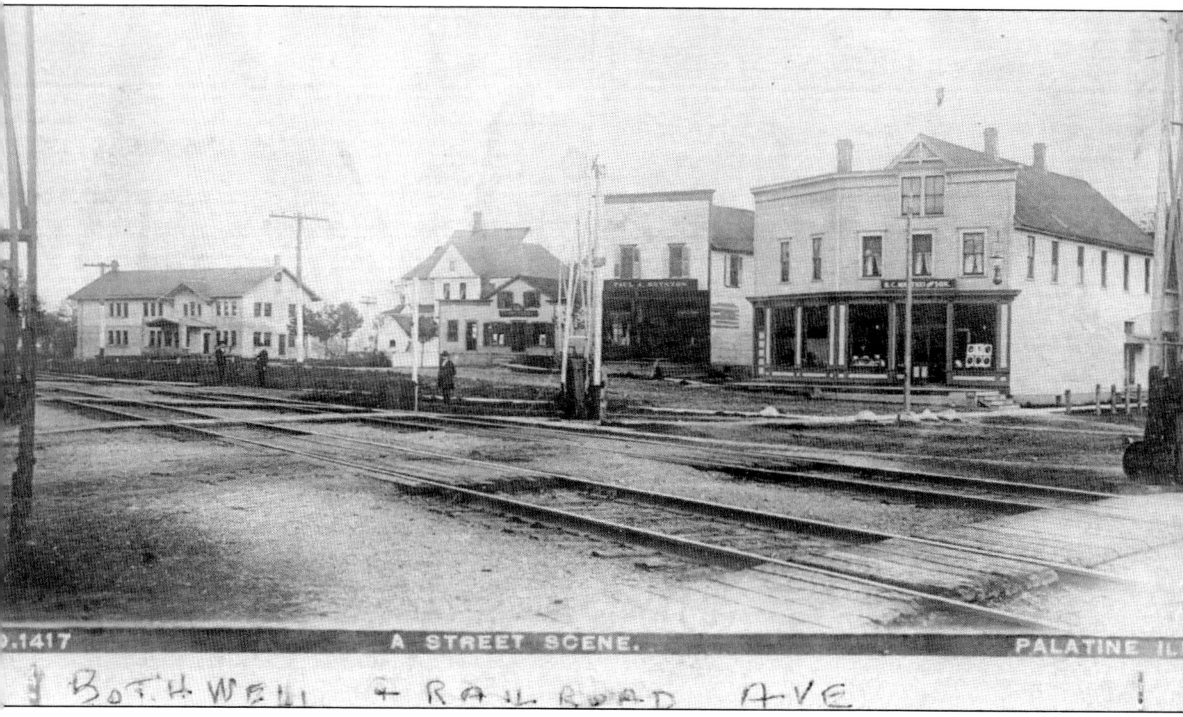

MATTHEI'S GENERAL STORE ON RIGHT. Henry C. Matthei came to Chicago from Germany as a boy. A visit to his sister Henrietta Schierding, wife of J.H. Schierding, brought him to Palatine, where he met his future bride, Emma Sutherland. In 1869, Henry went into business with his brother-in-law Henry Scherding and, later, his nephew J.H. ? in a store at the southwest corner of Brockway and Slade Streets.

Henry purchased his partners' interest in 1873 and built the Matthei General Store at the corner of Bothwell and Railroad Streets, which he remodeled and enlarged in 1901. On his retirement, he turned the store over to his sons George and Philip, who operated it until 1937. Paul and Irene Wilson bought the building in 1940 and opened Wilson's Ben Franklin.

Stanley Pepper acquired the location, razed the wooden building, and erected the Pepper Block in 1947, which opened with 13 stores in 1948.

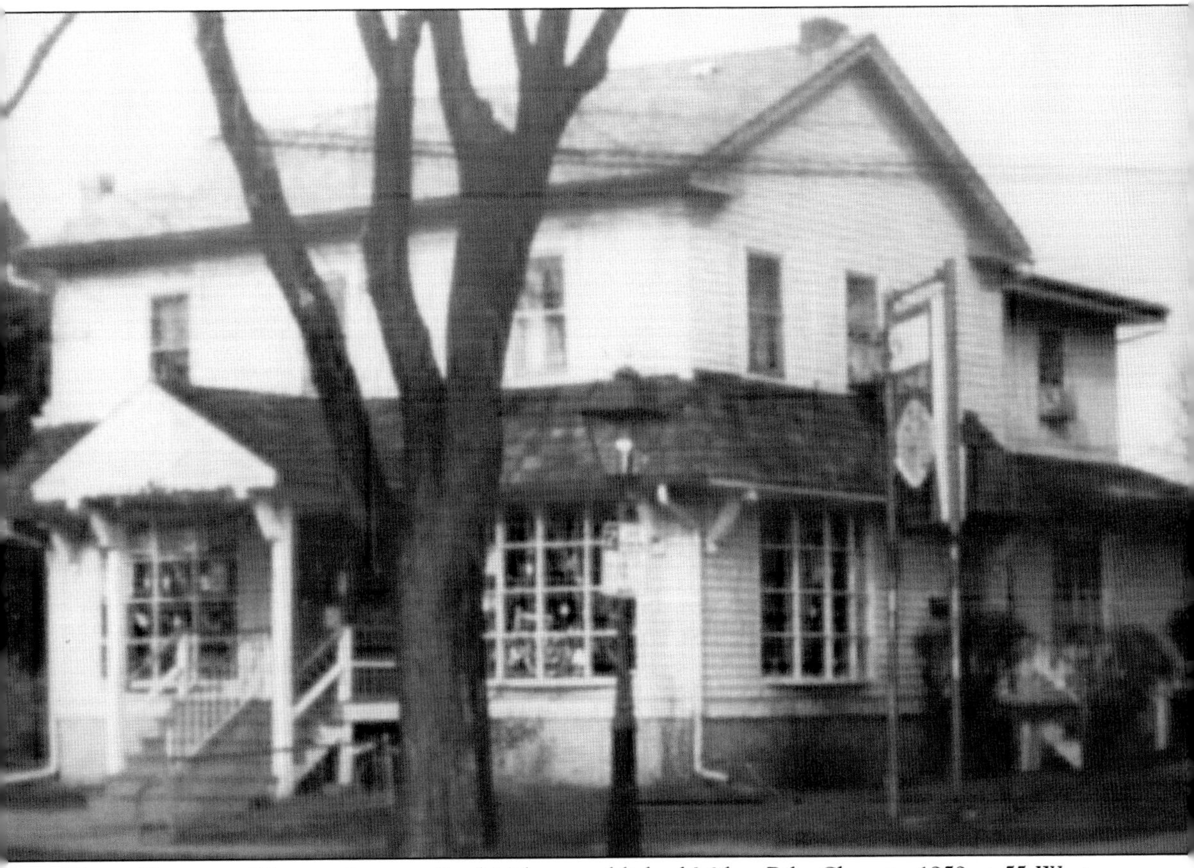

MIKES BIKES ON WILSON STREET. Fred Mikes established Mikes Bike Shop in 1959 at 55 West Wood Street when he bought the business from Gil Smith, who had another job and only operated the store part-time.

Customer service was Fred's main priority from the start. He had been trained as an auto mechanic after high school, and was trained as an aircraft mechanic during World War II.

People were amazed that Fred was going to have regular business hours for a bike shop. At first, the business did not provide a living, so Fred started to repair other things, and his wife, Harriet, went to work to help the family.

By 1965, bikes were becoming very popular and business improved. Fred and Harriet Mikes decided to sell their house in Bensenville and were able to buy a building at 36 West Wilson. In this very old house, the first floor had been turned into a shop and the upstairs was an apartment for the Mikes family.

Fred's son Wayne bought the business from his father in 1979. Wayne moved Mikes Bike Shop to 155 North Northwest Highway in November 1987 to increase visibility. Wayne's son Matt also works at the shop.

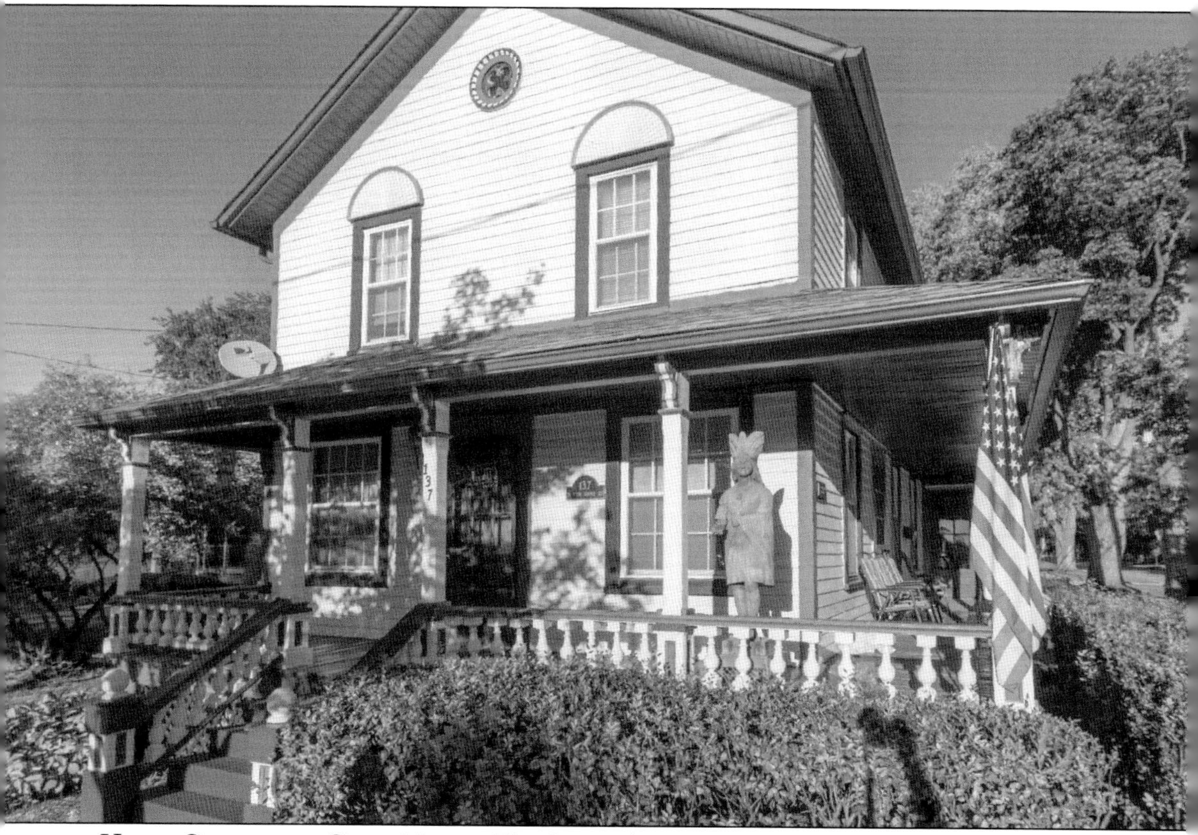

HENRY GODKNECHT, CIGAR MAKER. The Great Chicago Fire of 1871 brought Henry Godknecht to Palatine. He had been making and selling cigars in Chicago. After the fire, he needed a new location. His friend Ernest Prellberg, a Palatine tailor, offered him working space, so Henry moved his business to Palatine.

In 1873, Henry built a house at the northeast corner of Plum Grove Road and Wood Street. The family lived in the back of the house with a separate entrance. The two front rooms were used to hand-roll and sell cigars. Customers entered through the front door, walking past the "Pocahontas" cigar-store Indian statue that stood on the porch. At the time, images of Indians were used in advertisements for cigar shops.

Henry died in 1915, and his wife, Margaret, passed away in 1931. Their son Adolph Godknecht remained in town and served as mayor of Palatine. Their daughter Margaret lived in the house until her death in 1974. At that time, 100 years of artifacts and memories were auctioned off. Some of those artifacts, including the wooden Indian, were donated to the Clayson House Museum.

Thanks to the current owners, Michael and Rita Brzezinski, the house looks much as it did in the 1880s. Rita always refers to the room where Henry Godknecht rolled his cigars as the "rolling room."

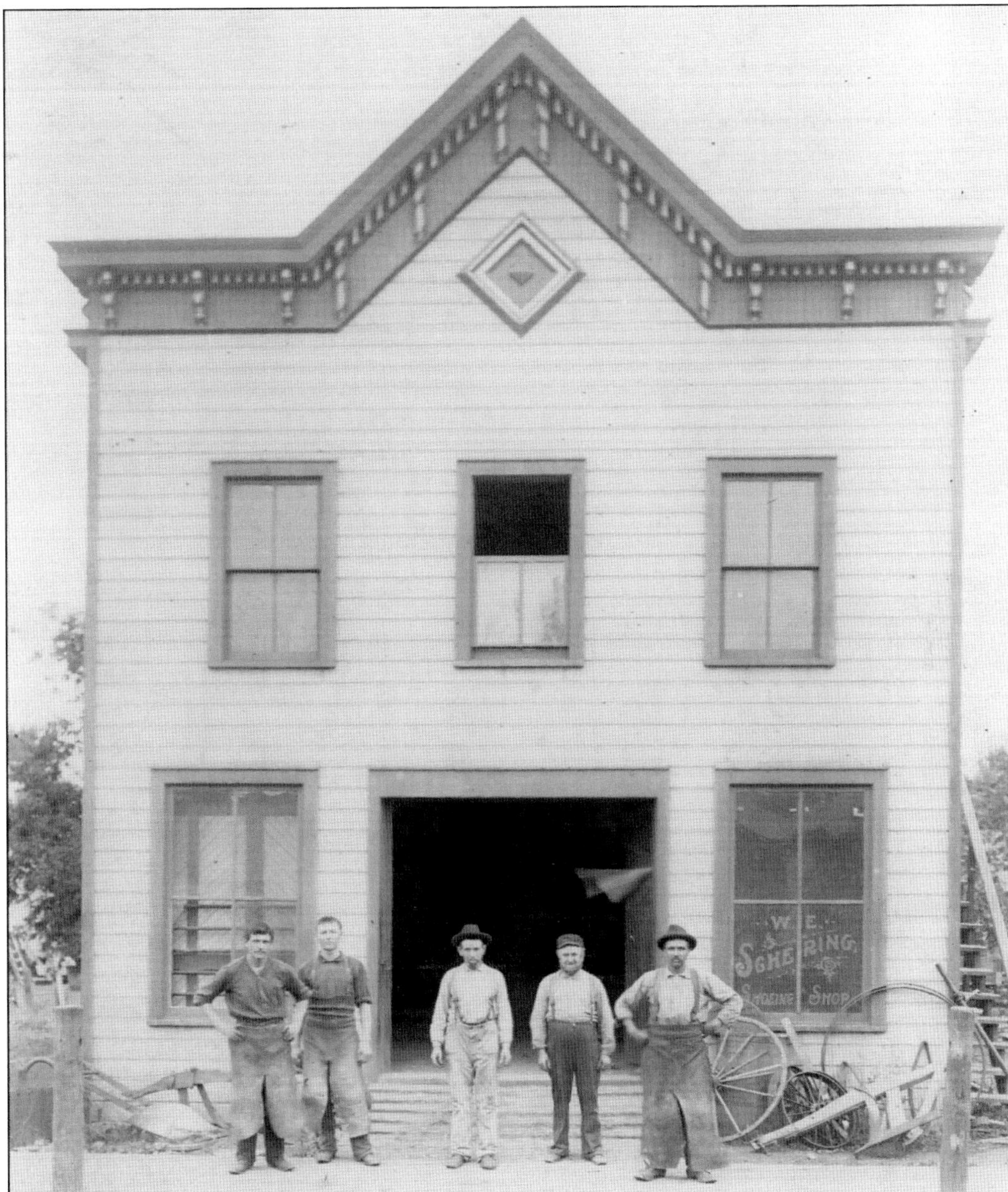

LOUIS NERGE, ELMER PETERSON, AUGUST KIMMET, CHRIS SCHERING, AND WILLIAM SCHERING (LEFT TO RIGHT). William Schering was born in Germany and came to Palatine in 1881. He served a blacksmith apprenticeship under Fred Harz. Later, he bought the Luerssen Blacksmith Shop on Slade Street. Schering raised the building 2.5 feet and the sidewalk a foot so people did not have to wade through six inches of water during heavy rains.

Schering shoed horses for the Cook County Fair in Palatine from 1914 to 1928. He also worked for farmers and the carriage trade, averaging about 58 shoes per day at 20¢ per shoe. Racehorse shoes were more expensive. On his best day, he fitted 108 shoes. When he retired in 1953 at age 85, Schering was the oldest active blacksmith in Illinois.

In 2001, the Music Store on Slade Street expanded into the former Schering shop. After the stripping away of three false ceilings and walls, remnants were found of the blacksmith shop.

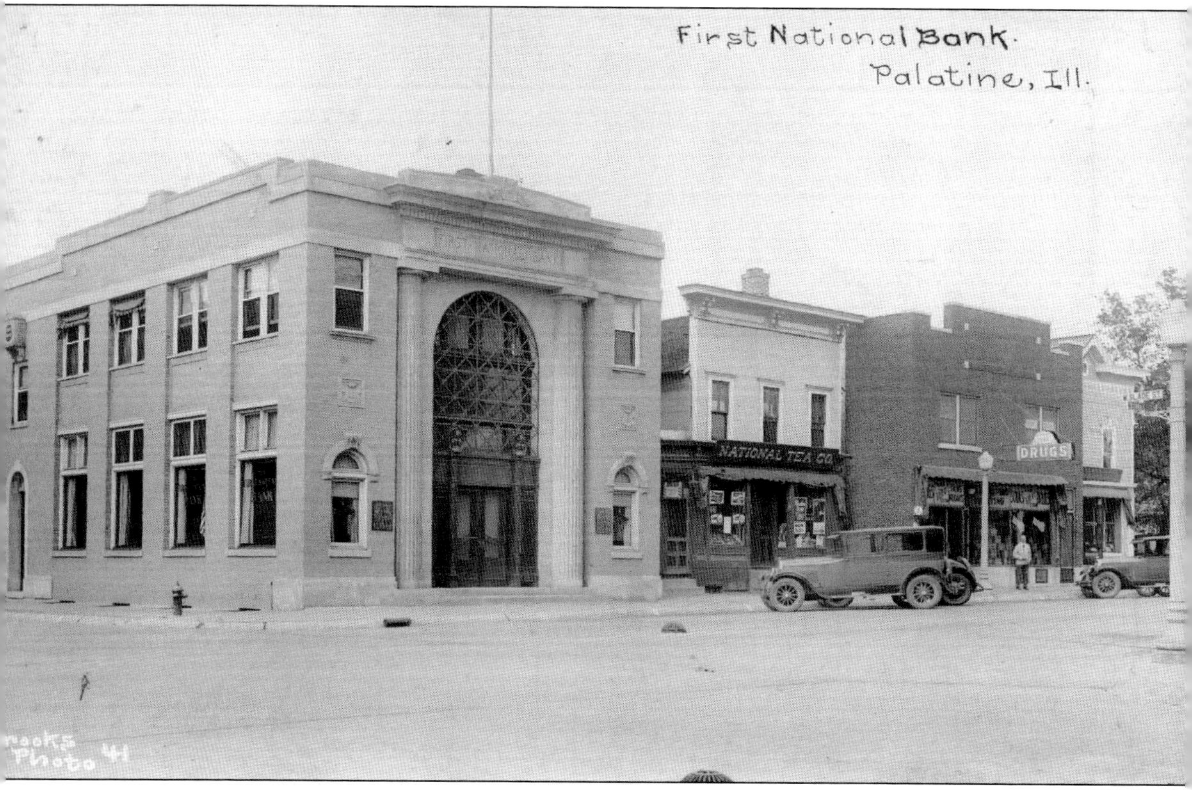

First National Bank of Palatine. Organization of the First National Bank of Palatine (left) began at a meeting on January 25, 1921, soon after the closing of Charles H. Patten's Bank of Palatine. The new bank purchased Patten's equipment, including his lease in the Batterman Building and the Patten property on the northwest corner of Brockway and Slade Streets where the bandstand stood.

The "magnificent new bank building," as described by the *Enterprise*, opened May 9, 1925. Features of the bank included two electrically protected vaults, one with "invincible" safety deposit boxes, a drinking fountain on the main floor, and two offices and reception room on the second floor.

The bank prospered until the stock market crash of 1929. Steady and continued drain of withdrawals caused the bank to suspend operation on January 30, 1932. The situation was not helped when it was revealed that Pres. Ralph L. Peck had embezzled $25,000 by converting principal and interest on mortgages received by the bank to his own use.

A new Palatine National Bank was formed in 1944 and moved into the 1925 facility where it remained until 1968, when the present building was erected on the site of the Comfort and Sons lumber mill and grain elevator. Today, the bank's name is BMO Harris Bank. The site of the 1925 bank is now a parking lot.

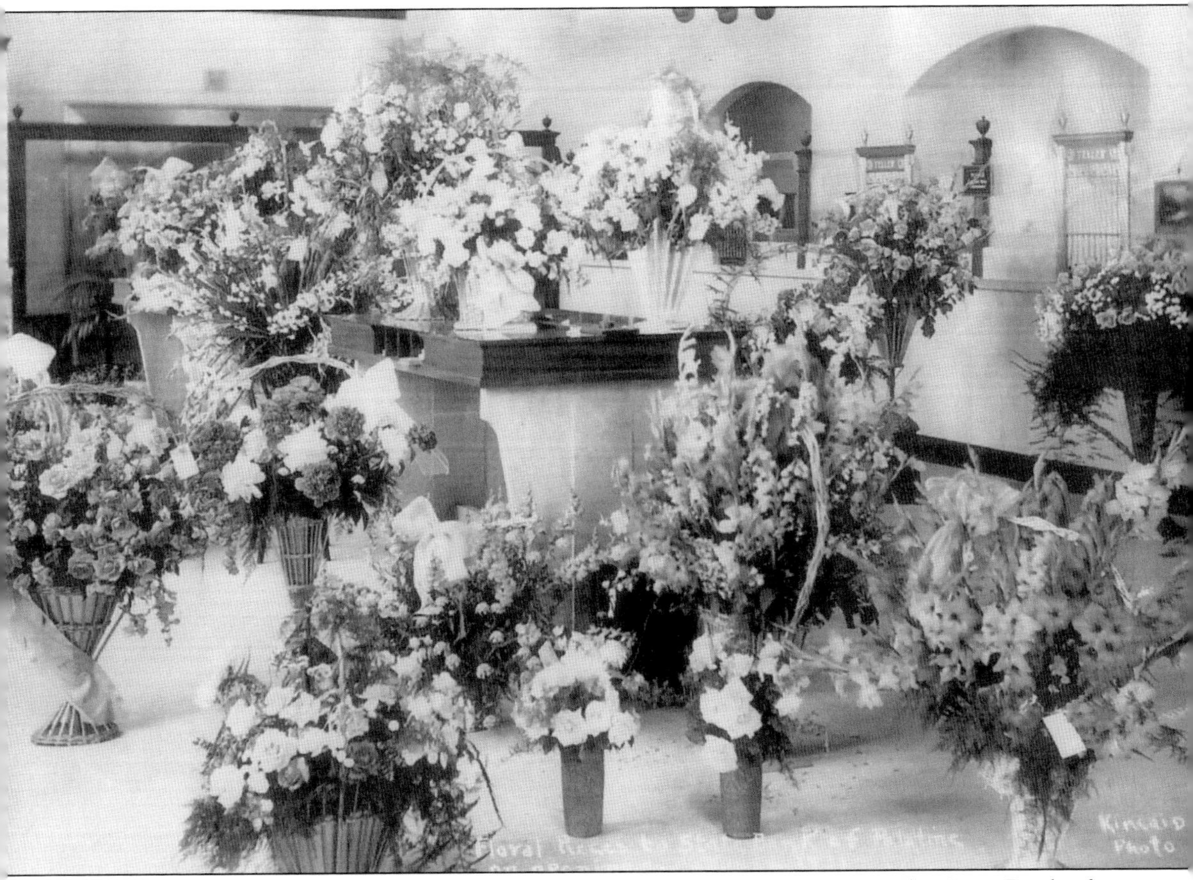

Flower Display at Opening of State Bank of Palatine, June 6, 1931. The State Bank of Palatine was organized March 25, 1919. It was located on the first floor of the extensively remodeled Kunze Tavern on the southeast corner of Slade and Brockway Streets, which has become known as the Starck Building. Dr. Starck's hospital on the second floor was entered from Brockway Street. Dr. Starck boasted that he provided the bank with the latest and finest furnishings.

The bank outgrew the Starck Building and prospered despite the Depression. On June 6, 1931, it celebrated the grand opening of its new building on the southwest corner of Slade and Bothwell Streets. Mosser Drug had been moved from the site, with the top half of the building going to Easy Street as a home. The lobby was decorated with an abundance of floral arrangements provided by the Palatine Village Garden Club.

In less than a year, the bank began faltering. On July 14, 1932, the State Bank of Palatine was closed temporarily for an examination by the state auditor. It never reopened. Attempts were made to salvage the bank, but on August 11, 1933, a receiver had been appointed with the intention of liquidating the State Bank of Palatine.

The building is still standing and has had many other uses.

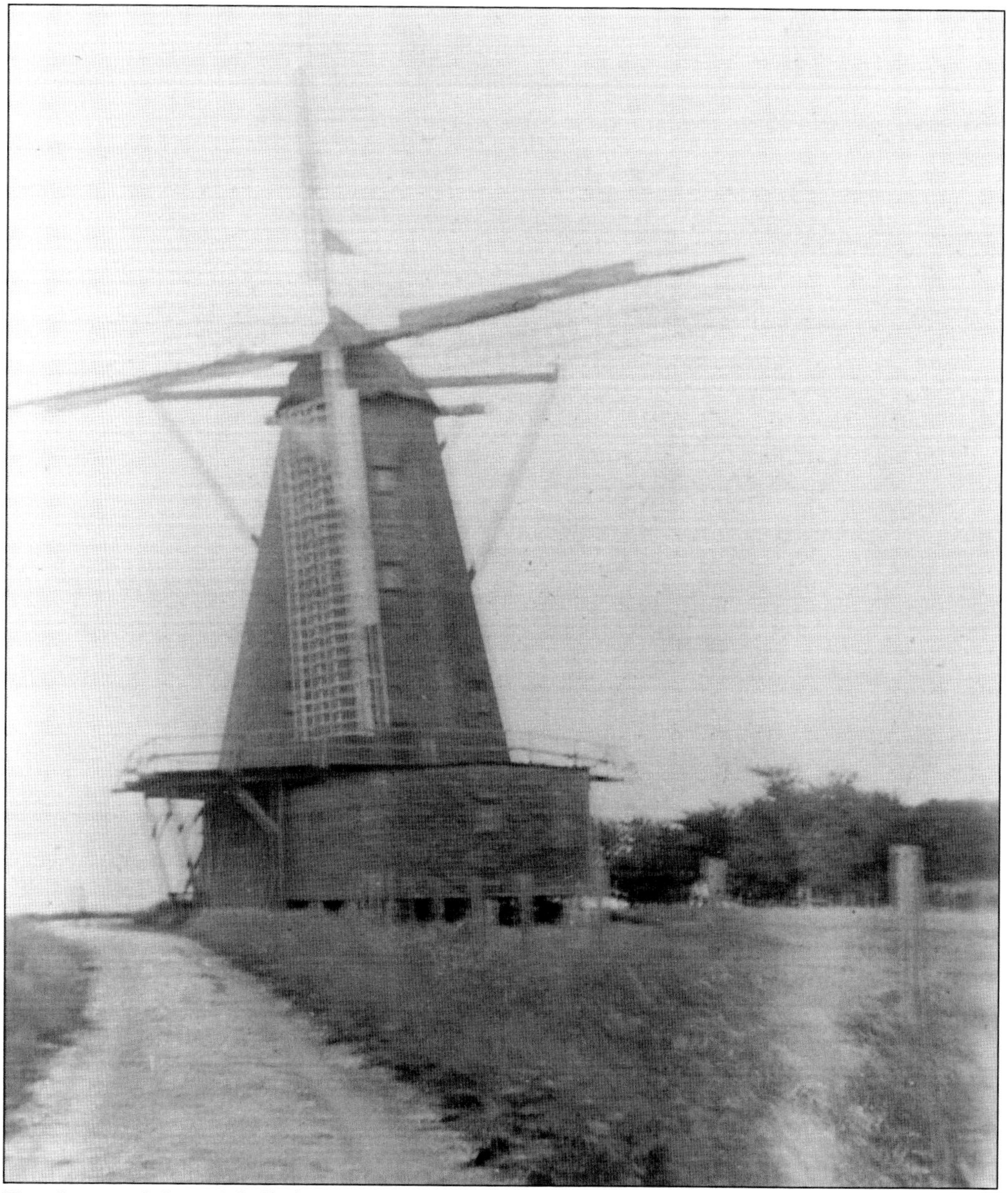

The Jahnke Mill. Of all the mills in Palatine in the 19th century, the most fascinating for children was the Jahnke Windmill. William Jahnke and his wife, Elise, came from Mecklenberg, Germany. He built the house and the mill, which was located about 200 feet behind the house in 1879 at Benton at Sherman Streets. Jahnke operated the mill for 15 years until the family moved to Chicago in 1895.

The mill was on a barren knoll on a dead-end road that was very muddy in the spring. Horse-drawn wagons loaded with grain moved to the platform where "the dusty miller" helped them unload. When a strong wind blew from any direction, the fans would go lickety-split.

The mill was dismantled in 1894 when the area was developed. The site of the mill has become the lovely garden of the 1940 Clarence Comfort house at 308 North Fremont. Clarence Comfort married Cora, Jahnke's granddaughter.

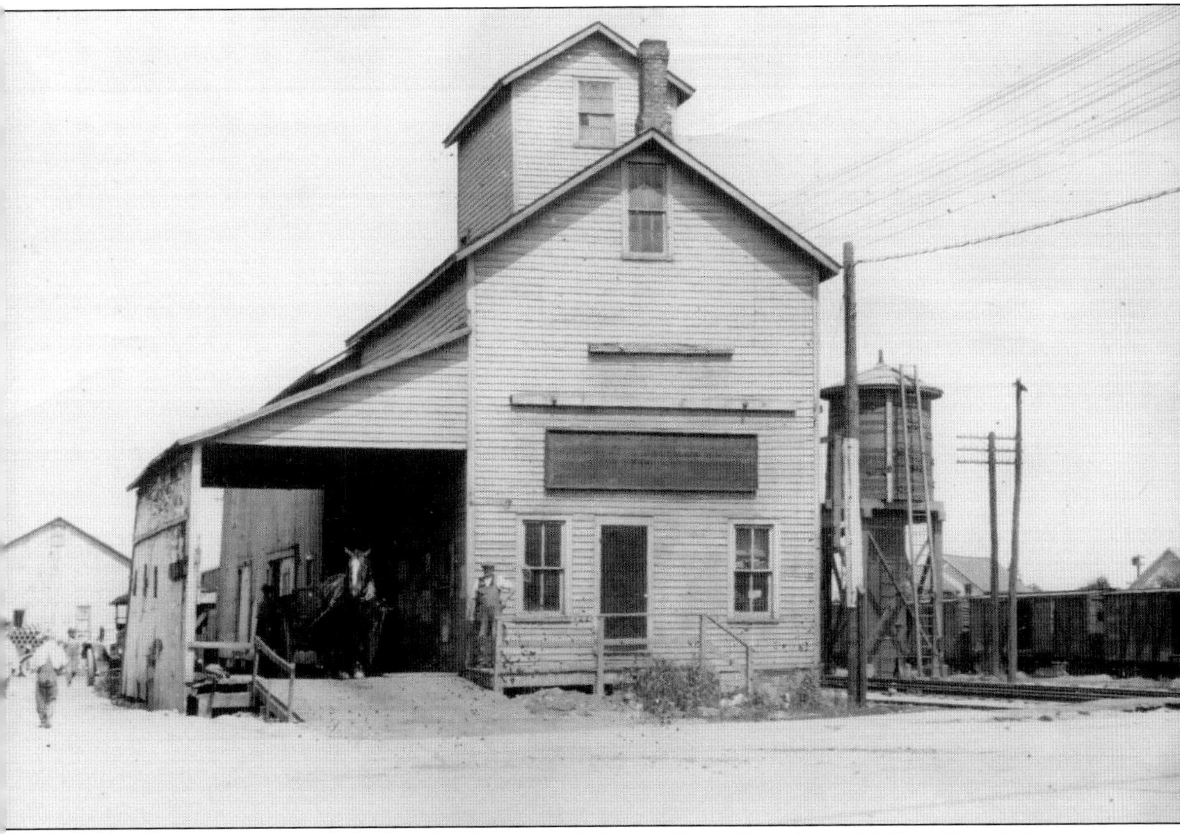

COMFORT AND SONS. Josiah Comfort came to Palatine from Canada in 1855 and settled on a farm northeast of town. His son Wesley Comfort married Emily Slade, the granddaughter of John Slade, who had arrived in Plum Grove in 1838 with several other pioneer families from Stockbridge, Vermont.

W.R. Comfort Sons was established in 1874 as Comfort and Slade by Wesley Comfort and his father-in-law, Joseph Slade. They operated a lumber mill and grain elevator next to the railroad tracks at Brockway Street. Farmers brought loads of wheat, corn, and barley for processing. A blindfolded horse traveling in a circle operated belts, which lifted the grain and stored it in bins to be shipped to market by Comfort when the price seemed right.

Wesley Comfort's sons Wesley Jr. and Clarence continued operating the business after his death. In 1929, they built a modern brick building as an office on their property. In 1968, Palatine National Bank (now BMO Harris Bank) razed the lumberyard facilities and built the present white marble bank building.

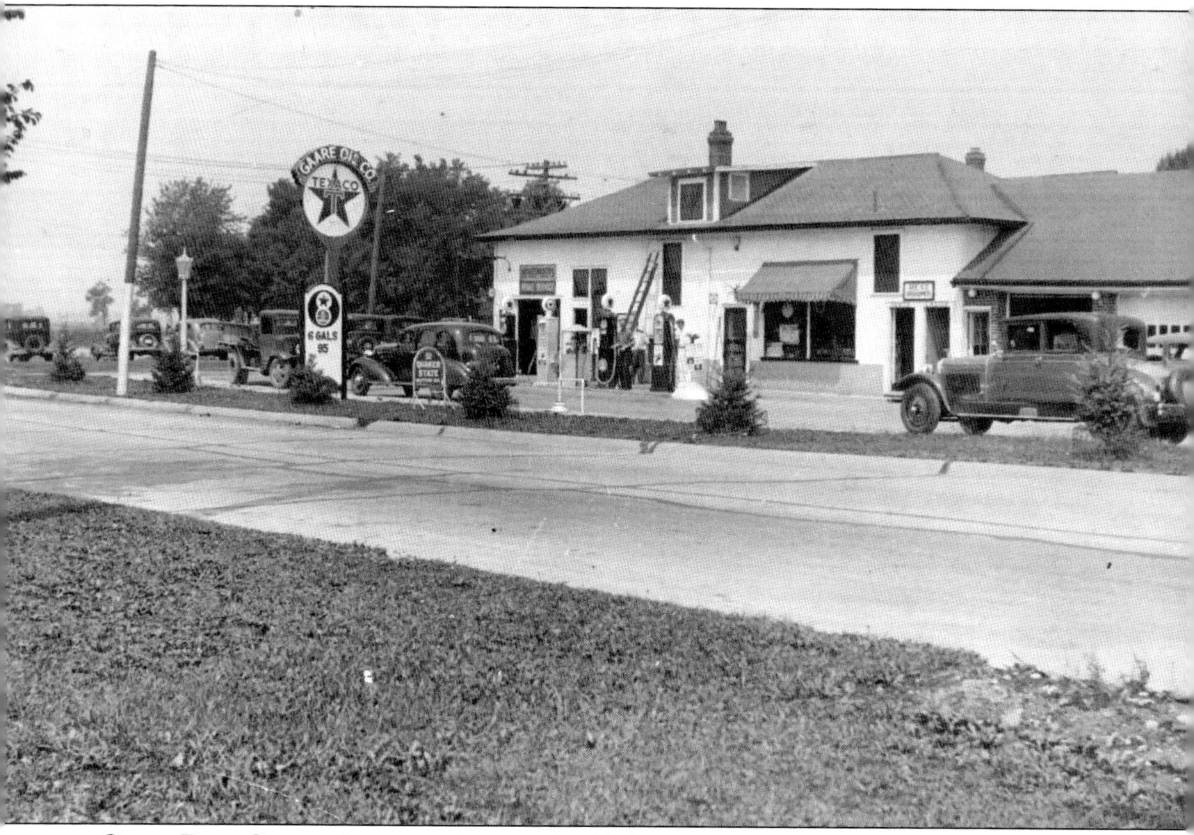

GAARE DAISY SERVICE STATION. Henry and Wilhelmina Gaare, originally from Germany, arrived in Palatine in 1901. He was a janitor at St. Paul Church. Their sons Charles and William "Bill" and two daughters, Elsie and Clare, remained in Palatine. Charles was a painter and decorator, sexton of Hillside Cemetery, and also worked for Bowman Dairy. Bill Gaare was employed by Comfort and Sons Lumber Company, the Cook County Highway Department, and Hines Lumber Company. He served as fire chief from 1949 to 1953.

The Gaare family lived and owned land on Smith Street, south of Hillside Cemetery. When Northwest Highway was routed down Colfax Street in 1925, the family built a Texaco service station, known as the Gaare Daisy Service Station. Henry's son Otto operated the station until he moved to Arizona in 1945.

Other operators ran a service station on the corner until the 1980s, when Total Auto Parts erected a building that later became NAPA Auto Parts. The Metropolitan Condominium now occupies the site.

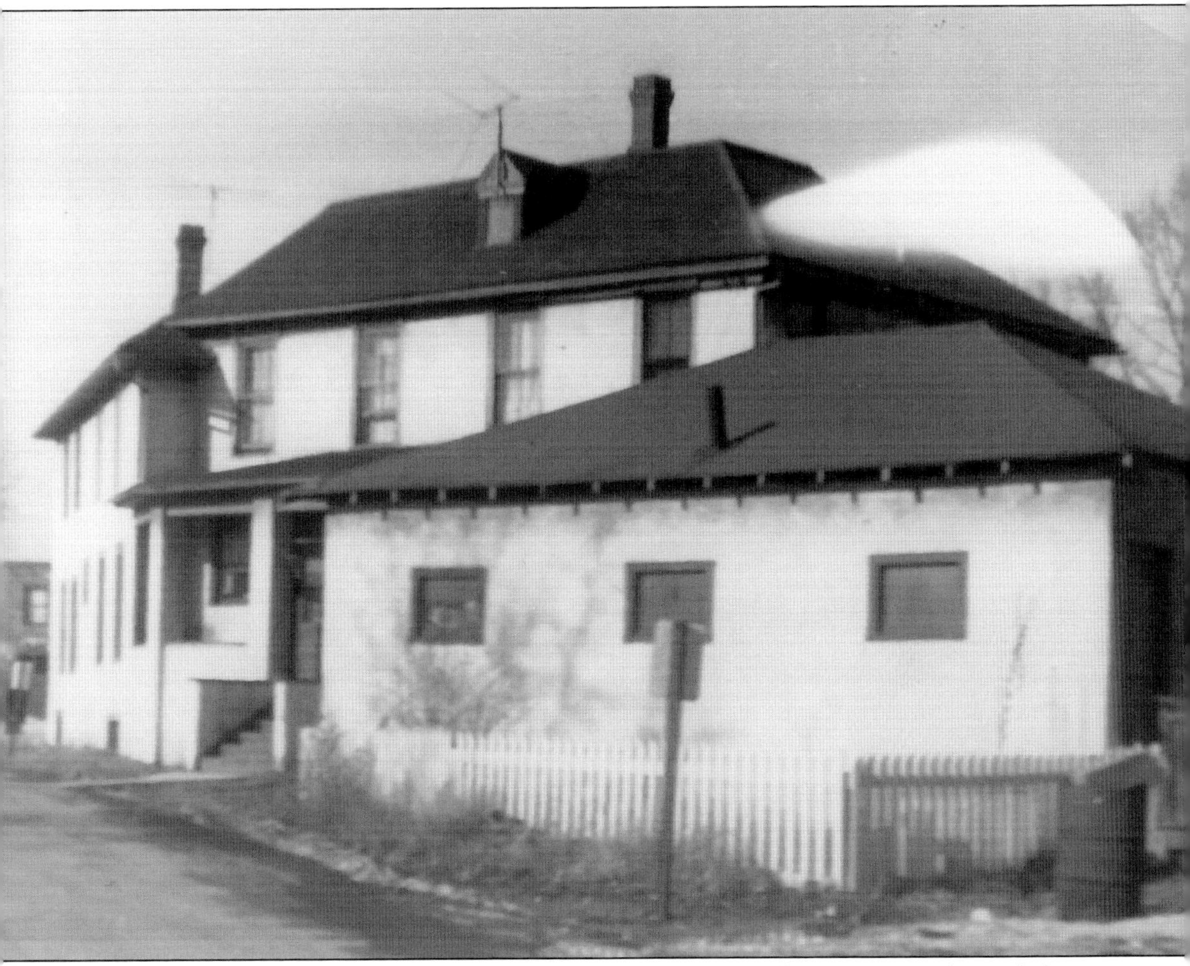

The Kuebler/Hunnerberg Hotel. The plot of land facing Railroad Avenue west of Lamplighter Inn was originally sold by Joel Wood in 1855 to Morgan Johnson who built a store. Rose Kuebler purchased the property as a hotel in 1867. She sold it to William Hunnerberg in 1879, and he and his wife, Elizabeth, ran the hotel until 1921.

There was a stable at the east end with a large hall upstairs used for dances, parties, and meetings. A tavern/restaurant was located at the west end. Older men often met there to play cards and have a drink or two, but no man was allowed to become drunk.

The hotel was filled most of the time with telephone linemen, railroad builders, and salesmen—also known as drummers, who used the hotel as their temporary headquarters while covering the surrounding area via wagons, buggies, and horseback. Mrs. Hunnerberg's reputation for cooking was renowned, and a guest could stay from Monday to Friday for $3 including meals.

The building has had various tenants, and in 1999, it was remodeled. Since then, there has been some kind of restaurant in the west corner of the triangle.

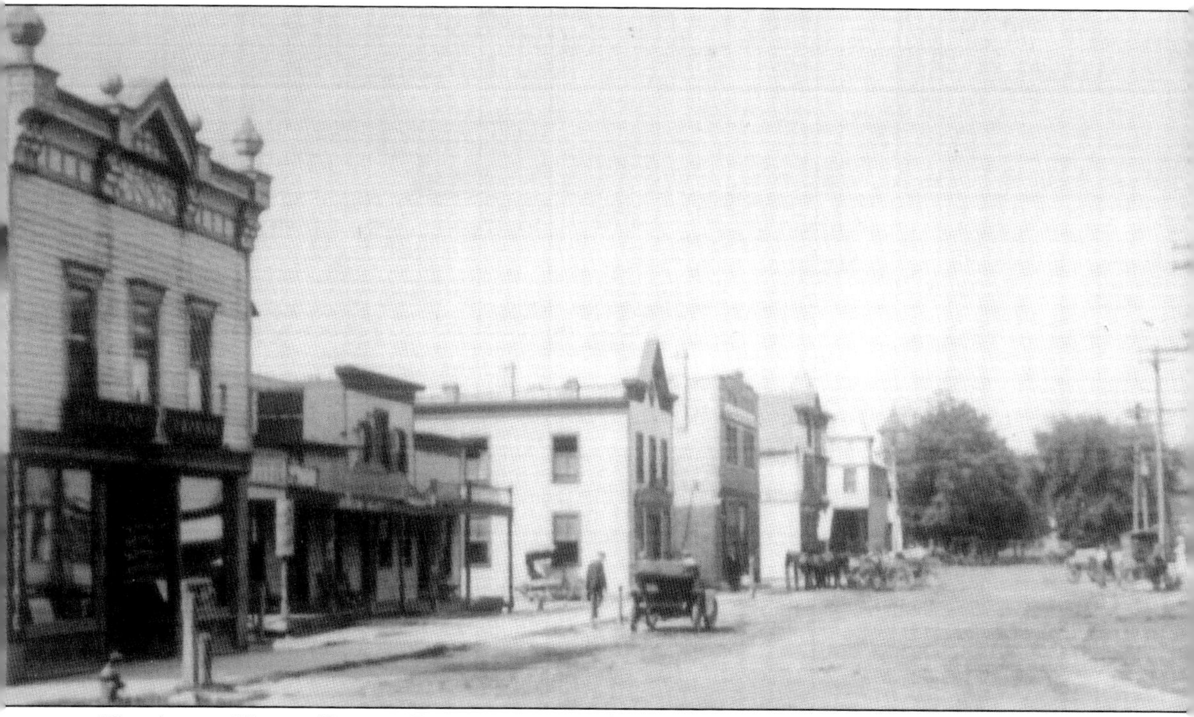

The Annex Hotel (Second Building on Left). Conrad Fink purchased the hotel on the south side of Slade Street between Bothwell and Brockway Streets in 1870. Conrad ran the tavern, and his wife, Minnie, cooked. After Conrad died in 1875, Minnie continued to run it with her new husband, William Ahlgrimm. In 1890, Ahlgrimm died, and Minnie rented out the hotel. In 1890, her daughter Minnie married Charles Seip, and they took over.

Minnie Seip roomed and fed as many as 50 people a day who came off the train. Room and board cost $3 a week. Three meals a day cost 25¢. Minnie specialized in oyster suppers for lodges. She was up at 5:00 a.m. every morning to bake bread, pies, and stews on the gas stove while overflow food was cooked on a wood-burning stove. A flowing well ran water into the hotel without the need of a pump, which made the hotel the envy of all other residents who had to haul water.

Seip tore down the old livery barn facing Bothwell Street in 1908 and replaced it with a dance hall, which was also used for Palatine High School basketball games before 1928.

The Palatine Athletic Club met on the second floor of Mosser Drugstore next door to the hotel, and the men would adjourn to the Seip tavern after meetings, thus coining the name "the Annex" hotel. With Prohibition and faster travel, the need for the hotel diminished, and it was sold to William Kehe and Louis Miller in 1932. They razed the structure and built five stores.

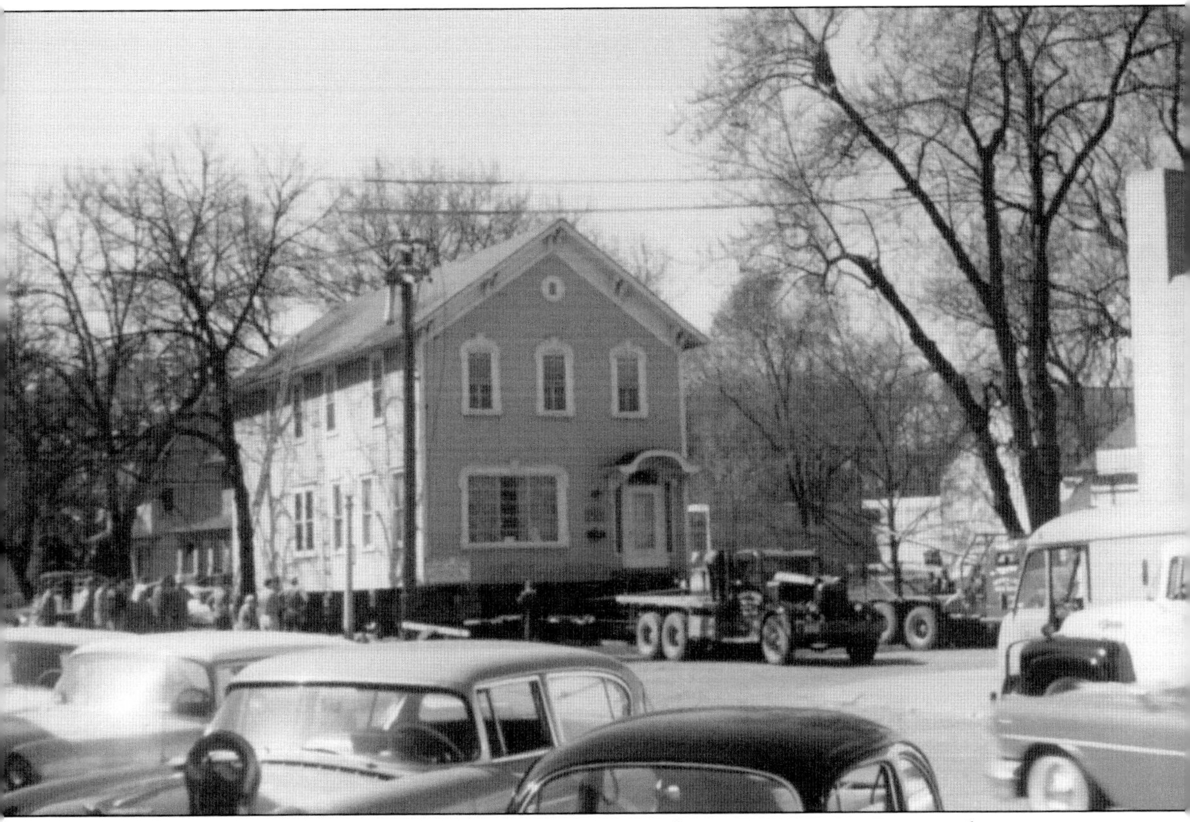

Moving the Mackenburg House in 1958. At a time when it was more economical to move a building than destroy it, the Haemker family was who people called to get the job done. Gottlieb Haemker came from Prussia in 1884. He had been in the house-moving business there and continued his trade in Palatine. He passed it on to his son Fred, Fred to his son Fred Jr., and Fred Jr. to his son Wilbert. Eventually, Willbert sold the business to Belding Corporation of Chicago and worked for them until his retirement.

Thanks to the Haemkers, many old structures in Palatine are still standing. The 1865 Dr. Mackenberg house was moved from Palatine Road to Wilson Street in 1958 and took two and a half days to move, which meant it stood in the middle of the street for two nights. The owners had left furniture and dishes in the house and claimed that not a dish was broken, no furniture shifted, and water even stayed in the fishbowl.

A house move attracted a lot of attention. When the Haemkers moved a house in Mount Prospect, at least 12 people offered to buy the house while it was still being moved. A large elevator that Ost and Abelman Lumber wanted moved was too large to be transported through the streets. So, Fred Haemker moved it over the railroad tracks after 9:00 p.m., and by 5:30 a.m., the railroad tracks were clear for the waiting trains.

As late as 1980, Haemkers moved a 1904 carriage house from behind the Palatine Township Hall at Slade Street and Plum Grove Road to the property of the Clayson House Museum on Palatine Road.

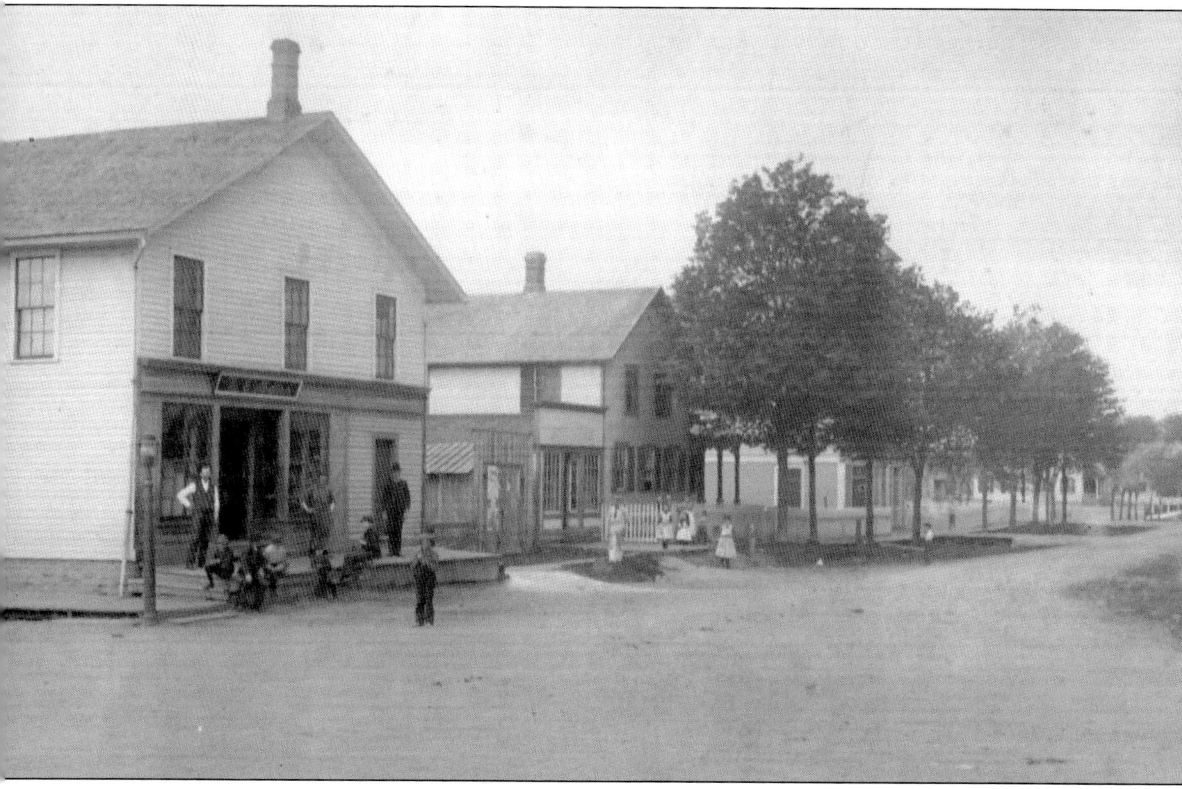

SMALL BUILDING IS PADDOCK PUBLICATIONS' FIRST OFFICE. Hosea C. Paddock was a teacher with dreams of creating a chain of local newspapers. He had unsuccessfully operated four newspapers before 1895, when, in 1898, he had an opportunity to purchase the *Palatine Register*, which had served the area since 1877. He had taken a $150 mortgage to cover the purchase price.

At first, Hosea and his son Stuart traveled to Palatine from Libertyville and stayed in the Hunnerberg Hotel for $3 a week. Hosea would travel into the country with his horse and buggy, meeting farmers and selling subscriptions. Meanwhile, 17-year-old son Stuart acted as compositor, pressman, reporter, and rewrite man. Stuart dropped out of Palatine High School in 1899 to work for his father.

Because so many of the farmers were from Germany, Paddock published a four-page newspaper that was half in German, a practice he discontinued during World War I as a patriotic gesture.

In April 1899, Paddock purchased the *Cook County Herald*, the oldest newspaper in Cook County, for $275. This began the expansion of the *Palatine Enterprise* of H.C. Paddock into the newspaper dynasty it has become today.

Six

Food and Libations

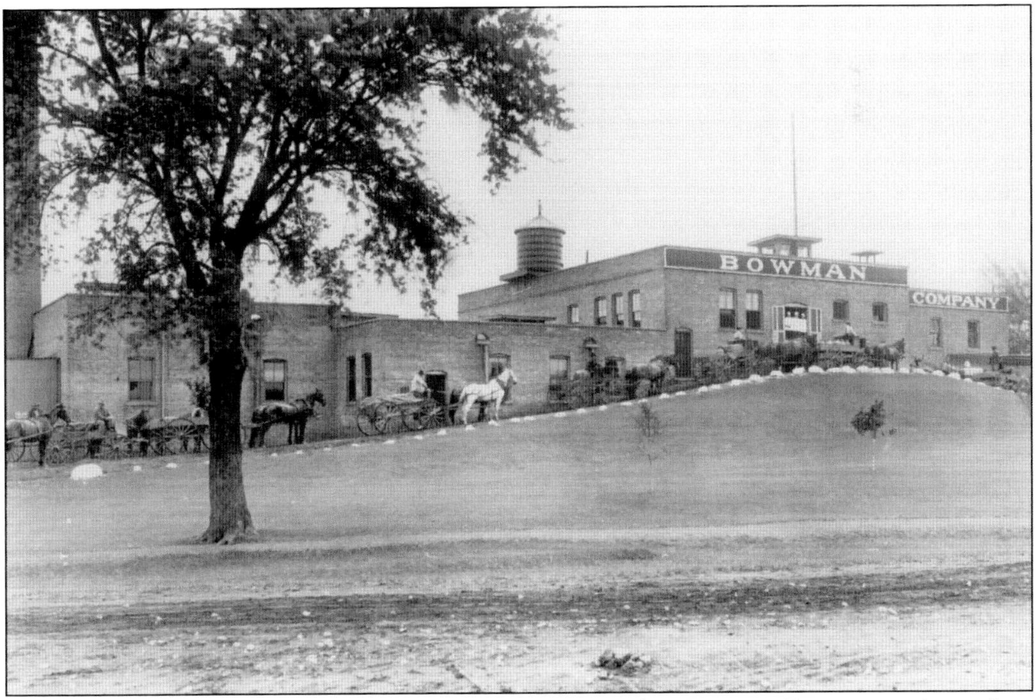

Bowman Dairy. Palatine farmers received a boon in 1906 when Bowman Dairy opened a modern facility next to the tracks on the east side of Smith at Wood Street. Bowman operated other plants in the Chicago area. Farmers could bring their milk directly to Palatine instead of bearing the expense of shipping by rail and the cost of equipment and cleaning. Bowman processed and bottled the milk and sent it by train to Chicago.

Farmers came with their horses and wagons to unload their milk. The Palatine, Lake Zurich, & Wauconda Railroad sent a daily train to Palatine from Wauconda with more milk.

When Bowman consolidated its bottling into one Chicago plant in 1930, the Palatine building was sold to Economy Fuse & Manufacturing Co. In the 1970s, the building was razed, and Wood Street Apartments were built as rental units, which have now become Park Towne Condominiums.

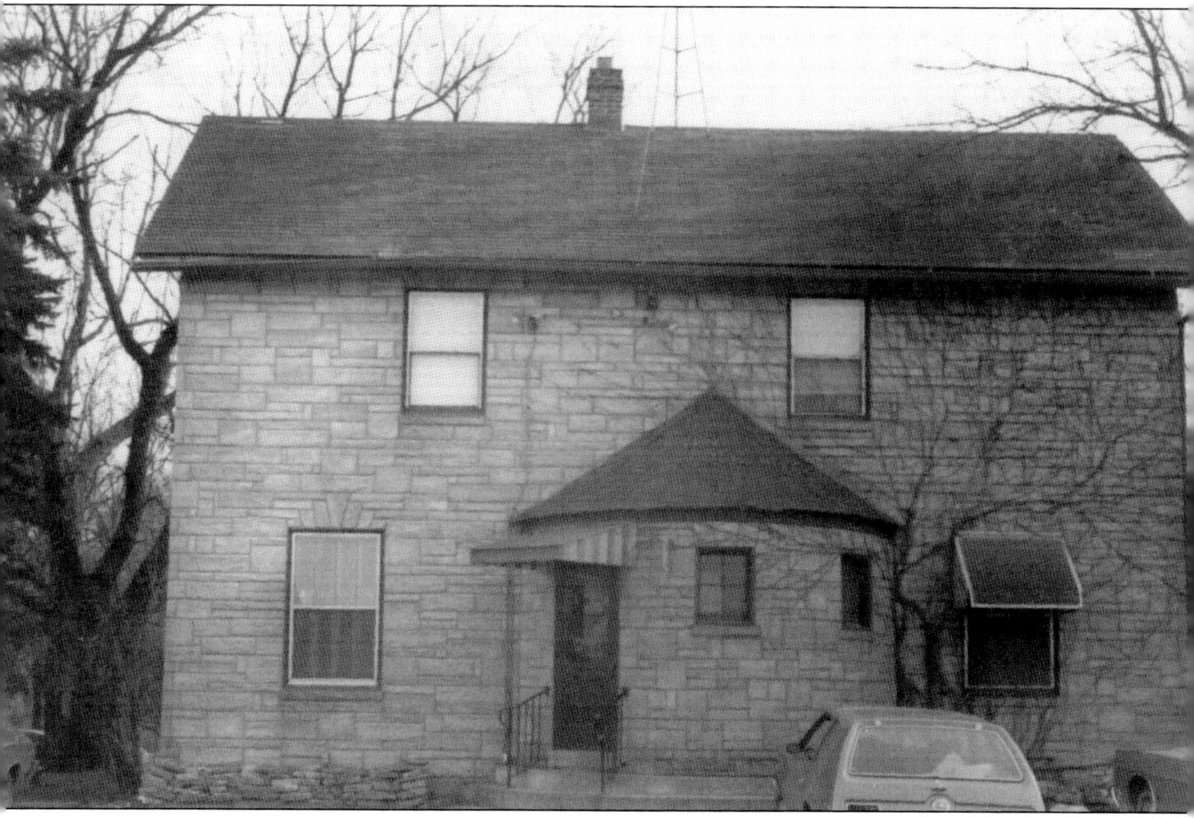

Brandt's Little Café on Northwest Highway. Joe and Romelda Brandt opened Brandt's Restaurant on the northwest corner of Palatine Road and Northwest Highway in 1954. They moved to Northwest Highway and Quentin Road in 1969 and became Brandt's Little Café. This had been the site of the 1870s Meissner home, also the Maple Grove Inn, which burned to the ground in 1930.

Haemker's moved a house from Baldwin and Roselle Roads to this site in the late 1930s. The house had been built in 1883 on the Flagg/Boss stock farm. During Prohibition, it was used by the Rodger Touhey Gang to make bootleg whiskey out of the grain that originally fed the cattle. When Arthur McIntosh bought the land and started to subdivide it for Inverness, he discovered the old house and had no use for it.

Before Brandt's, Nick and Al's Friendly Inn had occupied the building. Later, the George Grisco family continued operating it as Brandt's Little Café for many years. During that period, there was a fire in the building requiring restoration. Walt Oswald and Jim Iurio, both lifelong Palatine residents, now operate the restaurant.

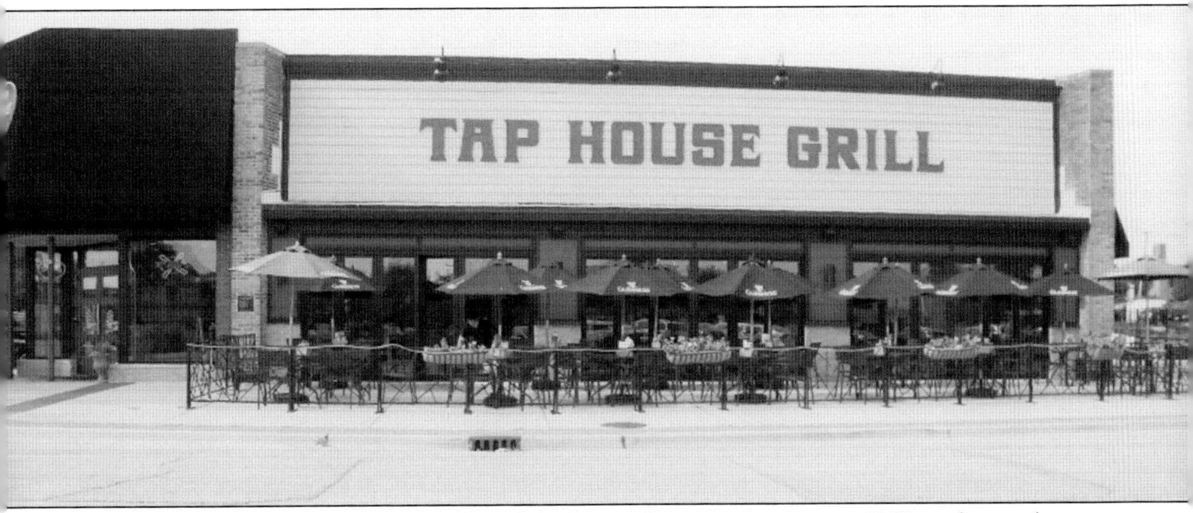

Jewel Foods/Tap House Grill. Jewel Foods built a modern grocery store in 1953 on the northeast corner of Wilson and Brockway Streets.

The mansion of Dr. William P. Schirding and his wife had been torn down. In 1928, Walter F. Swanson planned to develop the entire block from Bothwell to Brockway and Wilson to Wood Streets. The stock market crash of 1929 halted that project. For more than 20 years, the foundation for two buildings filled the site and it was not built on.

The Jewel store remained in the Wilson Street location until a larger facility was opened on South Plum Grove Road in November 1964. Seven houses on Plum Grove Road had to be demolished to build the new store. Most of these homes had been built before 1900 and some had barns behind them.

Jewel used the Wilson Street store for a few years as an administration center. Then it was occupied by S&H Green Stamps and the Ben Franklin Store for a while. As far as records can be found, it remained empty until Mia Cuchina restaurant opened in 1994. The village developed a plan for the whole block, bought the properties, razed almost all the buildings, and moved Mia Cuchina out. Then the stock market dropped in 2008, which once again brought a halt to an ambitious project. The building remained empty from 2006 until 2015, when it was rented to Tap House Grill.

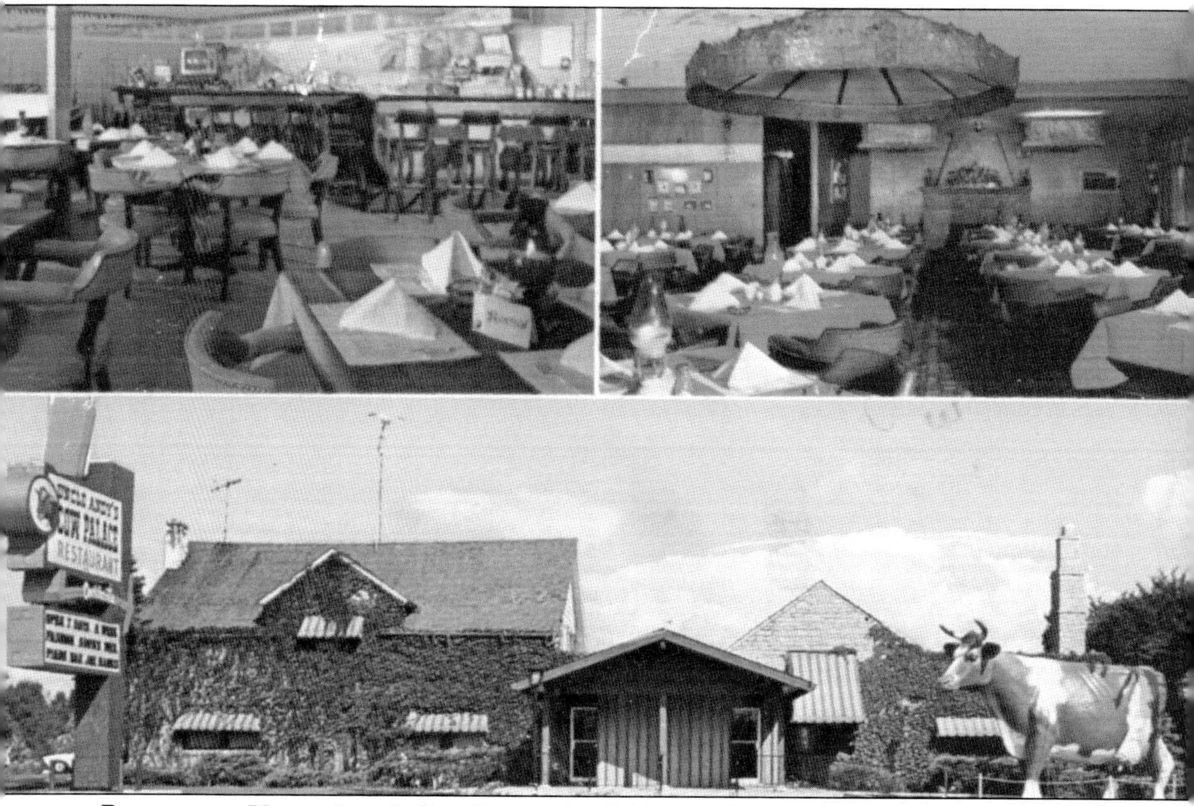

POSTCARD OF UNCLE ANDY'S COW PALACE. In 1946, several years after it was built, Jack Deynzer was able to open his restaurant and cocktail lounge, the Radio Club Farm, at Northwest Highway and Quentin Road. Shortages during the war had prevented its operation.

However, the building had been in use. North on Quentin Road, the one-room Wittenberg School District No. 13 was crowded with 93 children, so the restaurant had been become a schoolhouse.

Most Palatine area residents remember the business from the 1950s to 1970s as Uncle Andy's Cow Palace because of the huge statue of a cow that stood on the premises.

For a short time, it operated as La Romana (without the cow) and had been closed when the building burned down in January 1981. Quentin Corners Shopping Center was built on the property.

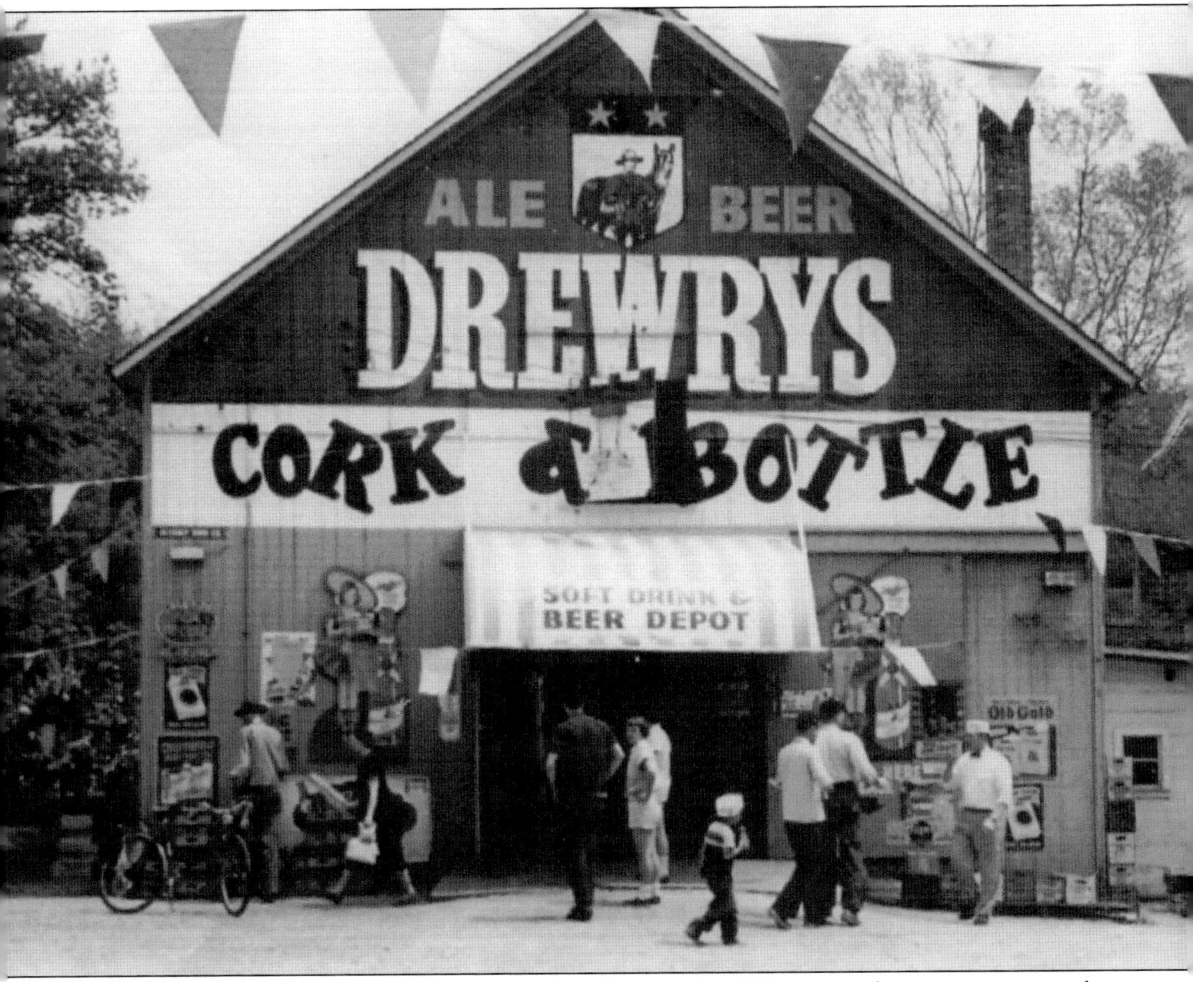

Cork and Bottle. Henry Schoppe operated an International Harvester farm equipment and Oakland and Ford auto dealerships in the garage at 11 South Brockway Street behind the house where his mother lived from 1892 to 1935. The house on the corner of Brockway Street and Palatine Road was removed in 1958 for a municipal parking lot to be built. Shortages during World War II led to the closure of the automobile garage.

After World War II, Charles Folkerts bought the building, and it became Cork and Bottle. Fred Korber Jr. and Ed Haseman purchased the business in 1954. After Korber retired to Florida, it was sold to Dobby Dobkin in 1963 and became Foremost Cork and Bottle. In 1971, Dobkin acquired the post office building to the south at 15 South Brockway Street and expanded and remodeled the store as Worldwide Liquors. Garfields Beverage Warehouse is the name of the store under its present owners.

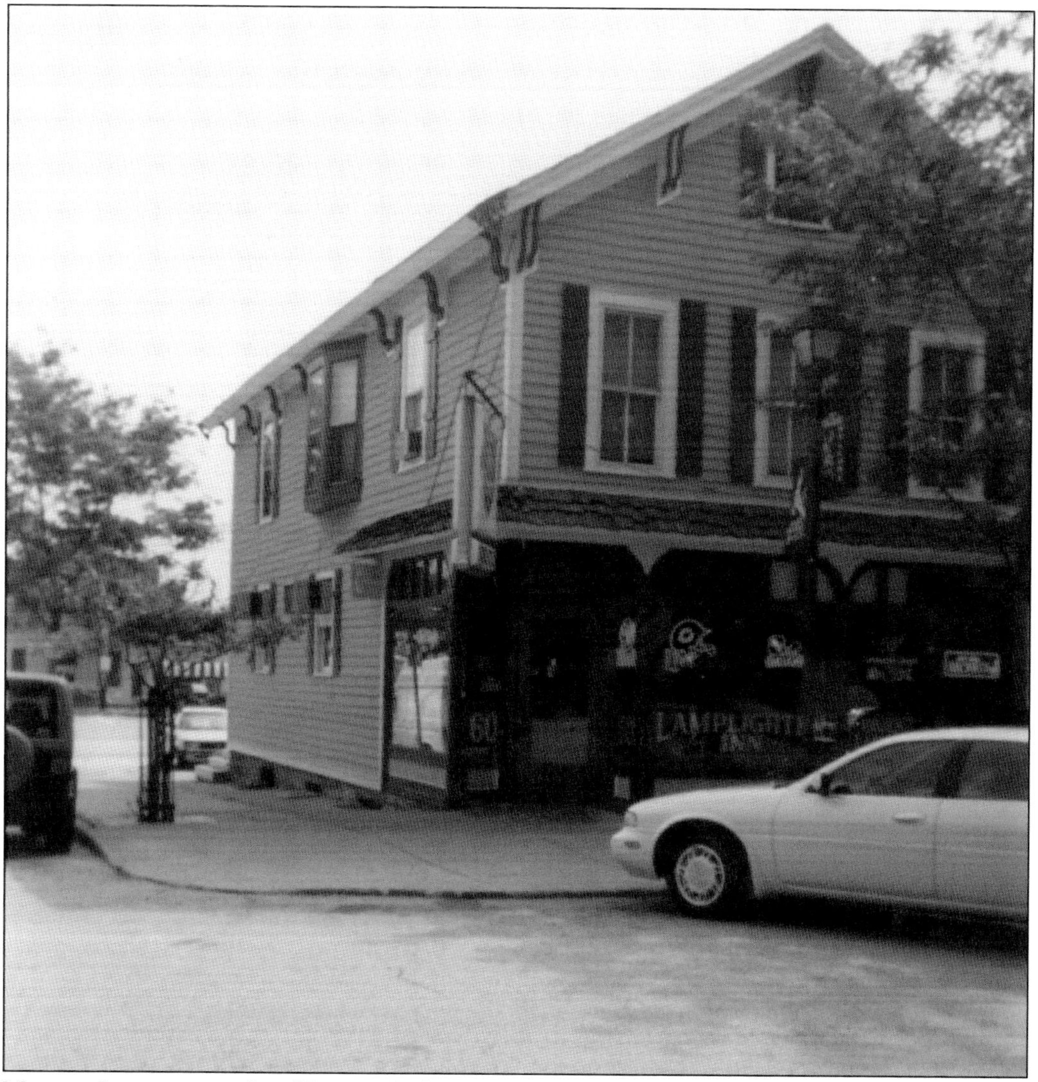

Modern Lamplighter Inn Tavern & Grille. Lamplighter Inn Tavern & Grille at the southwest corner of Wilson and Bothwell Streets is the oldest commercial building in Palatine. It was built in the 1850s and originally had three floors, with George Kuebler's barbershop in the lower floor at the rear.

During the Civil War and until 1868, older schoolchildren attended classes there. The Masonic Lodge No. 314 was organized there in 1859. The group purchased the top floor in 1885 for $800 and, a few years later, bought the rest of the building for $500. When members moved to their new lodge in 1904, the building was sold for $1,600 to Charles Rappolt, who operated a bakery on the second floor. The Palatine Methodist Church and Immanuel Lutheran Church both rented the top floor for short periods in the late 1800s.

In the early 1900s, the building was lowered, and the bottom floor became the basement. By 1934, the building belonged to Dick Sanford and was known as Dick's Tavern. The original front door was moved from the center front to the corner of the building. Everett McCrea and Al Zwirblis purchased the building in 1962 and named it Mac and Al's Bar.

The Bellanca family purchased the building in 1974, and it became the present-day Lamplighter. Recent renovations upstairs have revealed the old Masonic star–patterned ceiling.

Seven

Organizations and Churches

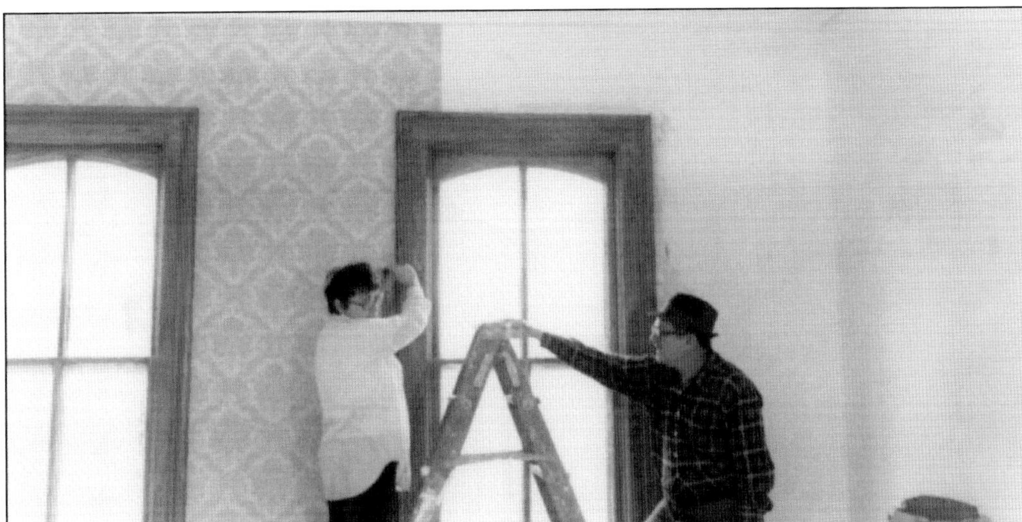

Marilyn Pedersen and Frank Regan Hanging Wallpaper in Clayson House. The George H. Clayson House at 224 East Palatine Road was purchased as a 1976 US bicentennial project by the Palatine Historical Society. The Palatine Library purchased the house for $48,000 with the proceeds of the sale of its Brockway Street facility, thus creating the George H. Clayson Historical Museum and Library.

Volunteer Marilyn Pedersen joined the society in 1975 and became the major force in the restoration of the building, which had been converted into apartments and was dilapidated both inside and out. Marilyn, along with Judith Gamoran, Frank Regan, and many other volunteers, raised more than $200,000 to hire a restoration architect and then restore the house.

Marilyn oversaw the extensive restoration. She and a group of volunteers provided a lot of the actual labor and raised money to furnish the house, which finally opened in 1979.

Marilyn did all this as a volunteer. In 1984, she became a part-time employee of the park district as coordinator and, in 1994, took on the job full-time. On December 31, 2015, Marilyn retired from being a full-time employee and cut back to part-time. It will not be surprising to see her once again working extra hours as a volunteer.

The Clayson House Museum is truly a community effort, as it is owned by the Palatine Library, building and grounds are maintained by the Palatine Park District, and operations and financing are done by volunteers (except for one employee). The museum is open Tuesdays and Thursdays from 9:00 a.m. to 4:00 p.m. and Sundays from 1:30 to 4:00 p.m. There is parking around the corner on the Oak Street lot.

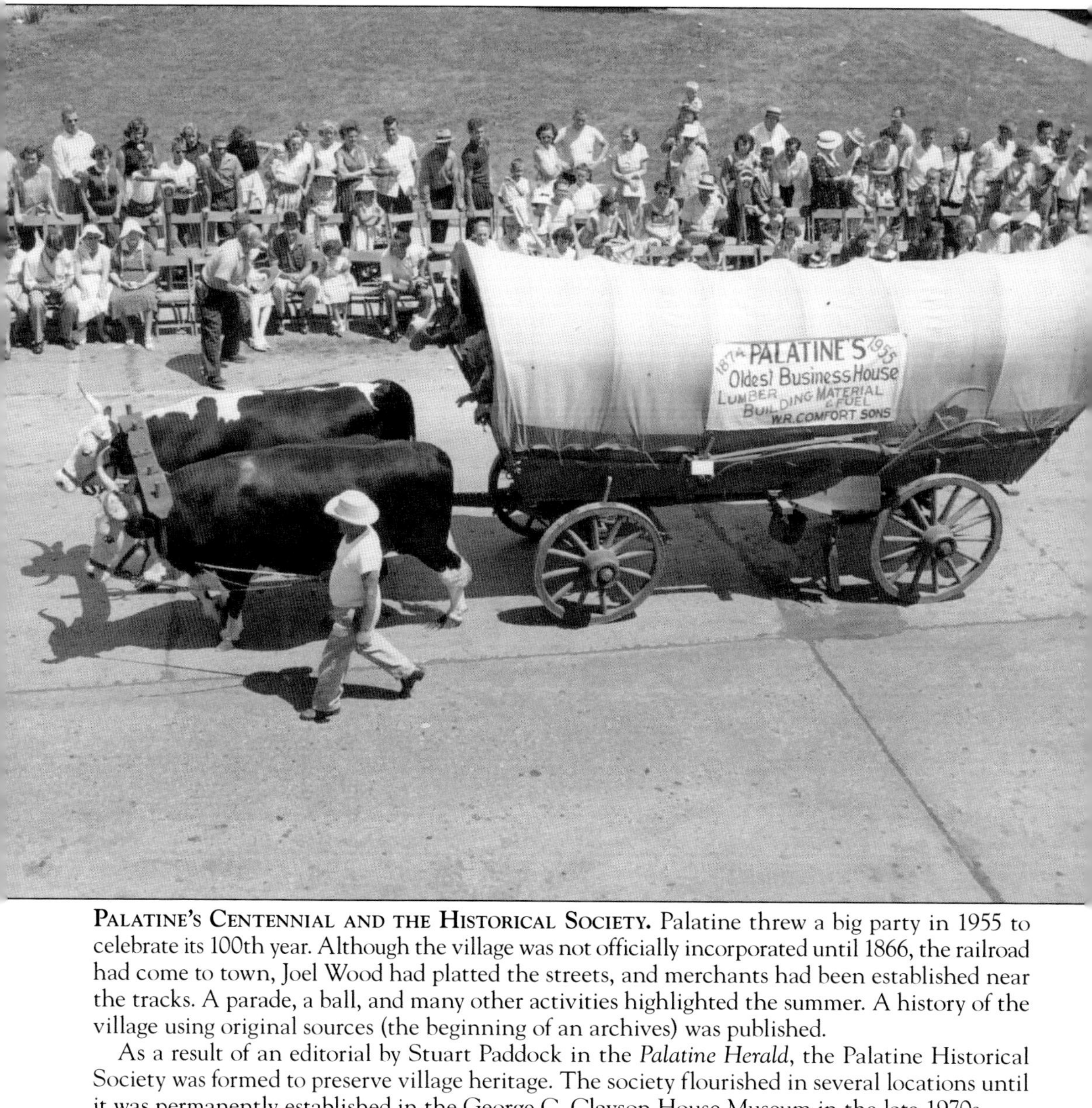

PALATINE'S CENTENNIAL AND THE HISTORICAL SOCIETY. Palatine threw a big party in 1955 to celebrate its 100th year. Although the village was not officially incorporated until 1866, the railroad had come to town, Joel Wood had platted the streets, and merchants had been established near the tracks. A parade, a ball, and many other activities highlighted the summer. A history of the village using original sources (the beginning of an archives) was published.

As a result of an editorial by Stuart Paddock in the *Palatine Herald*, the Palatine Historical Society was formed to preserve village heritage. The society flourished in several locations until it was permanently established in the George C. Clayson House Museum in the late 1970s.

Another celebration was held in 1991, marking 125 years since the official creation of the Village of Palatine. Once again, a lively summer included a ball, a Civil War reenactment, and other fun activities. The 1955 history was updated and republished.

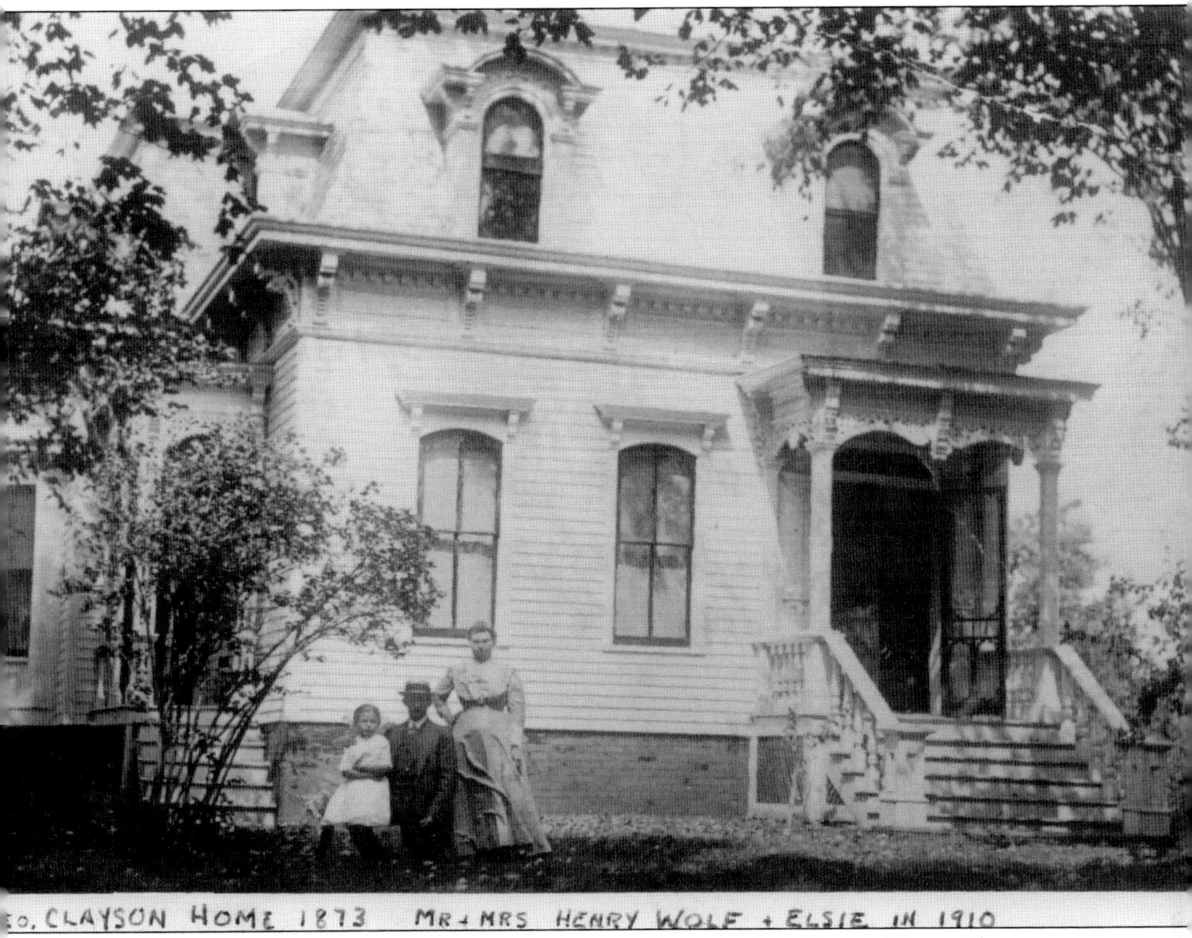

MR. AND MRS. HENRY WOLFE AND ELSIE AT CLAYSON HOUSE, 1910. George Henry Clayson was born in Cuba, New York, in 1833. He came to Chicago to work in 1860 and married Clarinda Harris of Palatine. He bought 10 acres of land in Palatine, which encompassed the entire block now bounded by Palatine Road, Northwest Highway, and Wood and Oak Streets. He used this property to grow fruit trees and grapes and built a house at 224 East Palatine Road in 1873 for $2,300 (now the society's museum).

The Claysons moved to Crystal Lake in 1887 and, eventually, settled in Phoenix, Arizona. Historical society member Marg Plank and her husband, Wally, discovered George Clayson's grave in the Pioneer and Military Park Cemetery there. The Planks donated a stone marker for the grave since there was none.

Henry Wolfe and family lived in the house longer than the Claysons. When the library purchased it for the historical society in 1976, it had been converted into apartments. The original wood siding was covered with composite material, and a hip roof had been added. It required extensive renovations to restore the structure to its original appearance, both inside and out.

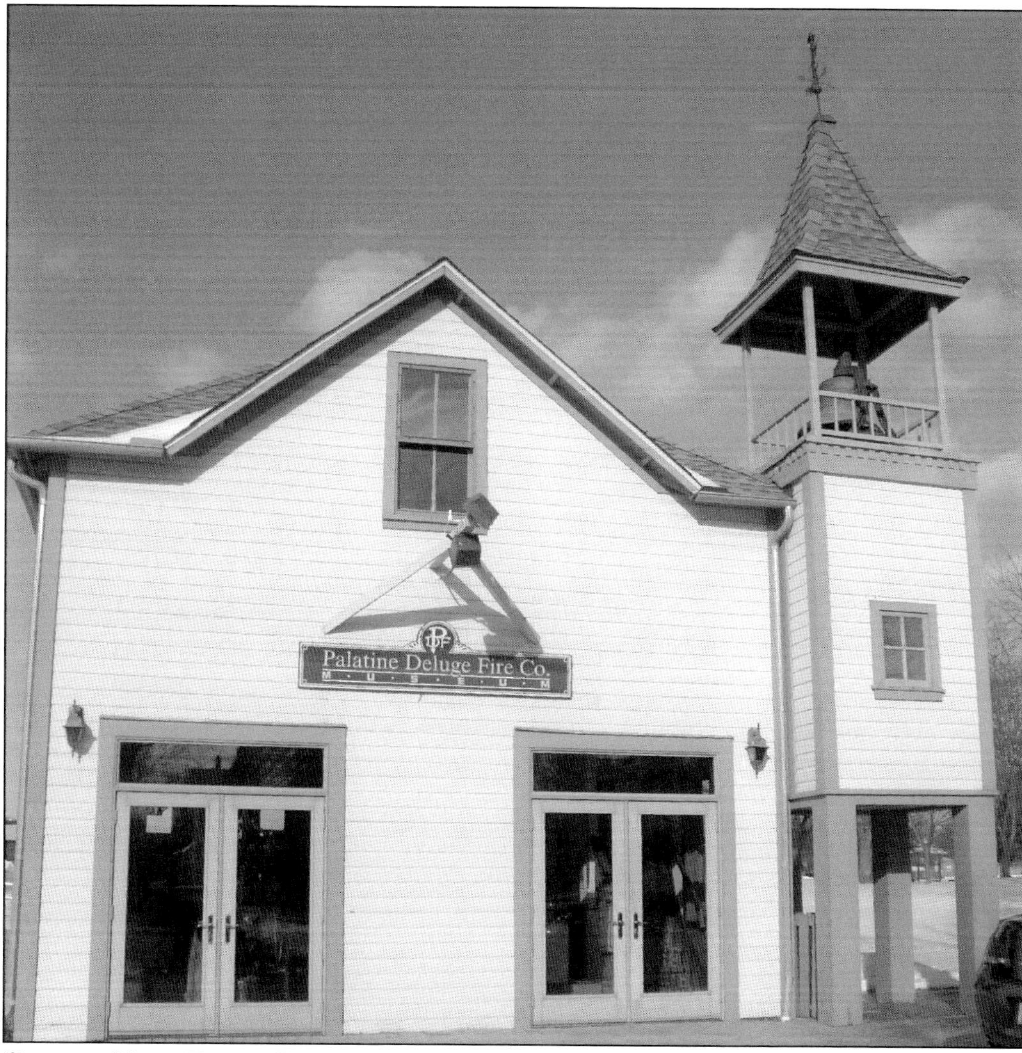

Carriage House Deluge Fire Museum. A two-story carriage house behind the Palatine Township Hall on Plum Grove Road was donated to the Palatine Historical Society. Fifteen thousand dollars was raised for Haemker Movers to place the building on the Clayson House property. An additional $60,000 was raised to remodel the building.

A bell tower (containing Palatine's original 19th-century fire bell) was erected on the side, so the museum would resemble Palatine's original village hall and fire station on Slade Street. The building was thermally conditioned to protect textiles and other artifacts stored on the second floor, and a handicap bathroom was installed.

Palatine's first fire engine and other firefighting paraphernalia sit on the first floor. Other displays include a piece of Schoppe's Store, a lady's emporium, a blacksmith shop, and old telephone equipment. A major attraction is a fully furnished Victorian dollhouse, which is decorated and lit at Christmastime.

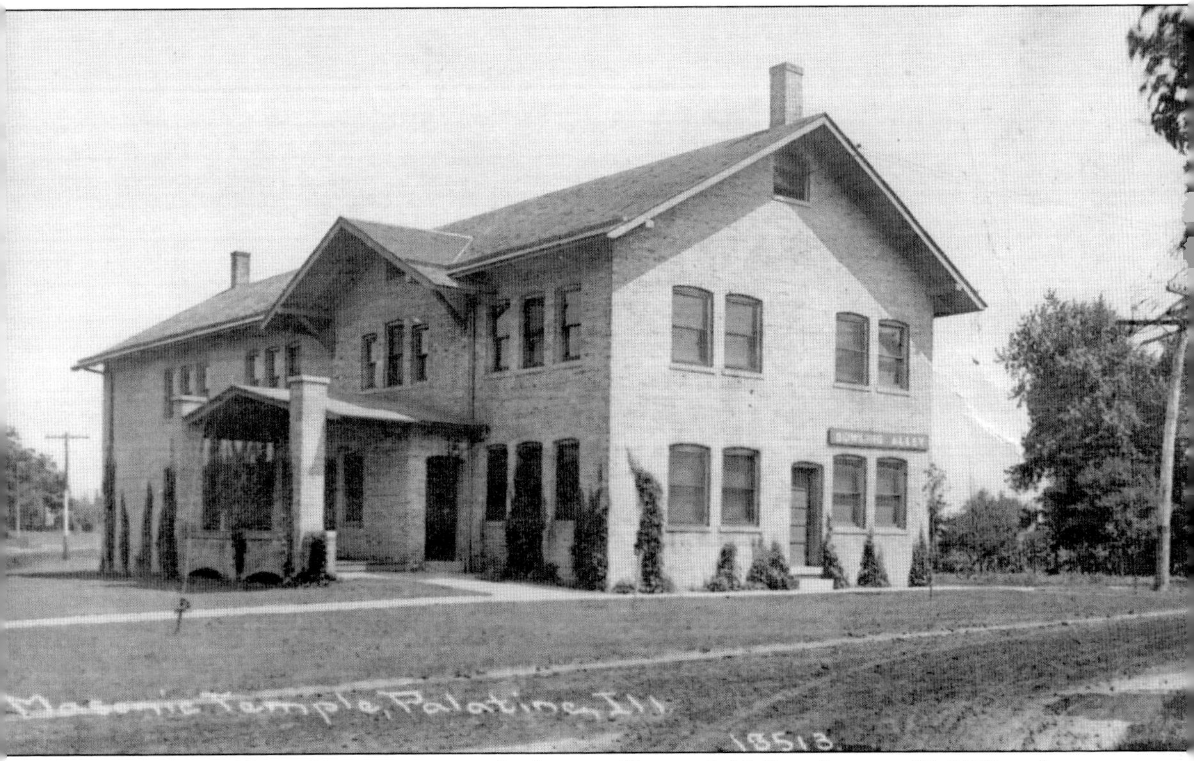

1904 Masonic Hall. Five men met at the home of Lucius J. Hall on January 15, 1859, to form a lodge of Masons. The first meeting was held in Palatine on February 1, 1859. Until 1904, the lodge was located in the building, which the lodge eventually owned, on the southwest corner of Wilson and Bothwell Streets.

In 1903, the lodge sold the building and purchased a triangular lot for $400, bounded by Plum Grove Road, Chicago Avenue, and the North Western Railroad tracks. It had held the stable for the Meyer Hotel across Plum Grove Road.

The building was dedicated April 29, 1905. It is remembered by many because of its striking blue color and location on the small lot. Over the years, it was home to many organizations besides the Masons. The Palatine Athletic Club rented the downstairs, which had two bowling lanes until they were replaced by a large dining room. Other occupants over the years were the Palatine Village Library, St. Philip's Episcopal Church, Christian Science Reading Room, Palatine Senior Center, Leader Newspapers, and others.

The cornerstone, removed in 2004 after 100 years, included newspapers, merchant business cards, coins, a roster of the lodge members, and more.

The village acquired the property in 2010 and razed the building, replacing it with a small park.

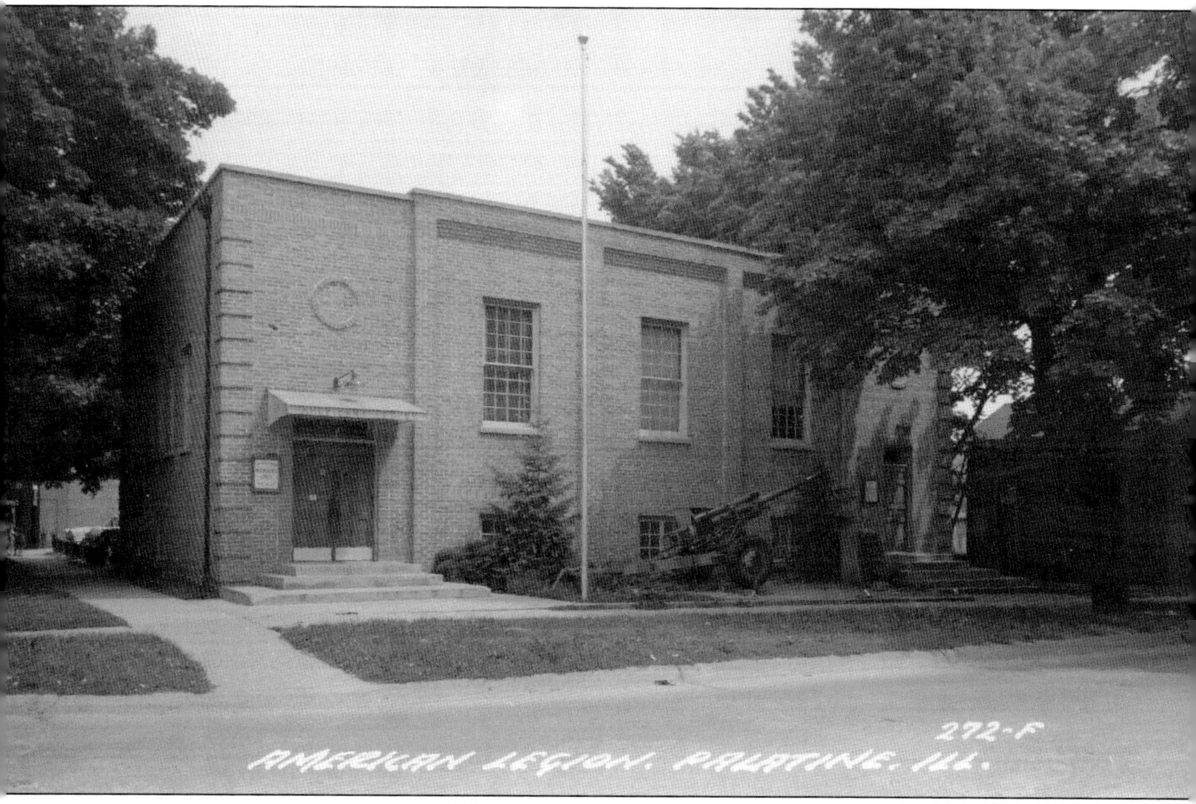

American Legion Post No. 690 and Women's Auxiliary. American Legion Post No. 690 was formed in October 1920, and the Women's Auxiliary was organized in January 1921. W.H. Brockway was a depot ticket agent. As the "boys" purchased their monthly train tickets, the story goes, he would ask them for an extra three bucks for Legion membership.

With a dream of building a home of its own, the Legion held fundraisers, which were mostly unsuccessful. The Women's Auxiliary was much better at raising money and saving, so it was that organization that purchased a piece of land for $4,700 in 1922. The two organizations decided to go fifty-fifty on the cost of the building. In 1948, with more profitable fundraising and generous donations of time and material, the building at Palatine Road and Greeley Street became a reality.

Sons of the American Legion was formed in 1936. Many of the sons became Legion members after World War II. All three organizations are active in serving veterans, participating in community projects, and keeping patriotism alive.

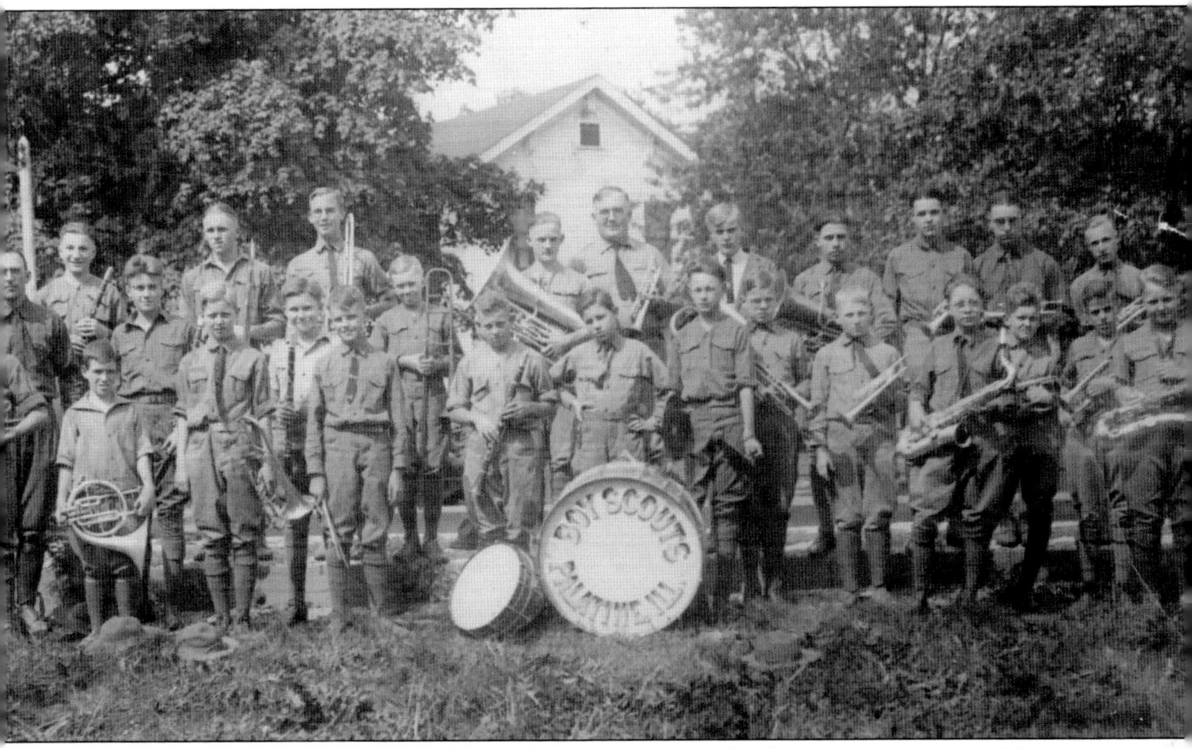

1920 Boy Scout Troop No. 1. Palatine Boy Scout Troop No. 1 was organized in 1919 with Scoutmaster Emory L. Kimball, principal of Palatine High School. George Minneberger, Harry Kincaid, and John Manz, who were Scoutmasters at various times, were assisted by a group of citizens. The Scouts conducted a successful campaign under Minneberger in 1920 to collect books to start a library.

Palatine Boy Scout Troop No. 9 was organized in 1924 and continued for many years. In 1946, the Palatine Lions Club set a pattern for other service groups by sponsoring Troop No. 9, which had reorganized that year under Scoutmaster Ray Mills.

Today, there are eight Boy Scout troops in the village of Palatine, but no Troop No. 1 and no Troop No. 9.

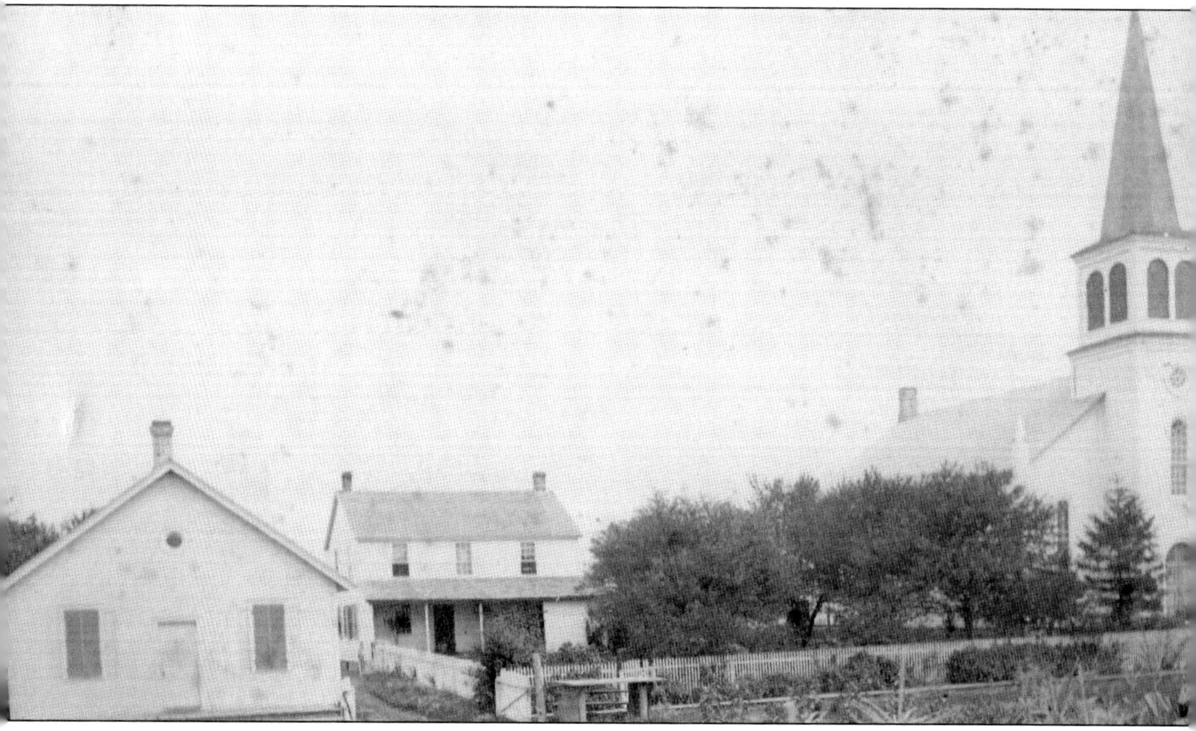

St. John's Church. St. John United Church of Christ on Algonquin Road west of Roselle Road is the oldest church building in Palatine. The congregation was organized in 1846 as the United Evangelical Congregation, Wickliffe, Cook County, Illinois.

A schoolhouse and parsonage had been built by 1865, and a new church was built in 1875 and renamed St. John. The schoolhouse and parsonage were destroyed by fire in 1882 and were replaced. Then, the church was struck by lightning and burned in August 1885.

By December of that year, a new church was erected, which serves the congregation today. The building was completely renovated in 1948. The church still has a hand-pumped organ.

Mount Hope Cemetery was created to the east of the church. About 1947, the schoolhouse was sold and moved to Palatine to become a home. The land was used to enlarge the cemetery.

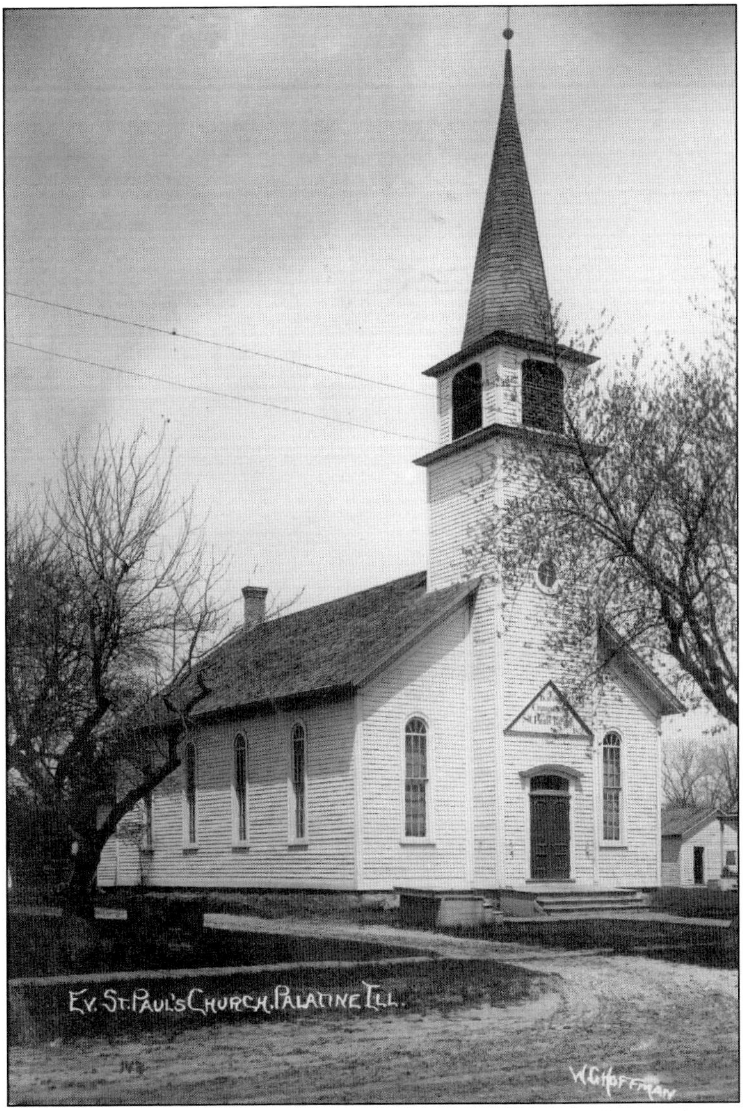

1872 St. Paul's Church. Many of the members of St. John's Church on Algonquin Road had moved to the village of Palatine, so Pastor Krueger began mission work in Palatine. A year later, the German United Evangelical St. Paul's Congregation was formed and met bimonthly at the Masonic hall at Wilson and Bothwell Streets.

The first wooden church was built on Palatine Road near Oak Street in 1872, and a parsonage was purchased. A schoolhouse, built in 1888, was used until 1925, when it was sold and converted into a residence on Route 53. The parsonage was partially destroyed by fire in 1897, and a new house was built and remained on the corner until 2012. The congregation owns a modern house across Oak Street.

The present brick building dates from 1925. An education addition was completed in 1955. Some of the church rooms were used as classrooms for a few years by an overflow of students from the Palatine Wood Street School.

The official name became St. Paul's United Church of Christ in 1957. Many early churches were founded by German immigrants, and services were held in German. Over time, English was introduced into the services until it became the predominant language of the church.

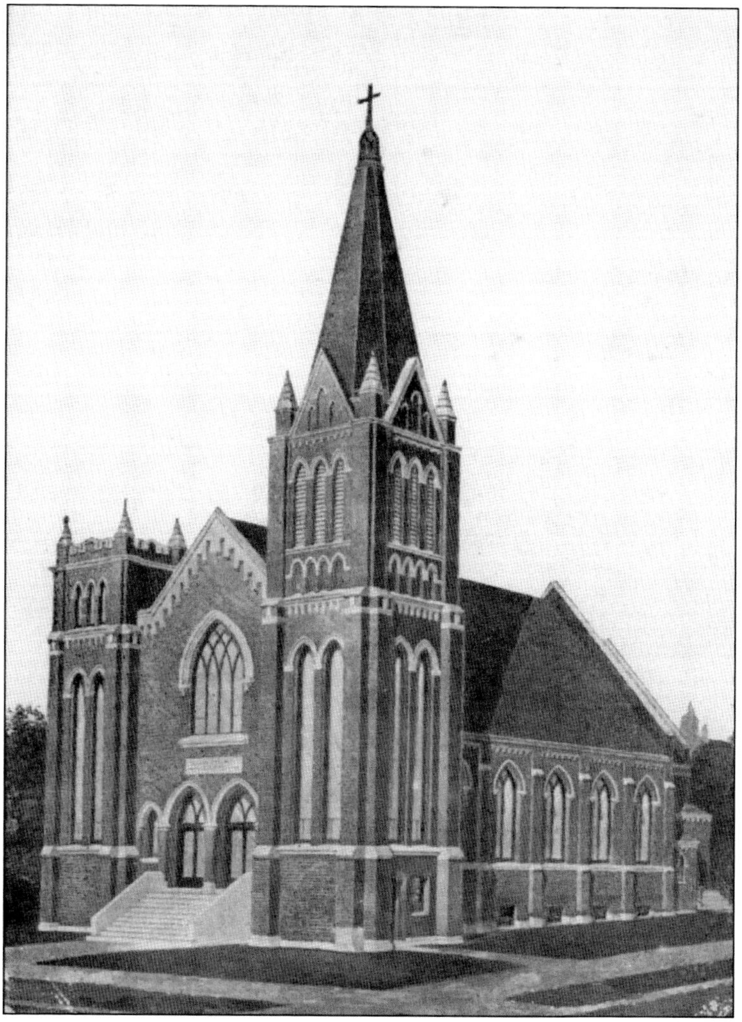

1914 Immanuel Lutheran Church. The story of Immanuel Lutheran Church is one of building, tearing down, rebuilding, tearing down, spreading out, and building.

Eleven families formed the congregation in 1869 and bought land south of Palatine Road at Greeley, which became a cemetery. The planned church was not built because of a lack of funds. By selling some of the property, they were able to buy a church building on Plum Grove Road north of Wood Street from the Disciple Church. A combined school and parsonage was built north of the church in 1870.

An impressive Gothic church arose on Wood Street at the corner of Plum Grove Road in 1914. The house there was moved west to serve as a parsonage. A 1926 school building was erected north on Plum Grove Road, and the original school became a home on Johnson Street, now demolished.

Lincoln Street from Plum Grove Road west to Bothwell Street was vacated so that the present church could be built in 1970. Land west of the church property was purchased, and several old homes were torn down. A new school was built in 1958 and has been added to. The 1926 school was remodeled at that time but was demolished in 1978. The old Gothic church on the corner was torn down, and the site is now a playground.

Except for a small area on Colfax, the Lutheran church now owns most of the property bounded by Plum Grove Road and Bothwell Street and Wood and Colfax Streets.

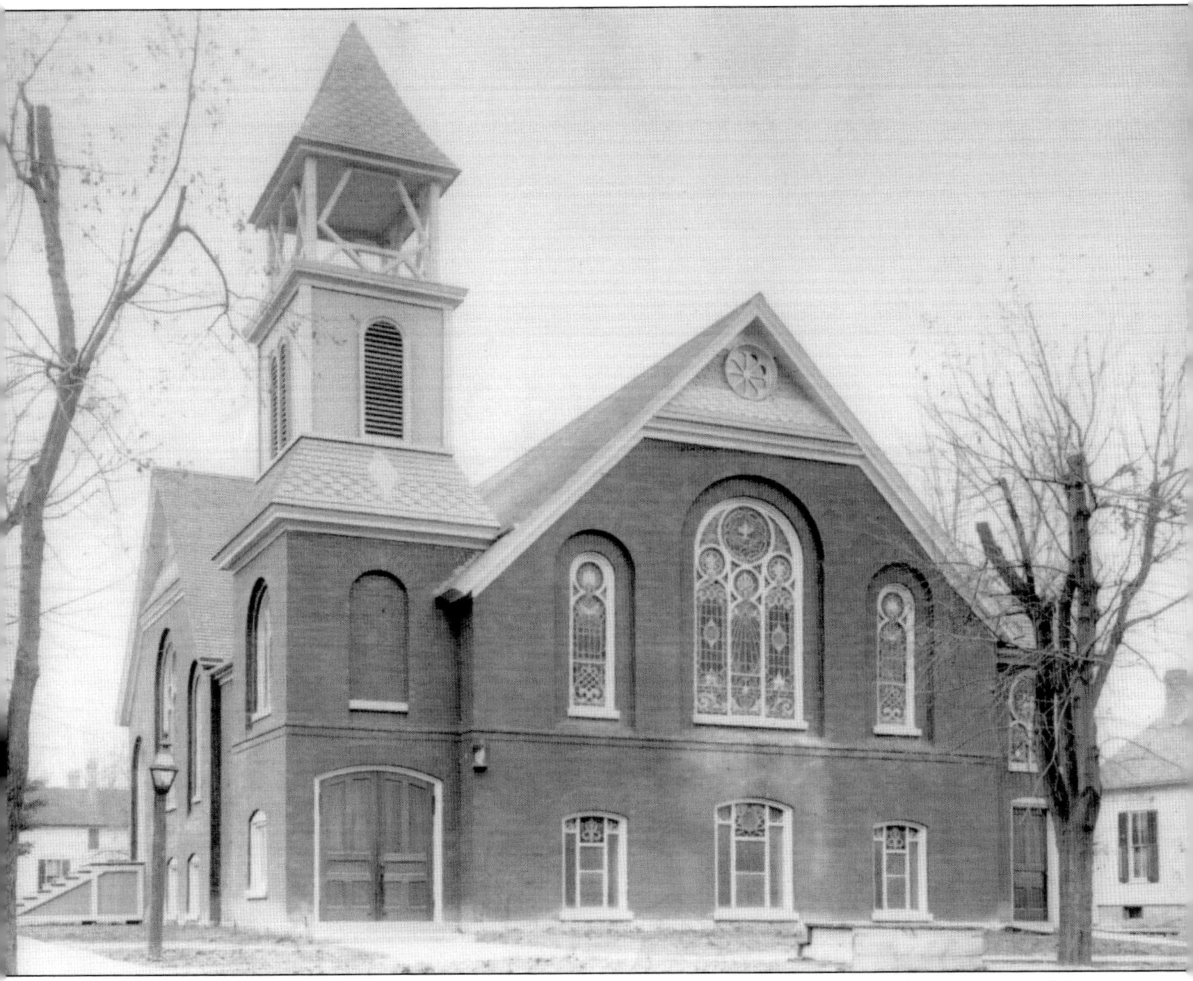

First United Methodist Church. Early Methodists settled in Deer Grove and were served by circuit riders who held monthly meetings from 1835 until 1857. A white-framed Methodist Episcopal church was built in town in 1858 at the southeast corner of Wood Street and Plum Grove Road at a cost of $1,500 on land donated by Joel Wood. A parsonage was built to the south in 1885.

From 1858 to 1863, revival meetings brought increasing numbers of converts. The church had a library of 1,200 volumes, the only library in town until 1920. Some residents attended two churches to take advantage of the books. A special class was organized in the 1860s to teach English to new German immigrants.

Rev. William Smith, a retired Union army chaplain, became pastor in 1891. He designed the redbrick church and served until it was completed in 1895. An addition was built in 1952. The old frame church was sold and moved to the rear of 207 North Hale Street, where it was used as a pigeon loft.

A new sanctuary was built at the corner of Slade Street in 1958, and an education wing was added on the north in 1969 (where the parsonage had stood) to connect with the 1895 building. Though the north church was restored in 1976, the structure was razed and replaced with a new building in 2006.

Other organizations have used the Methodist church's facility over the years, including for graduation services of the Palatine School.

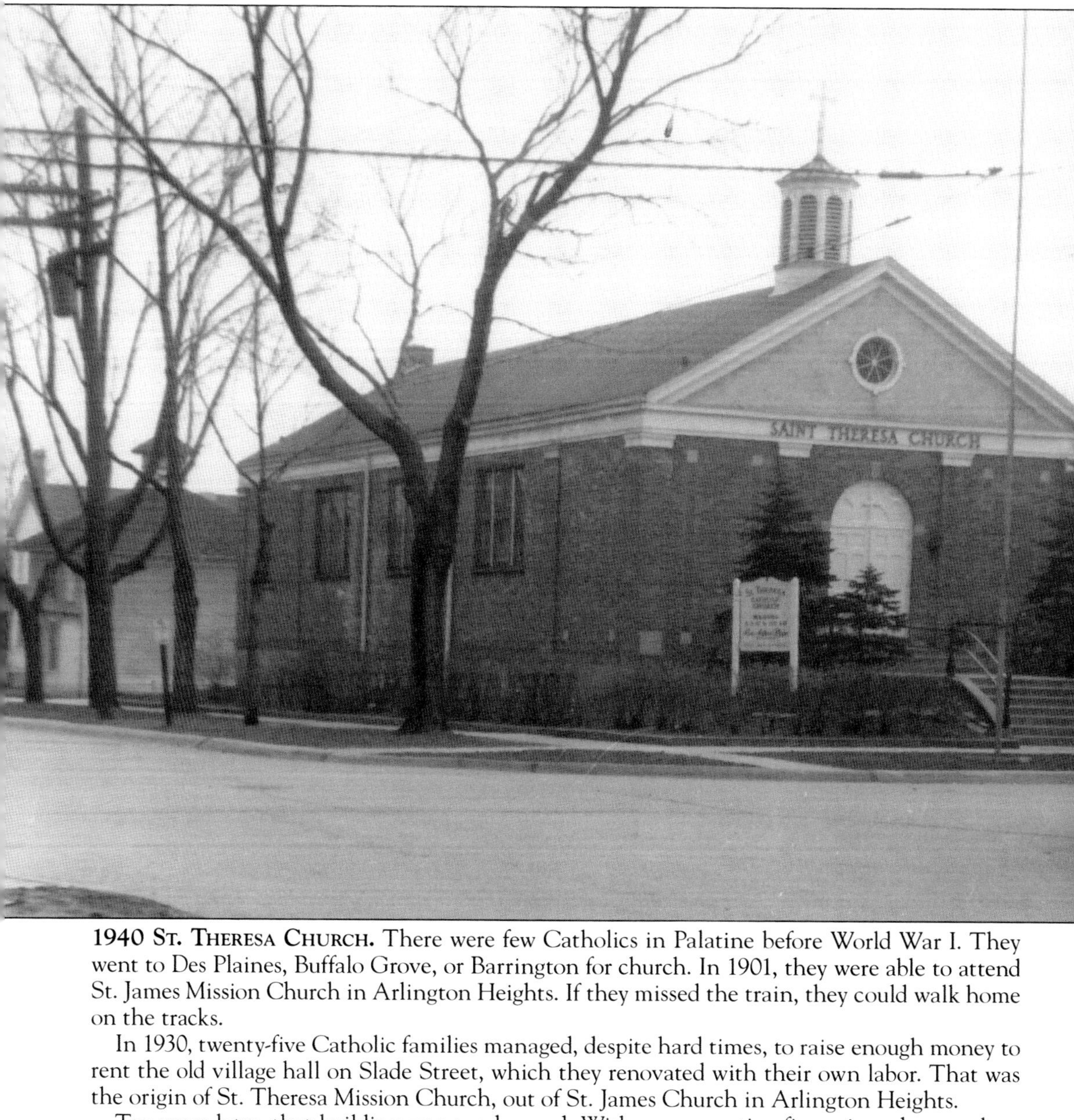

1940 St. Theresa Church. There were few Catholics in Palatine before World War I. They went to Des Plaines, Buffalo Grove, or Barrington for church. In 1901, they were able to attend St. James Mission Church in Arlington Heights. If they missed the train, they could walk home on the tracks.

In 1930, twenty-five Catholic families managed, despite hard times, to raise enough money to rent the old village hall on Slade Street, which they renovated with their own labor. That was the origin of St. Theresa Mission Church, out of St. James Church in Arlington Heights.

Ten years later, that building was condemned. With some creative financing, the members bought two lots on the southeast corner of Wood and Bothwell Streets and built a small brick building, St. Theresa Parish Church. At that time, the parish encompassed what are now St. Thomas Parish, Holy Family Parish, and part of St. Hubert's Parish in Hoffman Estates.

The population explosion in Palatine after World War II included many Catholics. The small church was crowded and lacked space to add on. St. Theresa School opened on North Benton Street in 1954. A chapel to seat 500 people was created in the basement until the parish could erect a church in 1961.

The old church then became Santa Teresita, the only Spanish-language church in the area. In the mid-1990s, the church name was changed to Mission San Juan Diego, and about 2003, it was moved to the former Scandinavian Club near Highway 53.

Eight

Entertainment and Sports

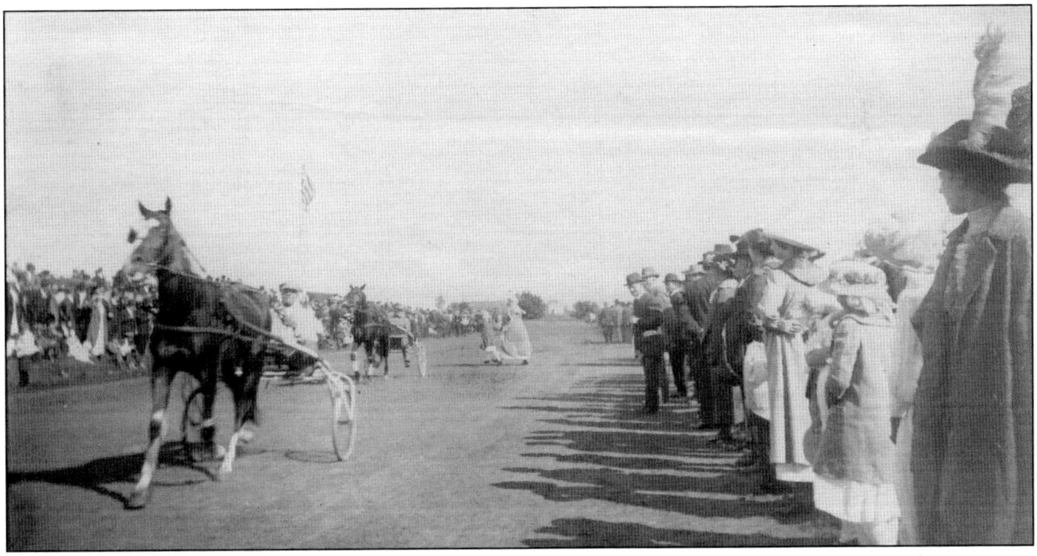

Harness Racing in Palatine. In the early 1900s, Charles E. Dean Sr. was one of America's leading horsemen. His 118-acre farm was north of Chicago Avenue (Palatine Road) and east of the city limits (present Northwest Highway). About 6 assistant trainers and 30 to 40 stablemen worked annually on the Dean farm for winter and spring prep of as many as 80 horses.

The Deans raised enough oats and straw on the farm and leased land to supply the grain and bedding for track prospects and 50 to 75 turnouts and broodmares that populated the paddocks and pastures. Dean's sons Charles Jr. "Chase" and Jerry were their father's helpers. Son Ben was a blacksmith and shod all the horses on the farm. Chase was also a harness racer.

Visitors arrived from every corner of the racing world to view the workouts, have a colt trained, to buy or sell a prospect, or to arrange to breed a mare with a stallion.

In 1916, the track was widened and a new grandstand built. The Cook County Fair Association leased the track and grounds one week each season for the next 12 years to hold an annual race meet and the Cook County Fair. Representatives of major stables came for the races, more in support of Charles Dean than for the meager purses. When the fair folded, harness racing in Palatine ended.

Both Charles and Chase Dean are members of the Harness Racing Hall of Fame.

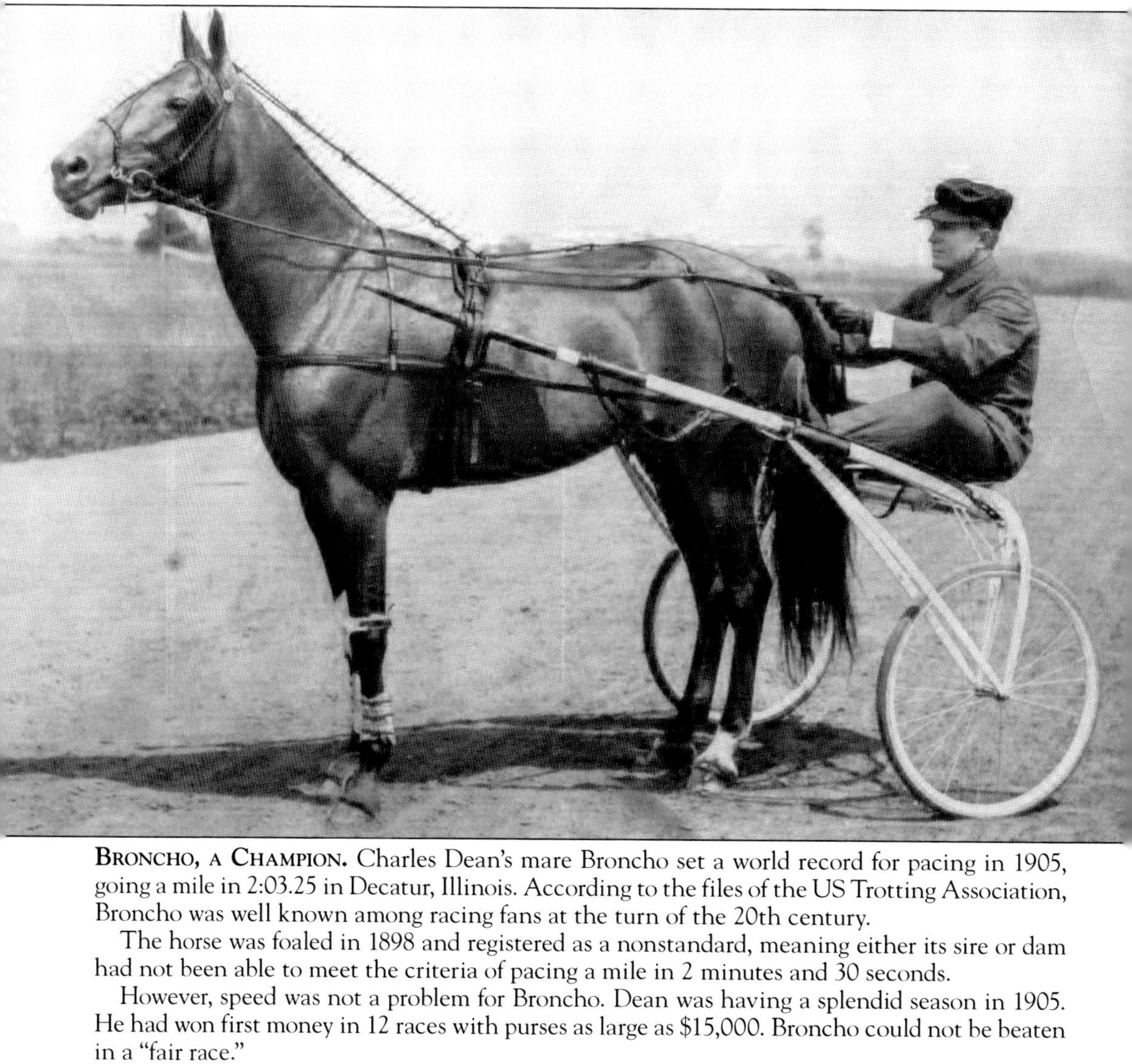

BRONCHO, A CHAMPION. Charles Dean's mare Broncho set a world record for pacing in 1905, going a mile in 2:03.25 in Decatur, Illinois. According to the files of the US Trotting Association, Broncho was well known among racing fans at the turn of the 20th century.

The horse was foaled in 1898 and registered as a nonstandard, meaning either its sire or dam had not been able to meet the criteria of pacing a mile in 2 minutes and 30 seconds.

However, speed was not a problem for Broncho. Dean was having a splendid season in 1905. He had won first money in 12 races with purses as large as $15,000. Broncho could not be beaten in a "fair race."

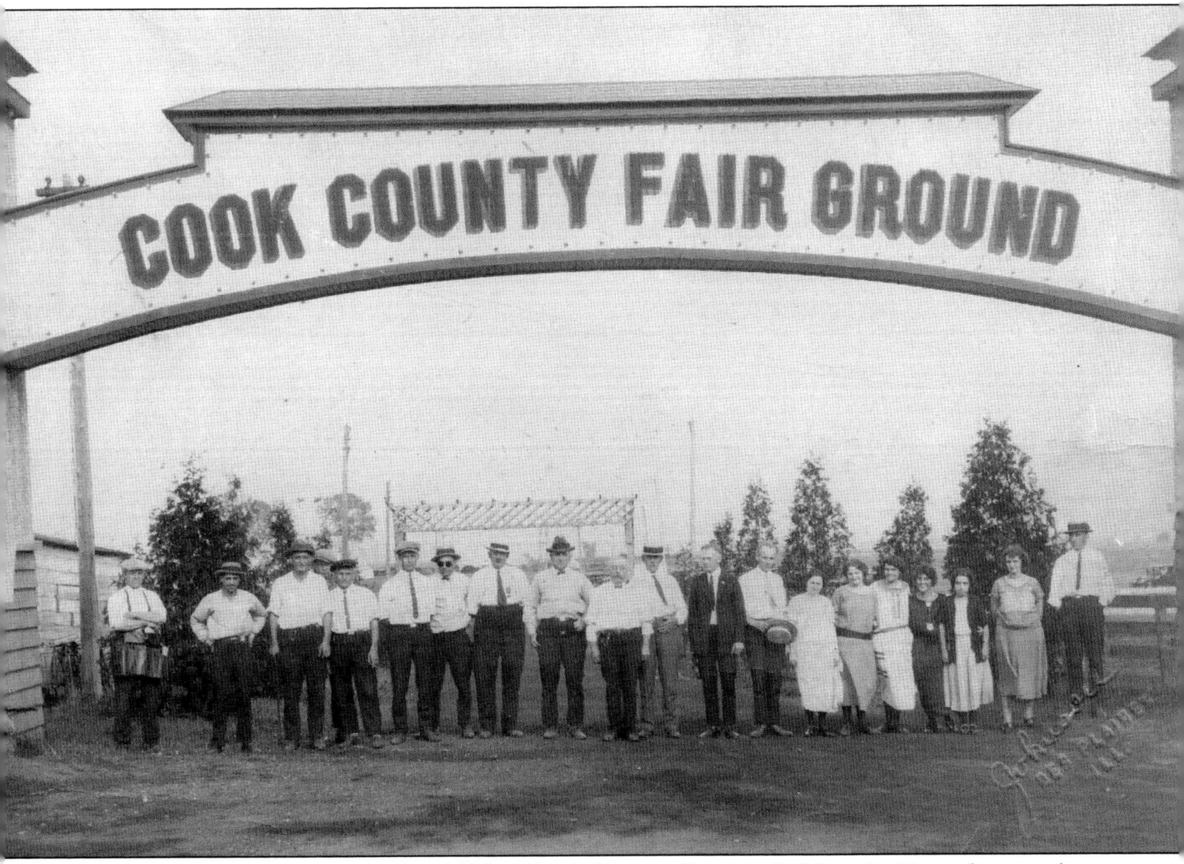

Cook County Fair. In September 1913, a Cook County Fair was held at the Dean farm at the southwest corner of Hicks Road (Northwest Highway) and Baldwin Road. The next year, the Palatine Commercial Association moved the fair into town, using a vacant store in the Batterman Building, Seip's Auditorium, a tent in front of Matthei's Store, a lot south of Schoppe's Store, and the Wilkening barn, with a racing program at Dean's farm.

The fair was such a success that it continued to be held until 1928 at Dean's farm. By 1924, it was six days of contests, exhibits, harness racing, auto racing, bands and dancing, clowns, and circus performers. Blue ribbons and monetary prizes were awarded.

A school department held a variety of children's handiwork. Farmers exhibited livestock and farm products. Fine arts included basketry, painting, decorating, and curios. Rural health nurses maintained a first aid and information booth. Farm and industrial machinery and new models of automobiles were displayed. On the midway, there were rides like the Ferris wheel, merry-go-round, and the Whip, as well as a Mystic show and an athletic show with wrestlers.

And what was the price for all this fun and excitement? A day's ticket cost 75¢, and the price was just 50¢ to come at night.

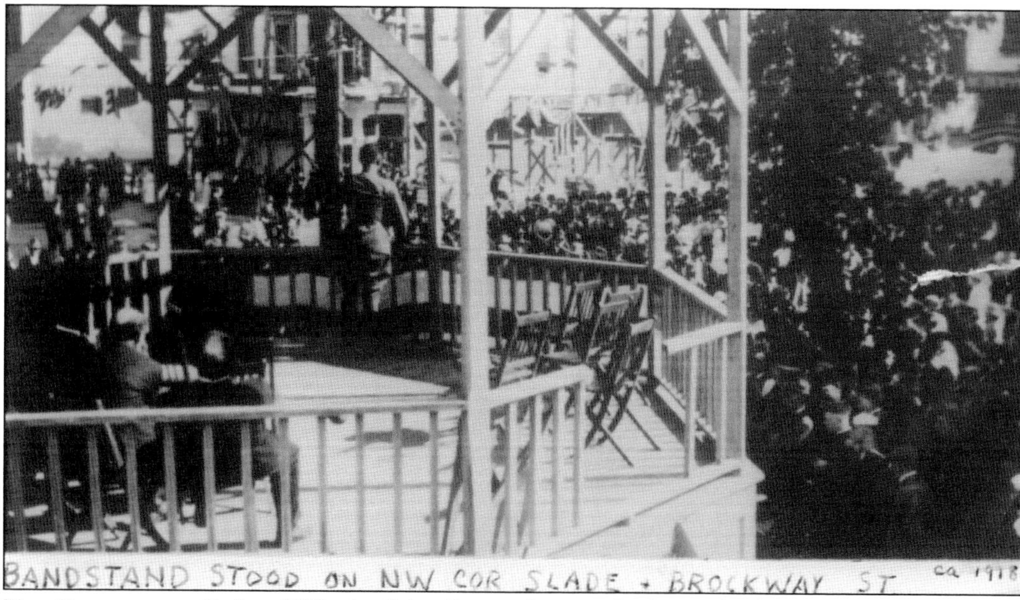

The Bandstand. Before 1910, the John Patten Store, which was built around 1857 and stood on Brockway Street at the northwest corner of Slade, was moved around the corner on Slade Street. A bandstand was built on the empty corner and remained there until it was demolished in 1921 so the Palatine National Bank could be erected there in 1925. The Palatine Military Band performed weekly concerts on the bandstand during the summer. The bandstand was used at other times for public occasions.

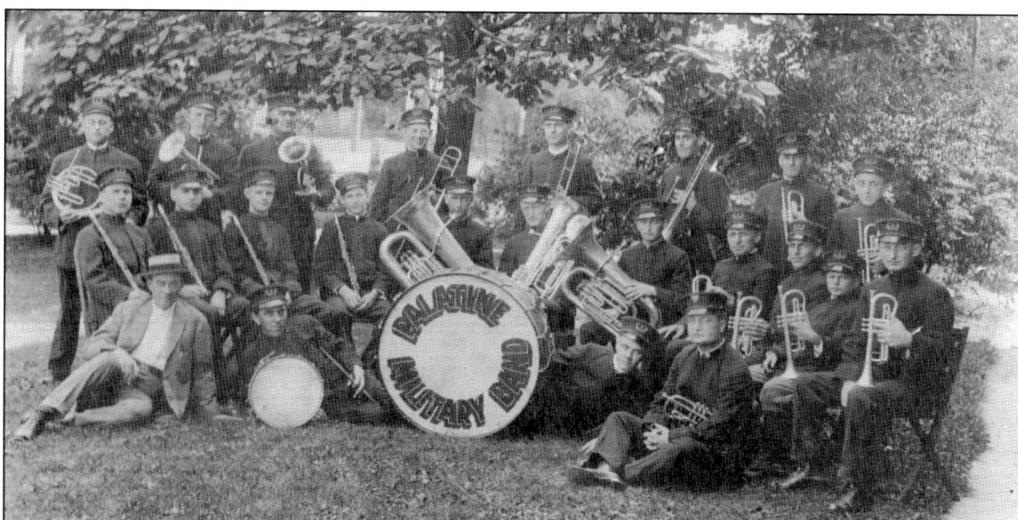

The Palatine Military Band. The Palatine Military Band was organized in the 1870s by J.H. Schierding, a mayor of Palatine, and remained active until 1935. The first practices were held in Knickrene's Cabinet Shop, later over Harmening's store, and then at Hunnerberg Hall.

On Friday evenings in the summer, the band played weekly concerts in the bandstand on Brockway Street from 1915 until the early 1920s, when the bandstand was torn down to build the Palatine National Bank. The band led the Memorial Day parade, and early on the Fourth of July morning, it toured the town on a hayrack, playing stirring music. The band was considered one of the best in Cook County. It won prizes and laurels in Chicago, Elgin, and other nearby communities.

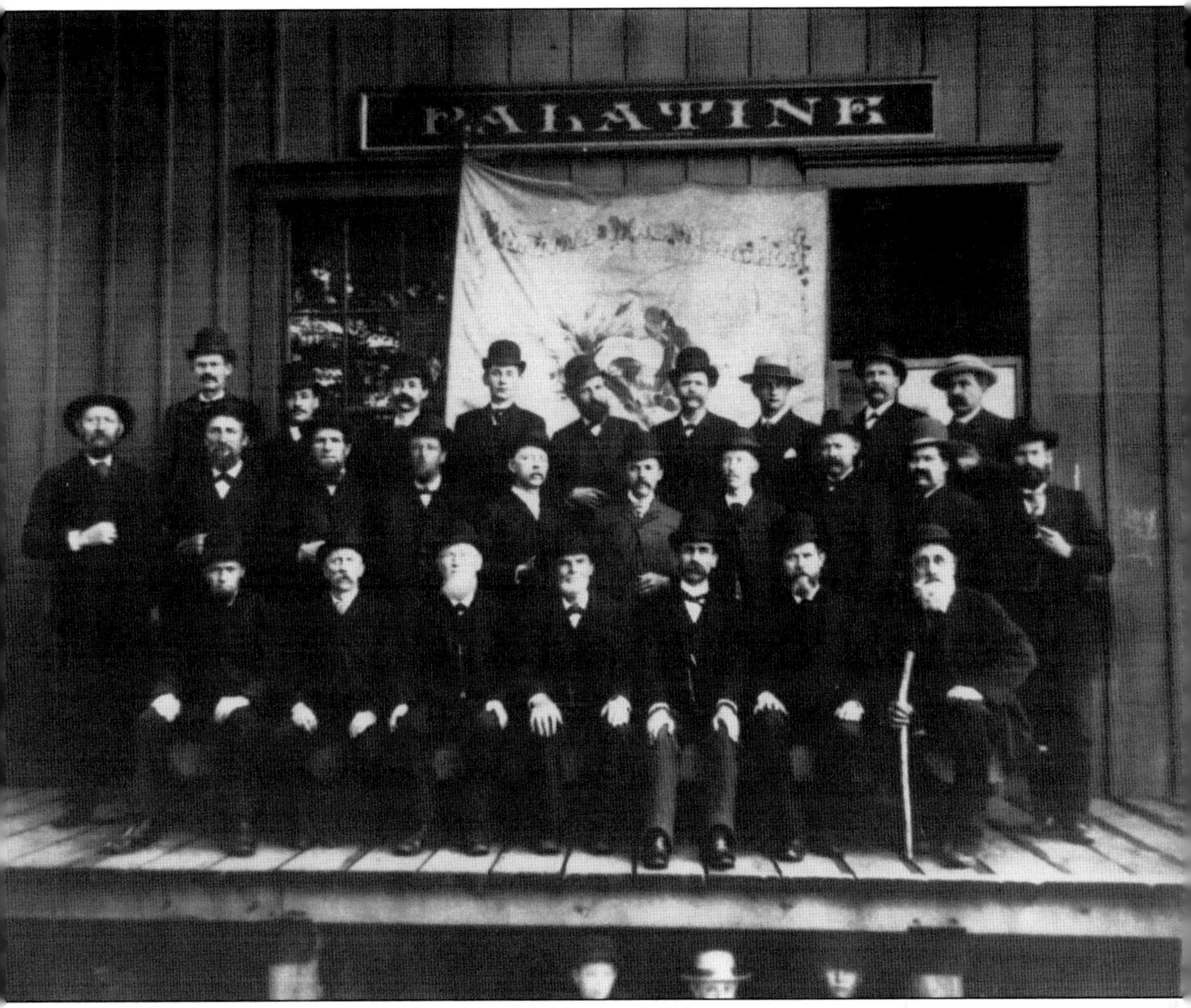

THE PALATINE MANNERCHOR. The people of Palatine did not lack for entertainment in the 1800s. The Palatine Mannerchor, or German Men's Singing Society, provided the community with outstanding entertainment, including original musicals and yearly and special event concerts. It also entertained residents of surrounding communities.

The group was well known in the area for its music, but the men also represented real community power. Members included leaders and businessmen: furniture maker Charles Danielson, cigar maker Henry Godknecht, the Prellberg tailors, the Kuebler Hotel owners, building and mill owner H.C. Batterman, village president J.H. Schierding, planing mill owner Henry Abelman, shop owner Charles Theis, and many other influential people.

The Palatine Mannerchor hired choir directors and met regularly on the third floor of the Batterman Building. When H.C. Batterman was president of the organization, the group planned and arranged the dedication of his building on November 27, 1884. That event included singing, speeches, and the Palatine brass band. Of course, the poster advertising the event was printed in German, with a small English translation at the bottom.

The Mannerchor membership and popularity reached a peak in the 1880s and 1890s. That coincided with the large German immigration into the area. Membership slowly decreased as fewer immigrants came to Palatine from Germany and fewer children of original immigrants spoke German.

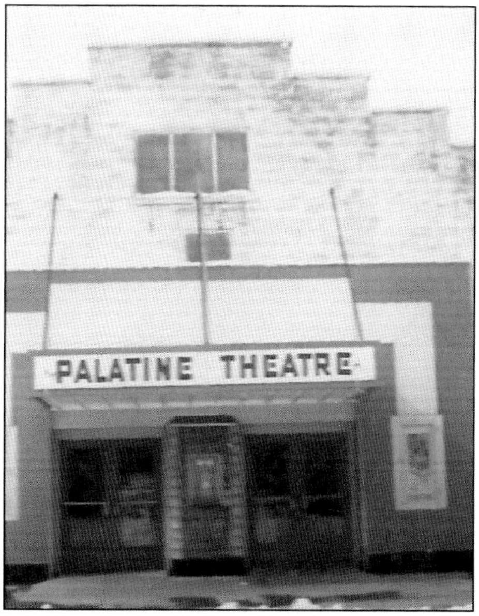

Palatine Theatre. Seip's Auditorium had replaced the barn behind the hotel in 1908. Beside dances held there, the hall hosted plays, meetings, radio programs, vaudeville acts, a circus show, movies, and Ku Klux Klan initiation ceremonies. The movie *Right Foot Forward* was filmed in downtown Palatine in 1920 and shown at the auditorium.

The hall reopened on September 25, 1936, as the Palatine Theatre. During renovations, it was fireproofed and the best sound system and a cooling system were installed. Charles Seips leased the facility. Over the years, the theater had many changes of managers and owners and was permanently closed and leveled in 1952.

Some of the highlights over the years were stage shows, food gifts to pay for admission in 1940, and scrap steel for admission in 1943 during World War II. Two films on sex hygiene, one for women and one for men, were shown separately.

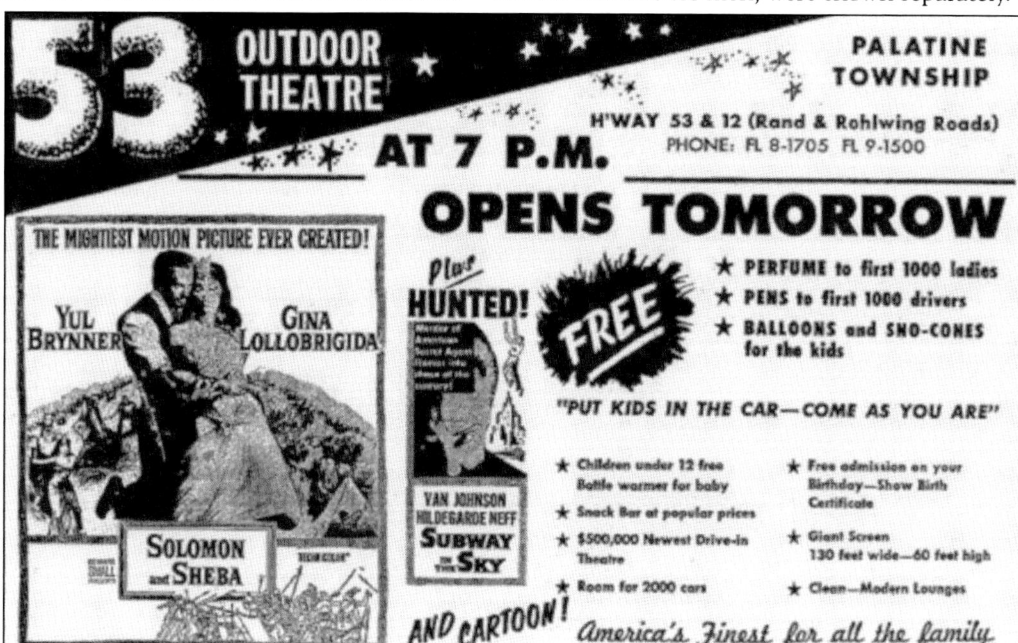

53 Drive-In Theater. The 53 Drive-In Theater was opened on the west side of Hicks and Rand Roads on April 29, 1960, by H. Schoenstadt and Sons, Inc., with one screen and a capacity of 765 cars. Jeffrey Kohlberg operated the theater for 25 years. Two more screens were added in the 1970s. At its opening in 1960, the theater boasted many modern features. Electric heating would be used extensively to keep the 53 Drive-In Theater in operation around the calendar. The concession building, administration building, projection booth, and ticket booths would be heated. By fall, wiring would be completed to install individual car heaters. Food service was available.

The drive-in played everything from commercial Hollywood fare to art movies, Z-grade horror films, and adult films. A Swap-O-Rama Flea Market opened there in 1976. The last movie was shown on September 21, 1986.

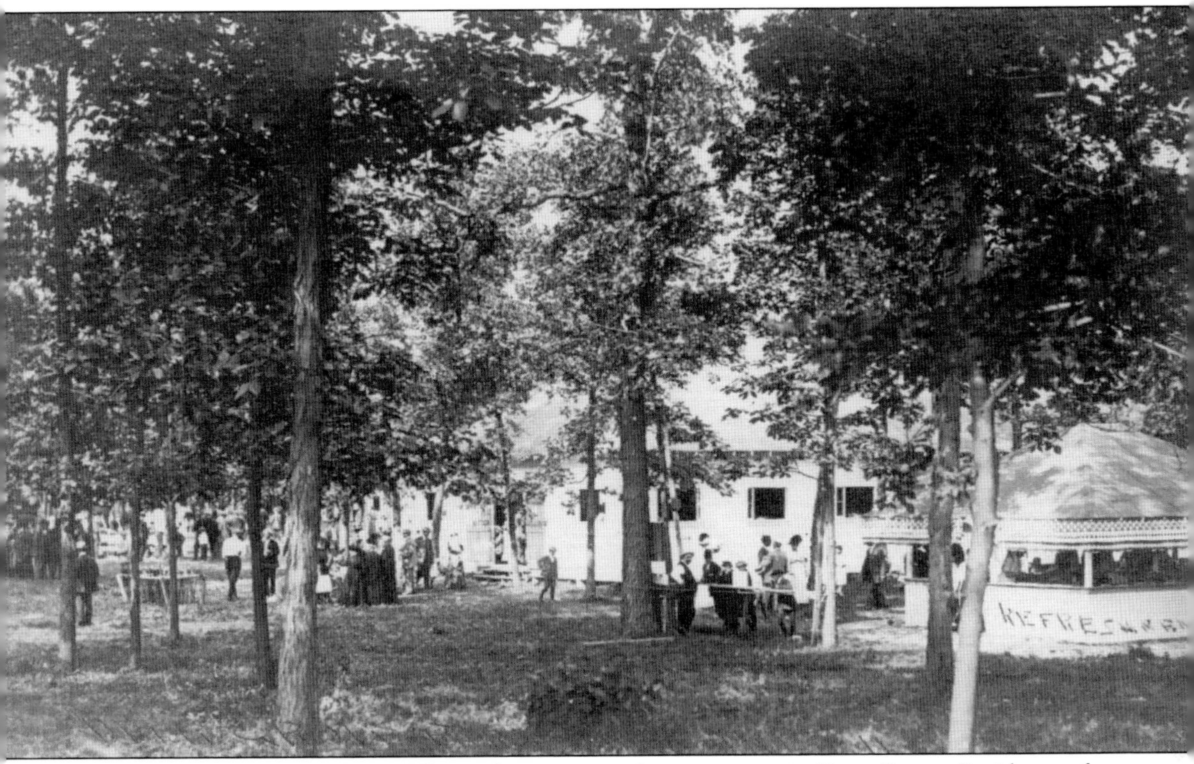

Deer Grove, a Private Park. The earliest area settlements were in Deer Grove. Residents of Palatine Township used the forest to collect wood for their stoves. Veterinarian Dr. John Wilson spent $5,000 in 1911 to develop 70 acres on the east side of Quentin Road into Deer Grove Park. The park flourished with the coming of the PLZ&W Railroad to transport people locally or those coming from Chicago by train to Palatine.

The park had a running track and a baseball diamond surrounded by bleachers on a sloping grass field shaded by trees. It could accommodate 500 viewers. There was a dance pavilion with a musician's stage. A refreshment parlor served ice cream and beverages, and a dining hall with a kitchen offered meals, although many brought picnic food. A well provided drinking water "of the purest crystal." A hitching cable would accommodate 600 horses, and there was room for 500 automobiles.

Fearing commercialization of the area, the newly formed Cook County Forest Preserve District began condemnation against 300 defendants to create Deer Grove Forest Preserve, the first park in the district, in 1916.

Many improvements have been made in the 100 years of the park's existence. Today, the park has trails for hiking, biking, cross-country skiing, and snowmobiling; facilities for ice-skating, sledding, and tennis; and picnic groves.

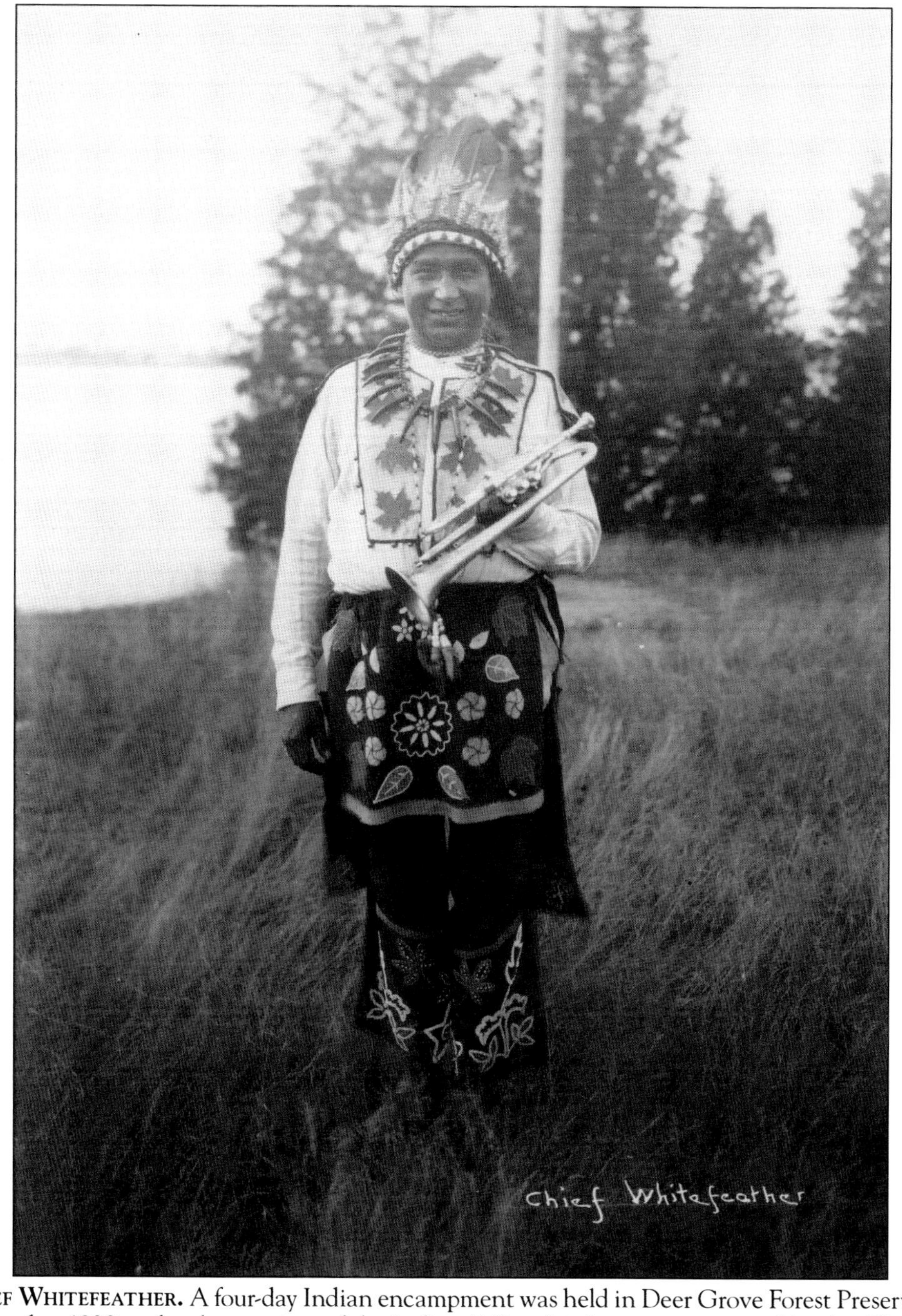

Chief Whitefeather. A four-day Indian encampment was held in Deer Grove Forest Preserve in September 1920 under the auspices of the Indian Fellowship League, sponsored by the Chicago Historical Society. Chiefs from surrounding states, representing all the tribes that formerly roamed Illinois, pitched their tents in the park. The ceremonies and dances were viewed by 60,000 people.

The activities were filmed and shown by the Pathe Weekly (newsreel) in Chicago theaters and in Siep's Hall in Palatine.

An Indian encampment was held again in 1921 and in 1923 with many visitors.

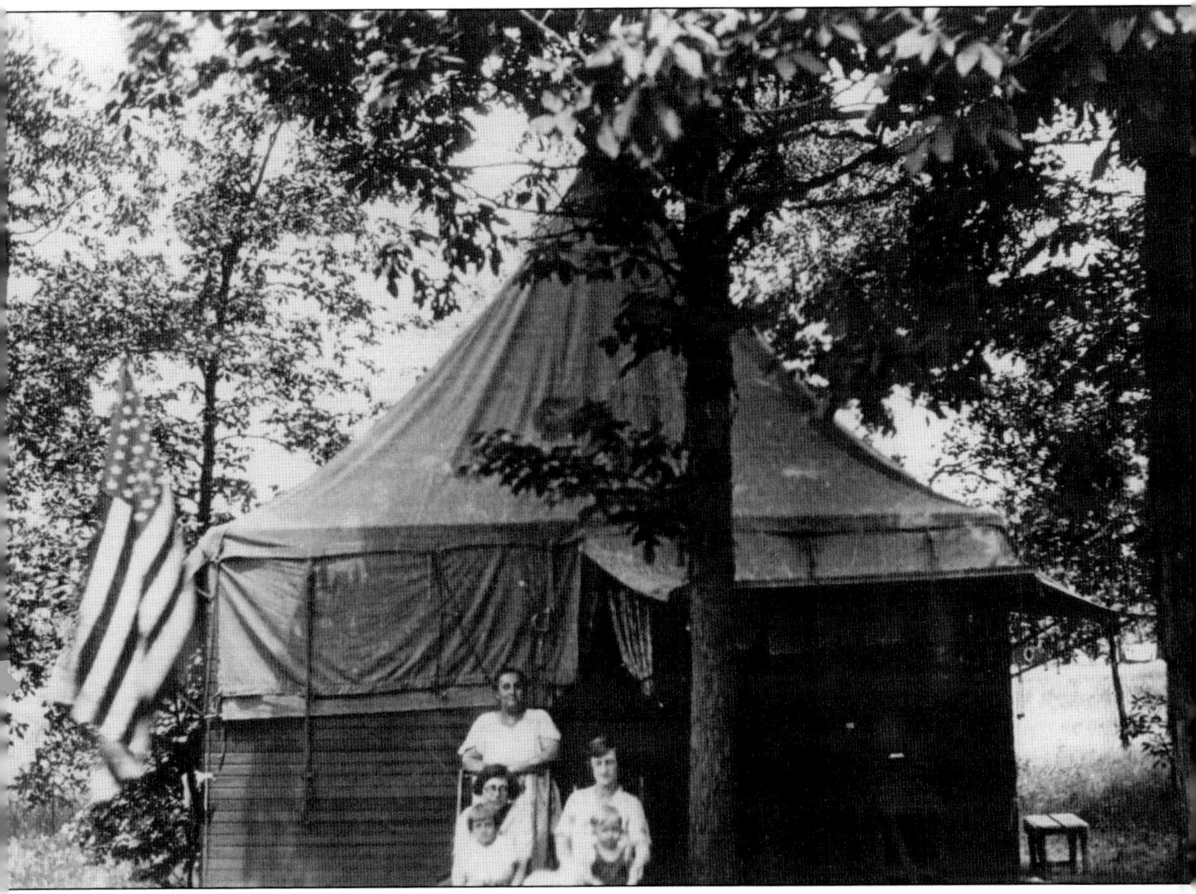

EDWIN BAUR FAMILY IN THEIR DEER GROVE COTTAGE. Before Deer Grove became a county park, some individuals who owned plots placed summer cottages on them. It is believed that they were originally built as treatment residences for tuberculosis sufferers in the days when the preferred treatment was to get plenty of fresh air.

The cottages had half-walls with siding on the bottom and screening on the top and a tent covering. They were 20 by 30 feet with a large living room, a small kitchen, two small bedrooms, and no indoor plumbing.

By the 1930s, the forest preserve wanted the cottages gone and some were moved to individual sites in the area around Deer Grove. Quite a few were moved south to the Plum Grove Road area in a subdivision named Teonia Woods, on the east side of Meacham/Plum Grove Roads and south of Algonquin Road. They were gradually improved, winterized, and enlarged. The traces of some of the cottages can be seen in the small homes that predominate in this subdivision, which is now part of Rolling Meadows.

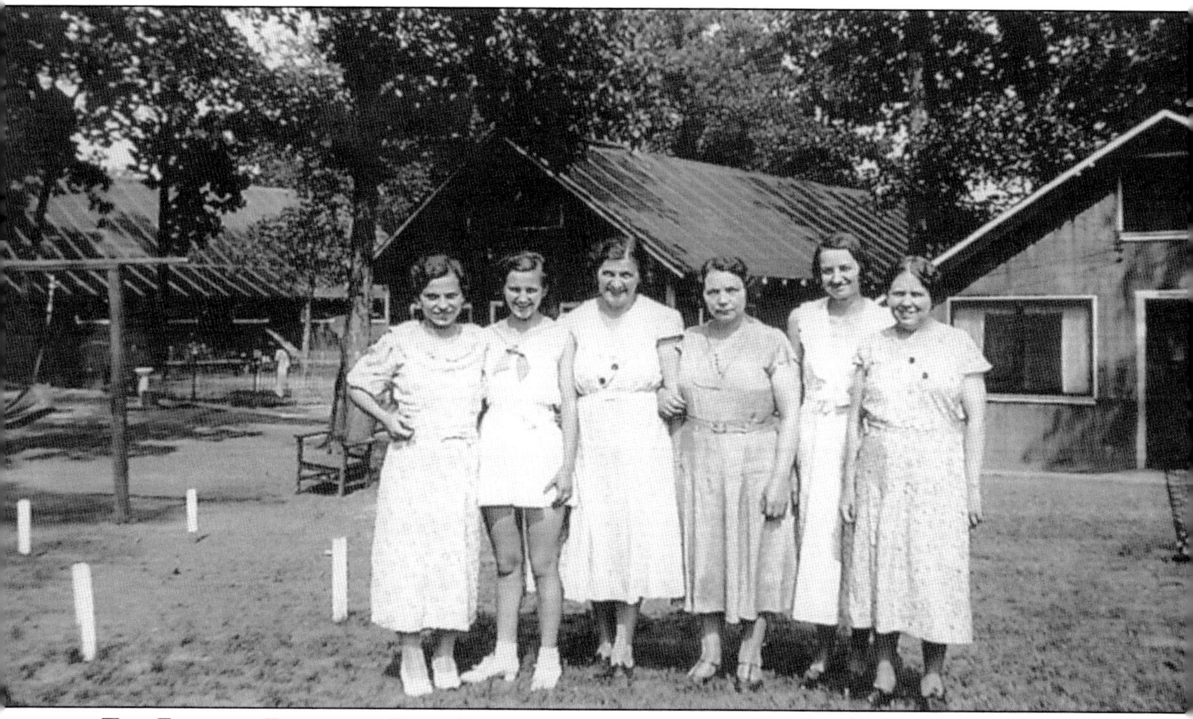

The Zielinski Family at Camp Reinberg in the 1930s. The Cook County Forest Preserve District purchased the 74.16 acres that were Wilson's Deer Grove Park for $11,416 in 1917. These buildings became the nucleus of Camp Reinberg, which was named after the forest preserve board's first president.

That same year, 600 children of poor parents and their mothers were given a 10-day outing at Deer Grove. Within a few years, the district had constructed two large dormitories, a huge mess hall and kitchen, bathhouses, toilets, and several small buildings. The camp was used by Boy Scout troops and local schools for one week to 10-day sessions and day trips.

In 1984, the Chicago Commons Association, which had been conducting a camp for disadvantaged youths, decided it could not afford to renew its lease. The Cook County Forest Preserve District took over the operation to be used primarily for hiking and camping activities, with no food service provided and no swimming pool.

In 2015, Camp Reinberg was opened to the public as a rental campsite. It has four heated and air-conditioned cabins that can each house 10 people; four smaller cabins available spring through fall; thirteen tent sites with picnic tables and fire rings; five RV sites; and an organized group campsite for up to 25 people.

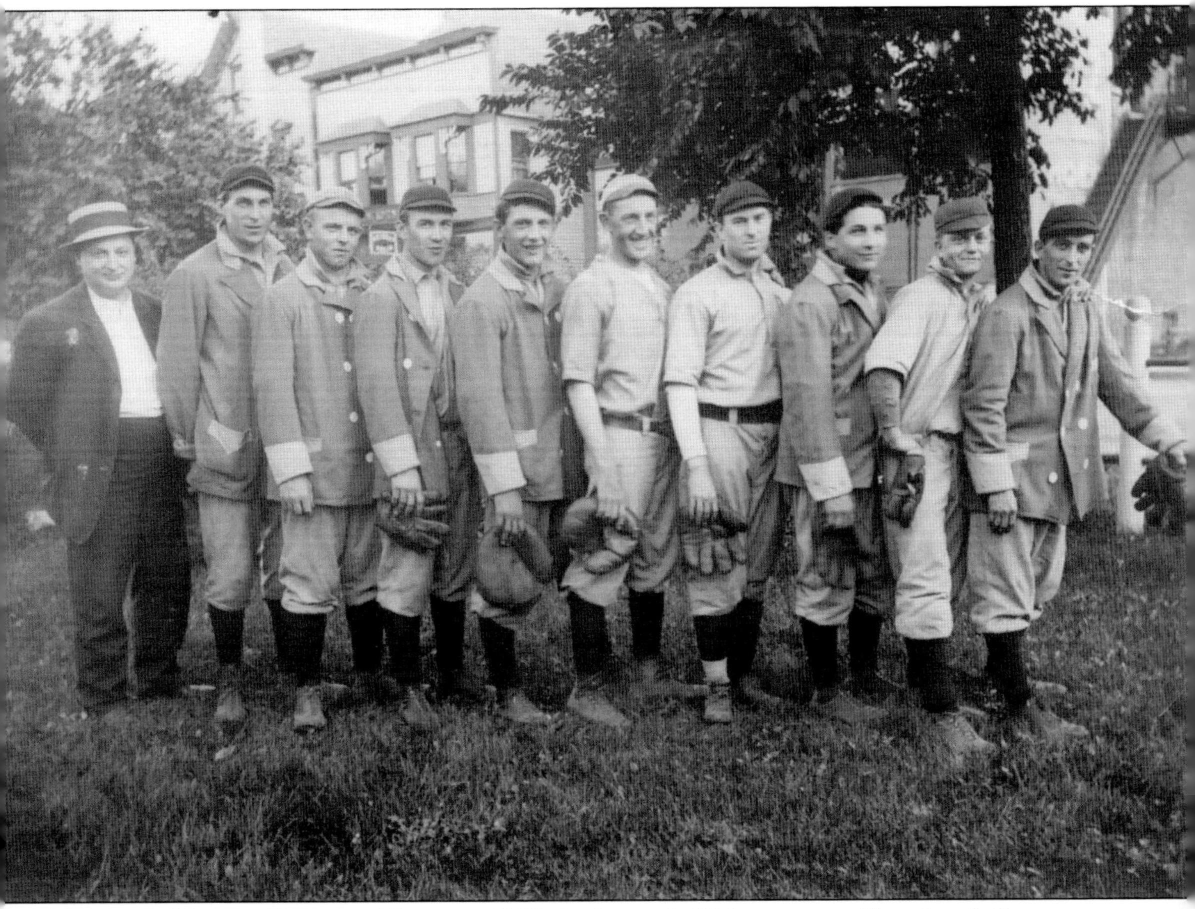

Palatine Village Baseball Team, c. 1910. In the early 20th century, village baseball teams, usually sponsored by local businesses, were a source of entertainment for residents.

In 1908, the Palatine Village Board ordered its baseball teams to provide an officer for ball games and stipulated that there would be no trespassing on property adjoining the field.

In August 1910, the Palatine Military Band played a concert and an ice-cream social was held to benefit the baseball team. Ice cream and cake cost 10¢.

An article in the *Palatine Enterprise* in 1905 described a scheduled baseball game in which the Arlington Heights team failed to show up at the last minute, with no explanation. The Palatine team had gone to a lot of expense in arranging the game and went "in the hole" for a large amount as a result. Since Palatine had a very strong team that year and would probably have scored an easy victory, they figured the explanation for the no-show was a "yellow streak" on the part of Arlington. The Palatine team vowed to only play teams that mean business.

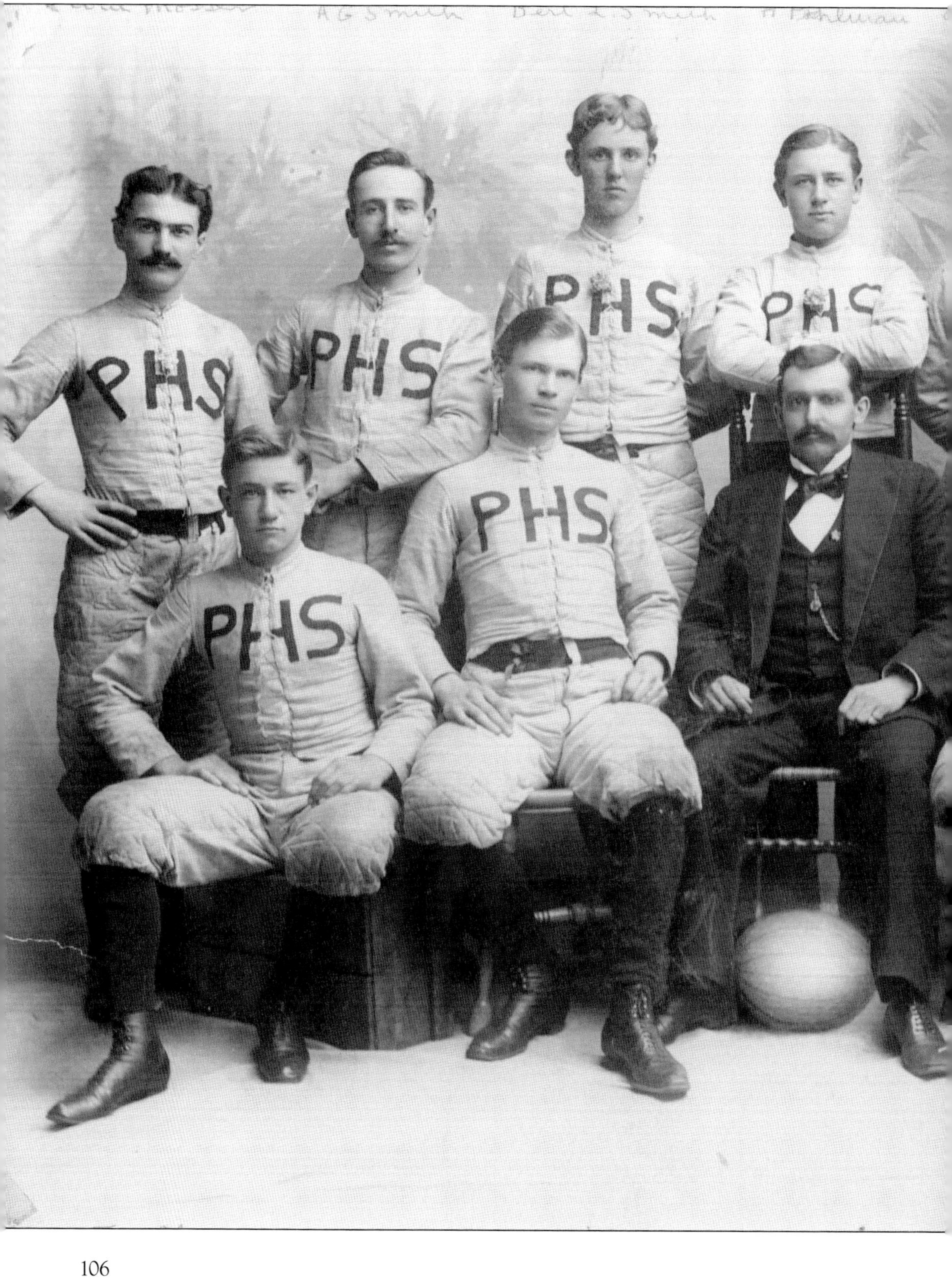
A G Smith
PHS

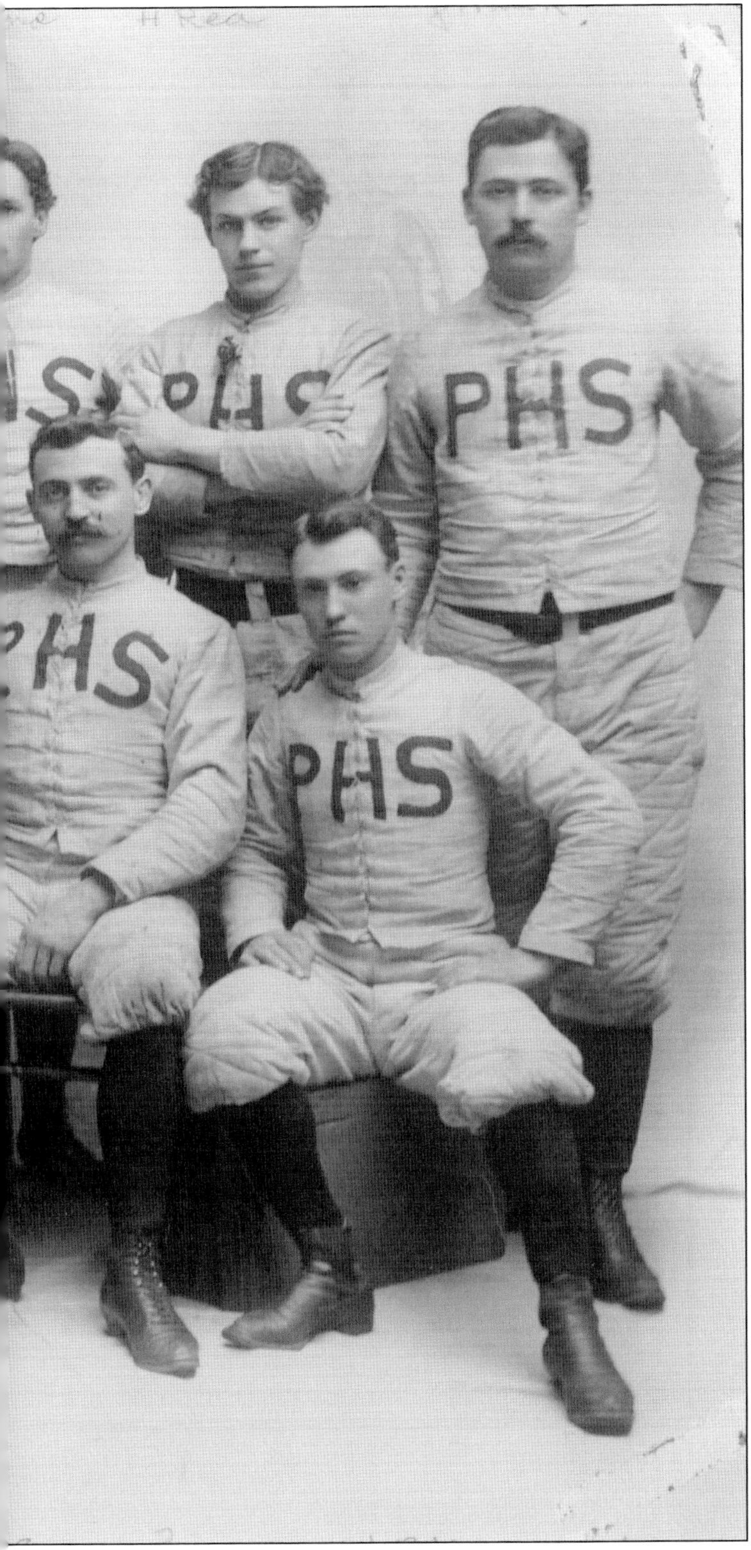

1902 Palatine Village Team. The Palatine Athletic Club was composed of men of the village whose aim was to provide sporting events for the town in the late 1800s and into the 20th century. They met on the second floor of Mosser Drugs until the Masons built their new hall in 1905 and occupied the second floor. To help finance the building, the first floor was rented to the Palatine Athletic Club. Beside a meeting room, the athletic club built a two-lane bowling alley, which was said to be the first one in the area, outside Chicago.

The football team they sponsored was composed of Palatine men and was pretty successful against teams such as Blue Island, Chicago Tigers, First Regiment Illinois National Guard, Barrington, and others. A.G. Smith, the Palatine correspondent for the *Independent* newspaper in Barrington, wrote descriptive articles about each of the games.

The club sponsored yearly family picnics with activities such as foot and bicycle races. It also held "Ladies Night" each January. At the 1896 affair, the Palatine Quartet sang several selections and dramatic recitations were given. The entertainment was followed by a light luncheon, which was served with popcorn and apples.

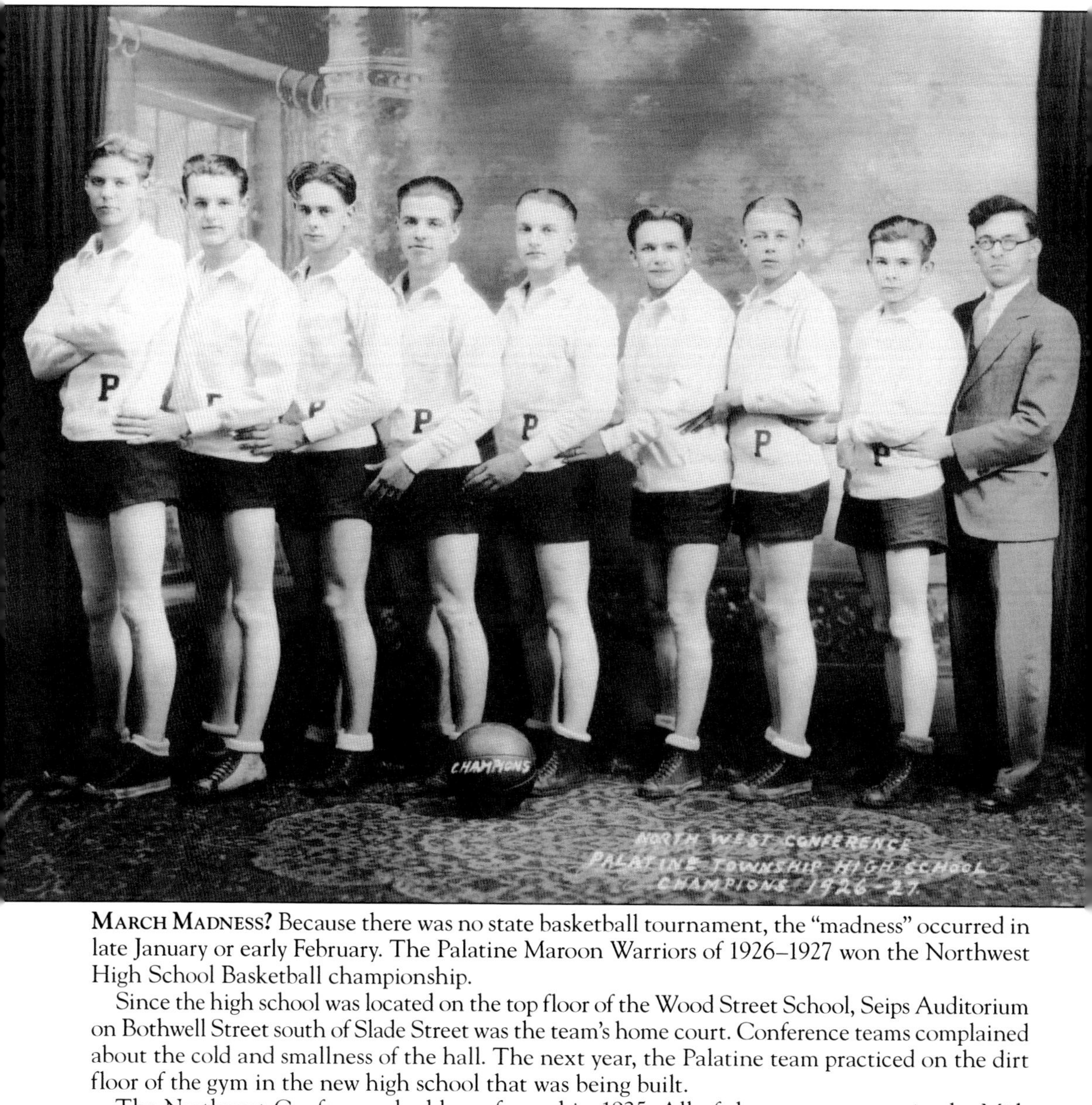

MARCH MADNESS? Because there was no state basketball tournament, the "madness" occurred in late January or early February. The Palatine Maroon Warriors of 1926–1927 won the Northwest High School Basketball championship.

Since the high school was located on the top floor of the Wood Street School, Seips Auditorium on Bothwell Street south of Slade Street was the team's home court. Conference teams complained about the cold and smallness of the hall. The next year, the Palatine team practiced on the dirt floor of the gym in the new high school that was being built.

The Northwest Conference had been formed in 1925. All of the present teams in the Mid-Suburban League except for Palatine, Barrington, and Arlington, did not exist at that time, so the teams came from schools in Antioch, Bensenville, Leyden Community, Libertyville Township, Warren Township, and Wauconda Township.

The 1930–1931 team played in its new gym. Unfortunately, Palatine came home from the championship game with a second-place trophy, having been beaten by Arlington.

An interesting thing about games of that era were the low scores. Palatine scored the most points of the season with 34 against Leyden. However, a more typical score was the 28-17 in an earlier game.

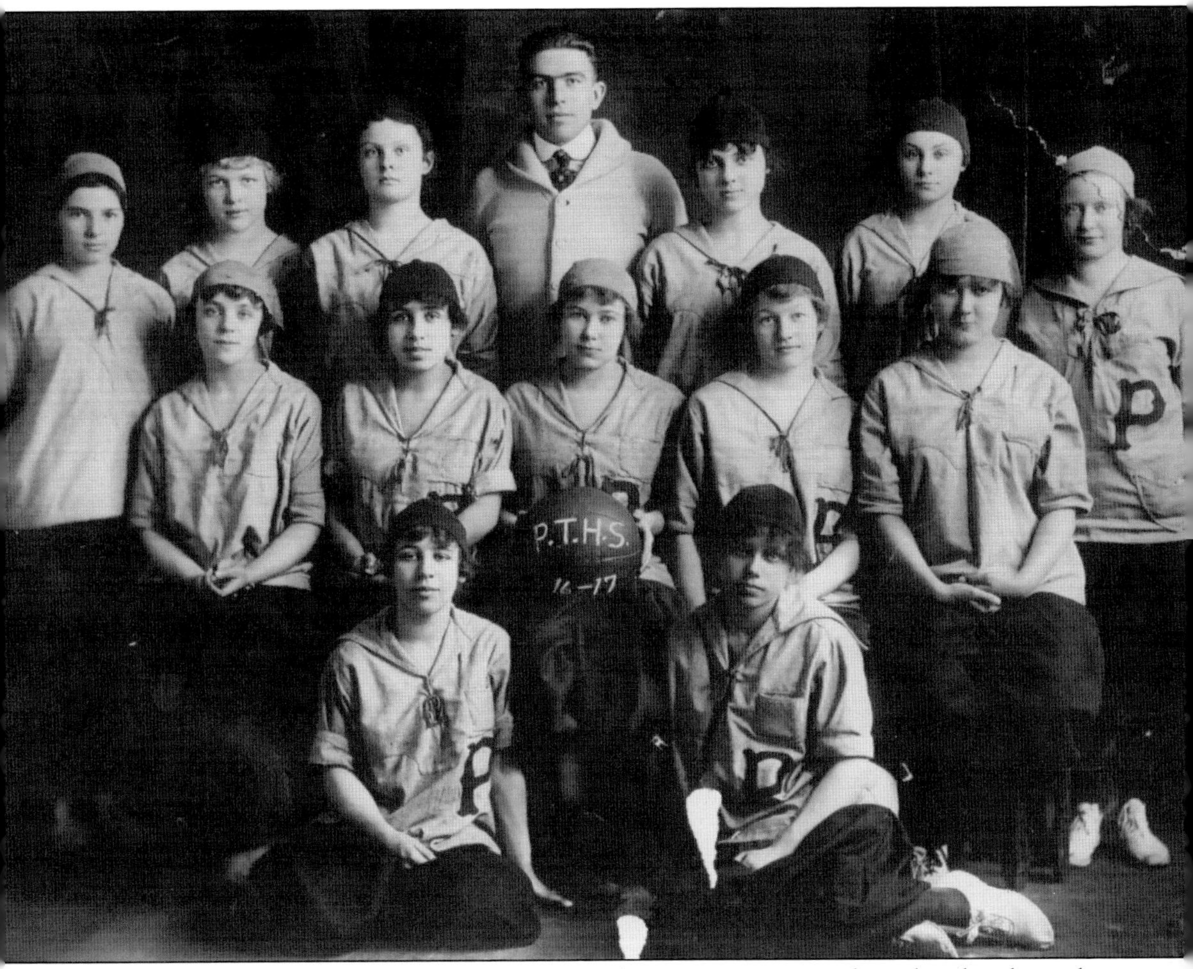

EQUAL OPPORTUNITY PALATINE HIGH SCHOOL. The government may have legislated equal opportunity sports in 1972, but Palatine High School was ahead of the game. The historical society has this wonderful picture of the 1916–1917 Palatine Township High School girls' basketball team. The young women probably practiced at the old Hunnerberg Hall because the Wood Street School did not have a gymnasium.

The players and coach are pictured here. They are, from left to right, (first row) Mildred Smith and Dorothy Timmerman; (second row) Ruth Schering, Myra Smith, LuLu Simmons, Edna Timmerman, and Jennie Hanns; (third row) Madge Gibbs, Helen Matthei, Helen Swick, Coach Heinz, Dorothy Gibbs, Grace Vogtm, and Frances Daniels.

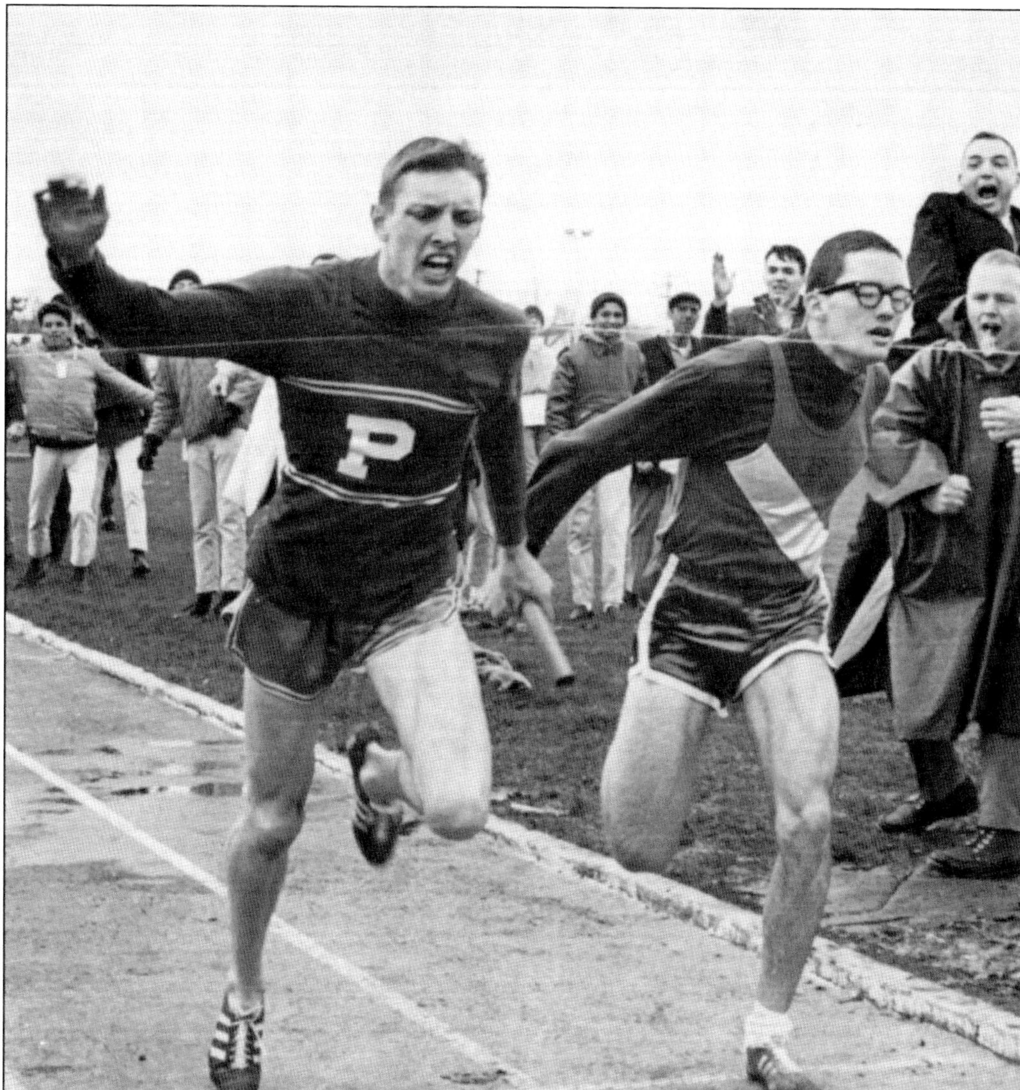

GORDON DREYFUS, 1965 STATE MILE CHAMPION. The 83rd Palatine Relays were held on May 6, 2015, which makes it the second-oldest continuously held track event in the state of Illinois.

Carl Megel was coach of the football, basketball, and track teams at Palatine High in 1932. He had taken his track team to several relay meets, including Pekin, Springfield, and Wheaton. When the athletic talents of the Palatine track team, notably Ed Hahnfeld in discus and javelin, attracted attention, Megel decided to arrange a Palatine Relay meet on April 19, 1933.

Megel was assisted by Gerald McElroy, who had come to Palatine High School as a teacher in 1931. During the Depression, no funds were available for awards. Red, white, and blue ribbons substituted for trophies. Peter Vervloit made the hurdles in his high school shop.

Megel and McElroy were on the track at 5:00 a.m. on the morning of the meet to measure and line the lanes, set up standards, and attend to every detail.

The girls' division of the relays was started in 1976. The meet has been held at the Ost Field cinder track at the 1928 Palatine High, Conant, Fremd, and the 1977 Palatine High School.

Nine

PEOPLE

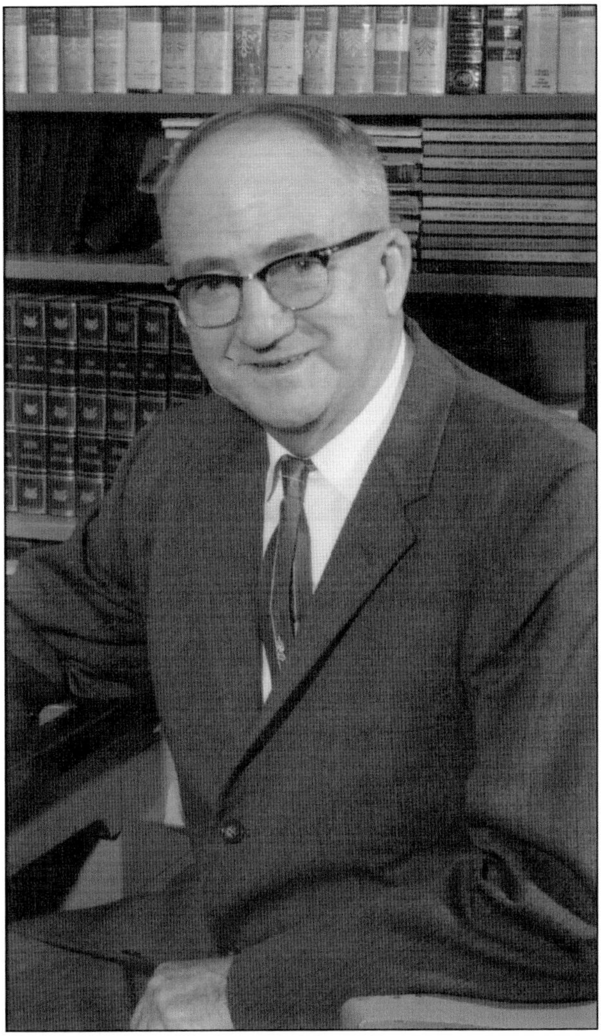

WILLIAM FREMD. As one of eight graduates from Palatine High School in 1920, William Fremd was known as "the smart one." He had grown up on a farm near Dundee and Rand Roads and later married neighbor Edith Baumann.

When he was 26 years old, he attended a school board meeting on a whim and wound up being elected to the board. For the next 44 years, he served on the boards for District No. 15 and District No. 211, including 20 years while simultaneously serving on both boards (1937–1957).

In 44 years, Fremd grew into a forward-thinking board member who secured the high school district's stability. He foresaw the beginnings of suburban sprawl and was the force behind the decision to purchase land around the area. Hoffman Estates and Schaumburg High Schools stand on former farmland purchased by the school district while Fremd served on the board. Fremd High School was named in his honor.

One year during the Depression when the school district only collected $1.40 in revenue, Fremd gave the school district $1,000. He was also one of the first people in the township to own a tractor because he was allergic to horses.

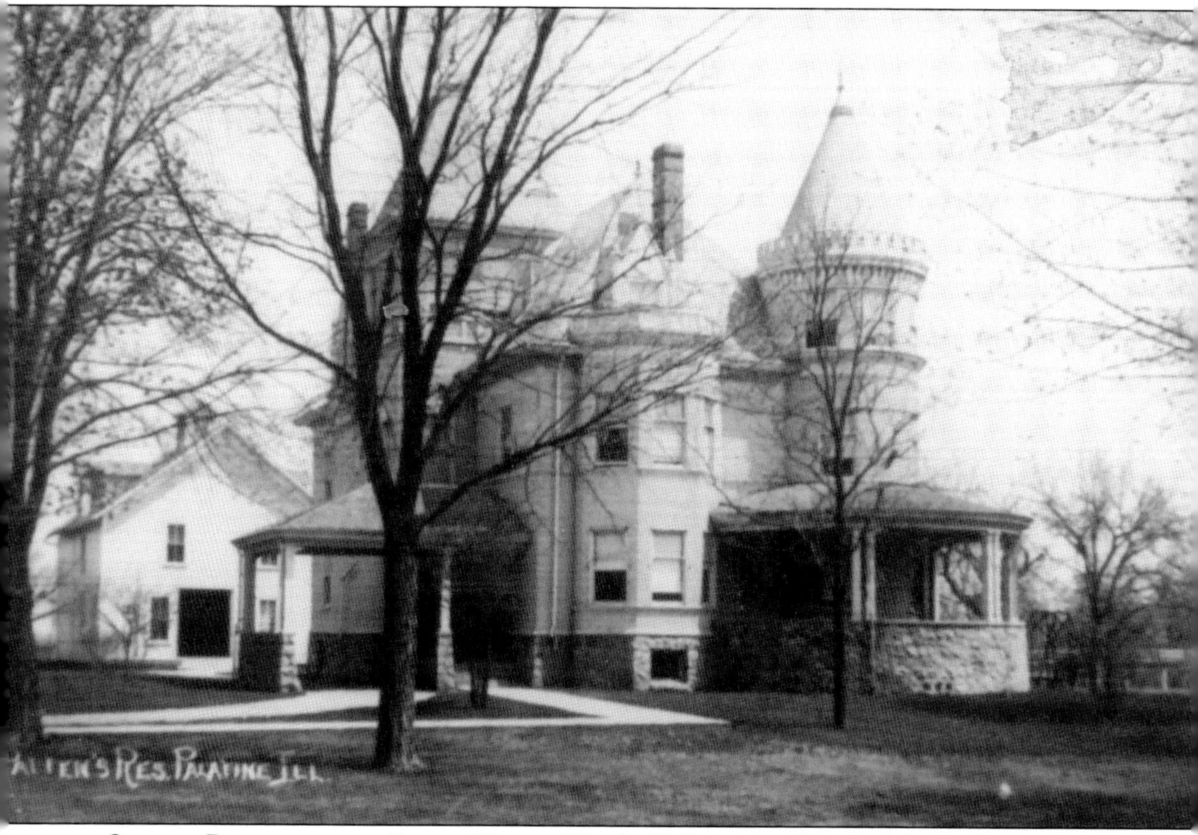

Charles Patten and the Patten House. Charles H. Patten was born to John and Lillis Patten a few months after they arrived in Palatine in 1852. With an inheritance from his father, he founded a bank in the Batterman Building, which, for a time, was the only bank in town. His bank closed when a new state law prohibited private banks, but he helped organize the First National Bank of Palatine and was a director for many years.

He was village president in 1894–1895 and is credited with building Palatine's first water system. Upon retirement, Charles and his wife traveled a great deal and spent winters in warmer climates. He died in 1929 and is buried in Hillside Cemetery.

Charles Patten is most remembered for the house he built in 1898 on a large lot at the southeast corner of Benton and Wood Streets. It was designed by a French architect. While he and his bride were on their honeymoon, the Marshall Fields Company came in and decorated the home, including putting murals on the ceilings of the first floor. The couple did not like them and covered them with a false ceiling.

The house remained in the family until 2004 when 90-year-old Barbara Patten, widow of Charles H. Patten's grandson Charles, died. It took six years and a million-dollar discount to sell the house to a family with young children. The six-bedroom Queen Anne–style house is one of the few mansions in town that has not been razed.

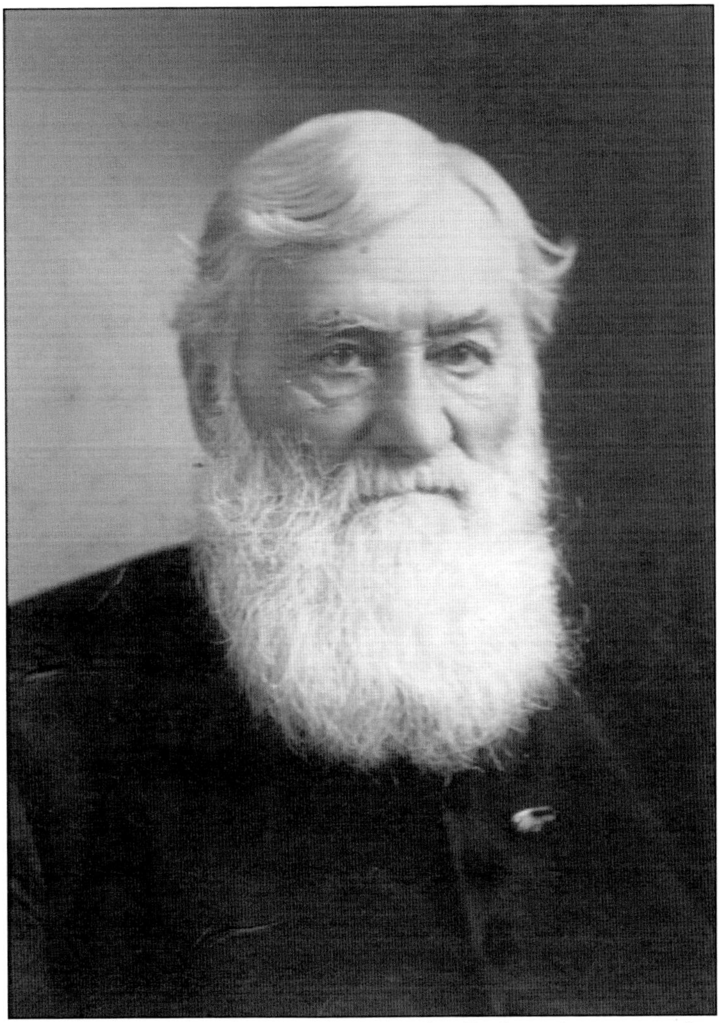

Judge James Bradwell. Myra Colby met James Bradwell when she was teaching in Elgin and James was there on business. The couple eloped in 1852 because Myra's family did not like James. She was the daughter of Abigail and Willey Colby, who had settled in Schaumburg. Myra had attended finishing school in Kenosha, Wisconsin, and Elgin Female Seminary for a year.

Thomas and Elizabeth Bradwell, James's parents, had lived in Utica, New York, in 1829; Jacksonville, Illinois, in 1833; Wheeling in 1834 (before the Indian treaty); and finally settled on a farm at Bradwell and Ela Roads in 1844. They were "landed gentry" and maintained servants to run their property.

In 1855, James was admitted to the Illinois bar. With the intent of working with her husband, Myra passed the Illinois bar exam with high honors in 1869. When she applied to practice law in Illinois, she was denied by the Illinois Supreme Court because she was a woman. She used her sharp mind and energy to found the *Chicago Legal News* in 1869 and was its chief editor until her death in 1894. Through her paper, she supported, lobbied for, and secured passage of laws that allowed a woman to keep her own earnings and granted the equal right of the mother to have custody of her children.

James had a stellar career as a judge, state representative, and president of the Chicago and Illinois Bar Associations. He had a wide variety of interests and was active in many organizations until his death in 1908.

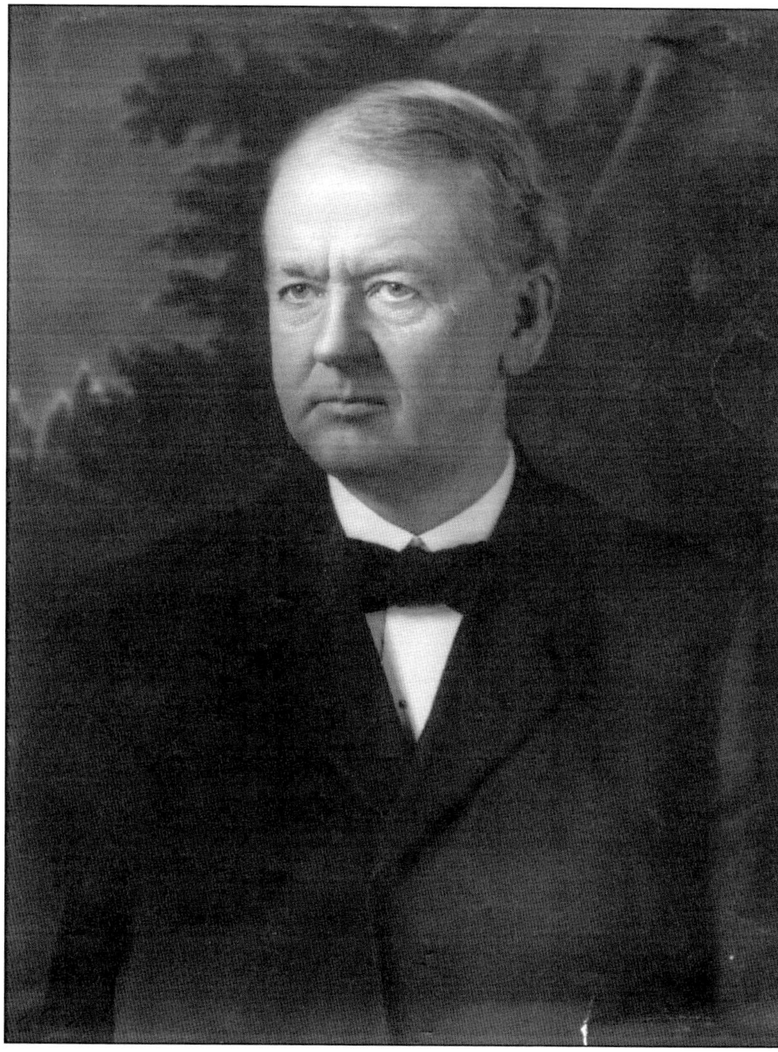

Charles Sidney Cutting. When Palatine High School District No. 211 built its first school on Wood Street in 1928, the auditorium was appropriately named Cutting Hall. The little gem of a theater looks much today as it did in 1928. The park district uses it for a variety of programs, and it is available to resident theater groups, dance recitals, and Palatine Village Band concerts.

Charles Sidney Cutting was born in Vermont in 1854. He attended the University of Oregon but did not graduate. He worked on a newspaper before coming to Palatine in 1874 as a teacher. Two years later, he married Anna Lytle, daughter of Palatine's first mayor; she was also a teacher.

Charles became principal of the Palatine school in 1875 and began a two-year high school course, at that time the only high school between Jefferson Park and Woodstock. Within a few years, the course of study had expanded to four years.

Charles began studying law, was admitted to the bar in 1880, and began practicing with Rollin Williamson of Palatine. Charles and Anna moved to Austin in 1895 (then a suburb of Chicago). He was elected a probate judge in 1900.

Although Judge Cutting was no longer principal of Palatine High when he began practicing law, he never lost his contact with the school. He served as lawyer to the school board until his death in 1936, often returning for graduation ceremonies and donating money to purchase books for the library.

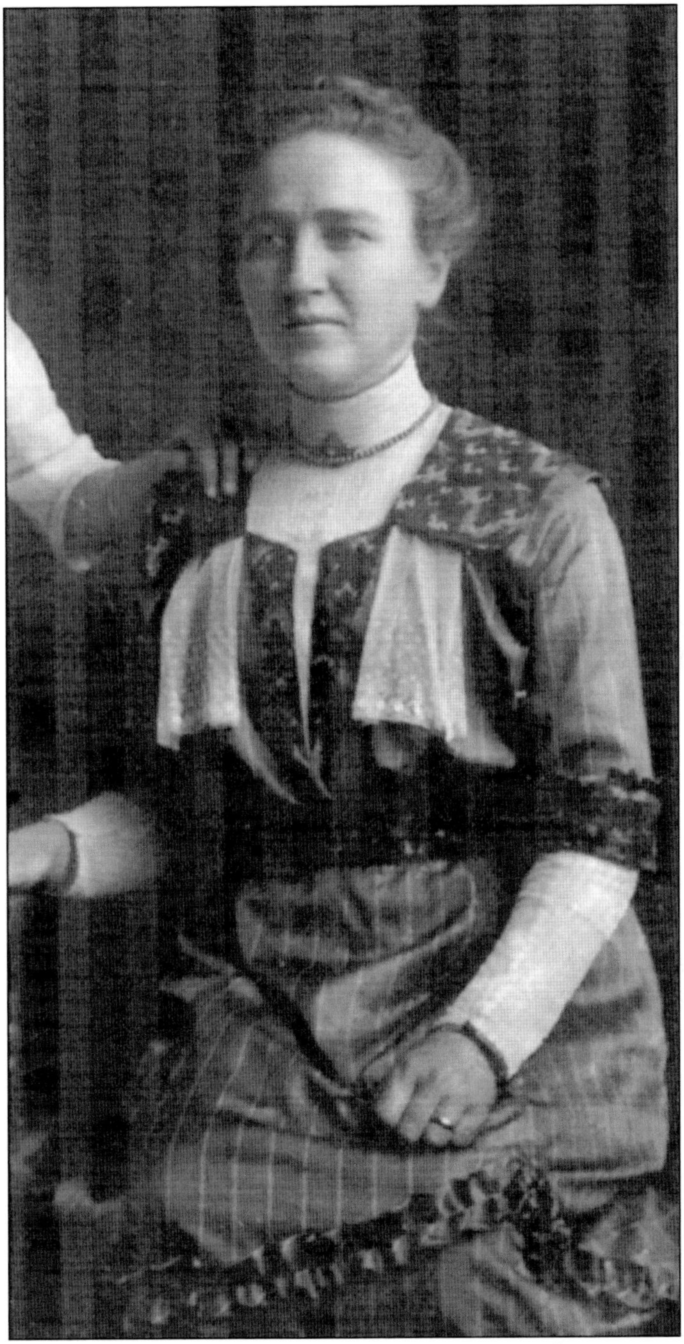

Martha Matthei. The first two Palatine women to vote in an election were Annie (Stuart) Paddock and Martha (Philip) Matthei. The year was 1914, six years before the Nineteenth Amendment to the Constitution granted women the right to vote.

In 1913, Illinois was the first state east of the Mississippi River to pass a women's suffrage law that allowed women to vote in local and national elections.

The March 1914 primary also carried the proposition "Shall Palatine be wet or dry." The dry voters lost by 283 votes, and 23 more women voted wet than voted dry.

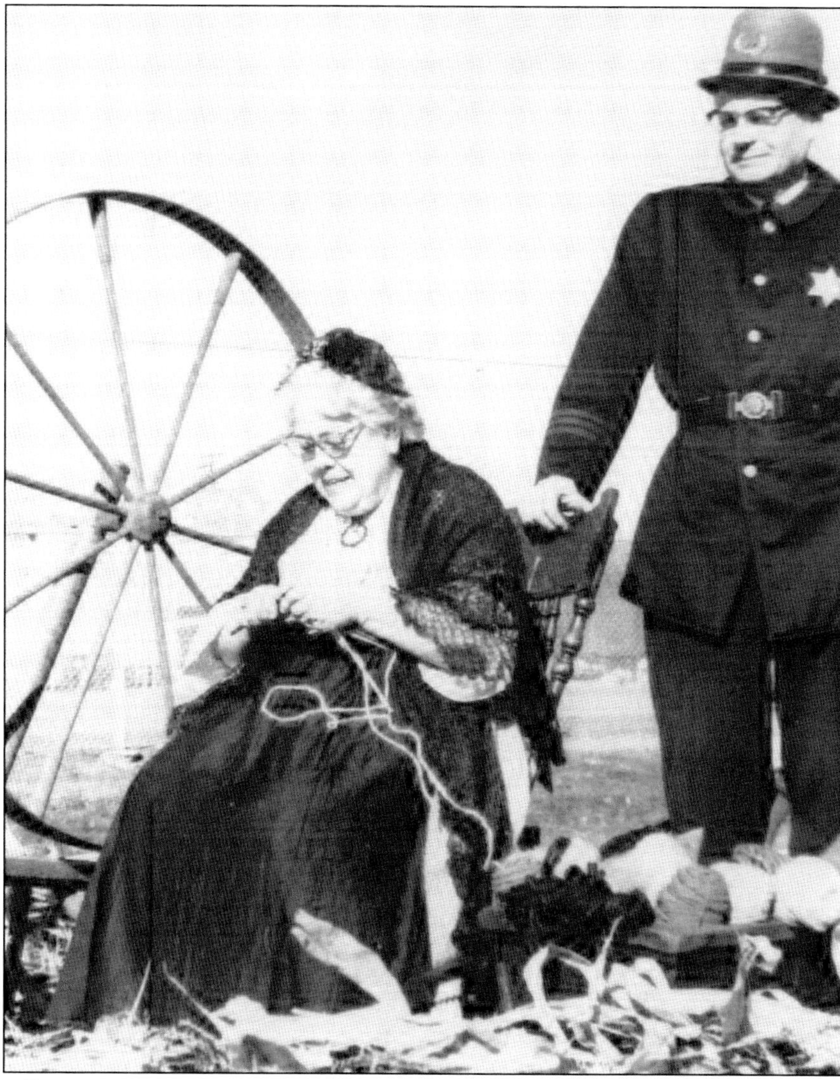

Florence Parkhurst and Avery Wolfrum, 1975. Florence Matilda Parkhurst, born to Albert G. and Gertrude Smith in 1902, grew up in the house at 303 North Brockway Street, which still stands. Florence was one of their eight children who spent their entire lives in Palatine. She graduated Palatine High School in 1921, married Chester McKinley Parkhurst in 1925, had one son, and was widowed in 1932.

Florence was a collector of things and information. The Florence Parkhurst Memorial Library in the Clayson House Museum is a testament to the wealth of material she left the historical society. For 46 years, she rode the train to Chicago, where she was a legal secretary. That train ride was spent reading history and creating documents about Palatine history.

She created notebooks of short histories of village families, their places of origin, marriages, children, births, deaths, and other pertinent information. Florence and Ray Mills of Palatine High School developed three walking tour books of Palatine, describing the residents of the houses.

Florence left memorabilia and photographs from her own life and from the organizations to which she belonged. Her collection included obituaries, birth notices, phone books, picture postcards, high school yearbooks, and other artifacts. After her death in February 1984, the Village of Palatine Board of Trustees passed a Memorial Resolution honoring Florence Smith Parkhurst.

Ten

Wars, Crimes, and Disasters

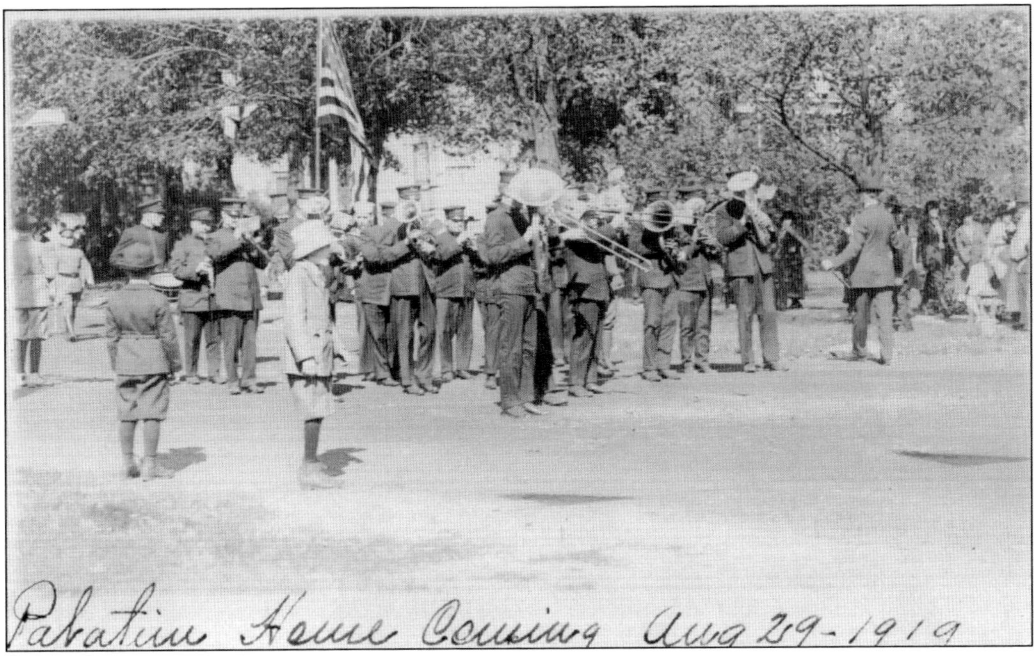

World War I in Palatine. Ralph Hildebrandt, the first Palatine boy to get into the fighting on the western front, was there at the very end. After recovering from his wounds, he rejoined his company on November 10, 1918, and at 5:30 the next morning, he went over the top. He was lying in a shell hole with bullets flying all around him when the "whistle blew" and the fighting stopped at 11:00 a.m.

Back home during the war, Liberty bond drives were conducted. Schoolchildren were organized into War Savings Societies to buy war stamps. Businessmen decided that to save fuel, they would close stores at 6:00 p.m. every day except Saturday. Exceptions were barbershops, ice-cream parlors, poolrooms, and drugstores.

A surgical dressing department was set up in the Patten Building, and the Red Cross sewing room was in the schoolhouse. J.A. Burlingame presided at a meeting in Seip's Auditorium where a new service flag was dedicated.

A World War I memorial plaque listing the names of 50 Palatine men who served was removed to the new American Legion building at 122 West Palatine Road in 1948. A "welcome home" parade was held August 19, 1929.

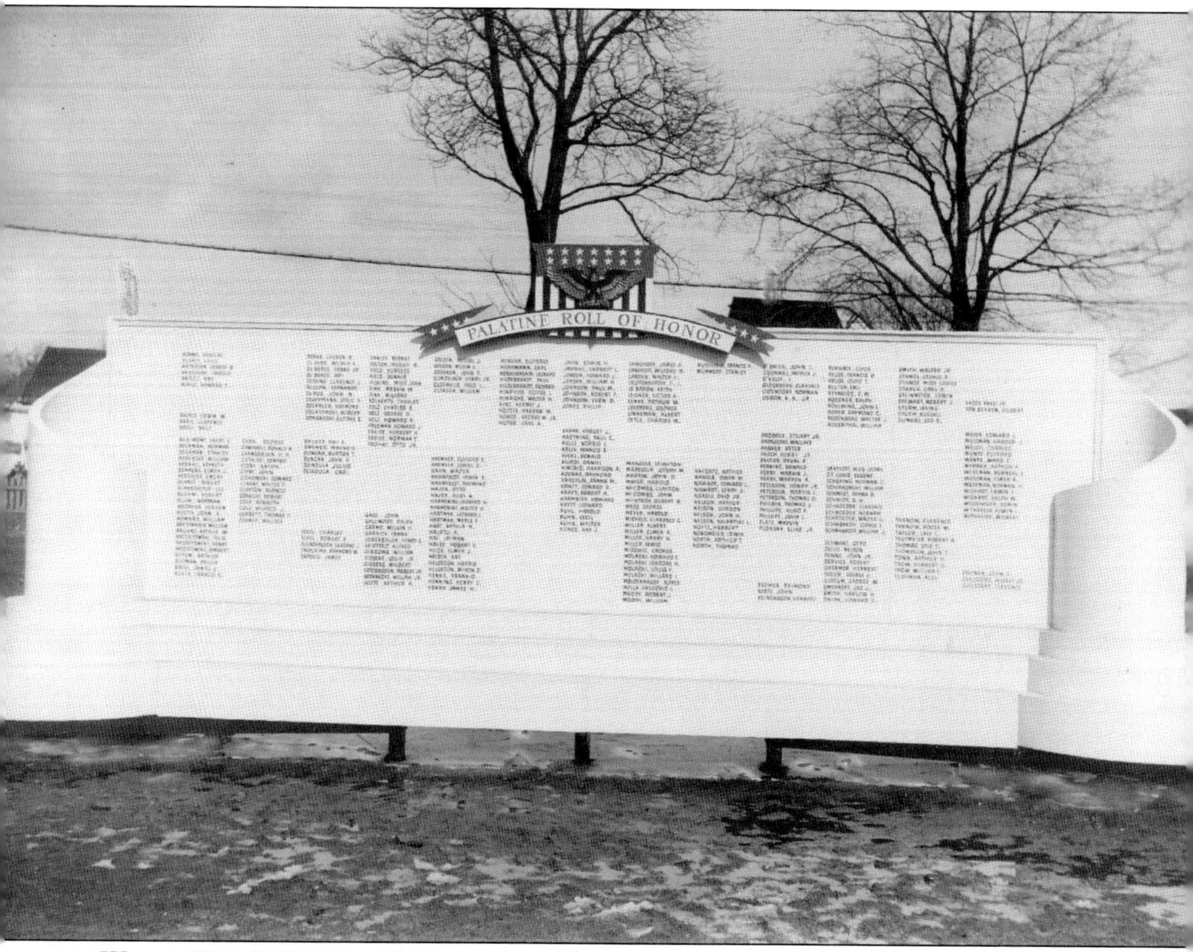

World War II Roll of Honor in the Triangle. Six hundred men and women from the Palatine area served in World War II. A total of 19 of them made the supreme sacrifice. A large wooden structure, the Palatine Roll of Honor, which listed all their names, stood in the triangle formed by Brockway and Slade Streets and the railroad tracks. Eventually, it had to be removed because of poor condition.

The first Palatine boy to die was John O'Brien, who had been raised by his grandparents, John and Hattie Umdenstock. He married Katherine Hans the same day he received his draft notice. He was a bombardier on a B-24 bomber in New Guinea, which was lost on November 6, 1943. He did not get to see the birth of his son that year.

A well-known Palatine man who served was Dr. Carl D. Starck, son of Dr. Carl A. Starck, founder of the Palatine Hospital. After the war, the younger Starck was in family practice in Palatine.

Harrison Kincaid taught mathematics and science at Palatine High School and was a basketball and track coach and director of athletics. He was commissioned as a lieutenant in the US Army Reserve in 1925 and was called into active duty as an instructor in 1943. He taught photography to bombardiers and was discharged after the war as a major.

On November 11, 1991, in a stirring ceremony, the Palatine Township Veterans Memorial on Northwest Highway at Wood Street was dedicated to veterans of World Wars I and II and the Korean and Vietnam Wars.

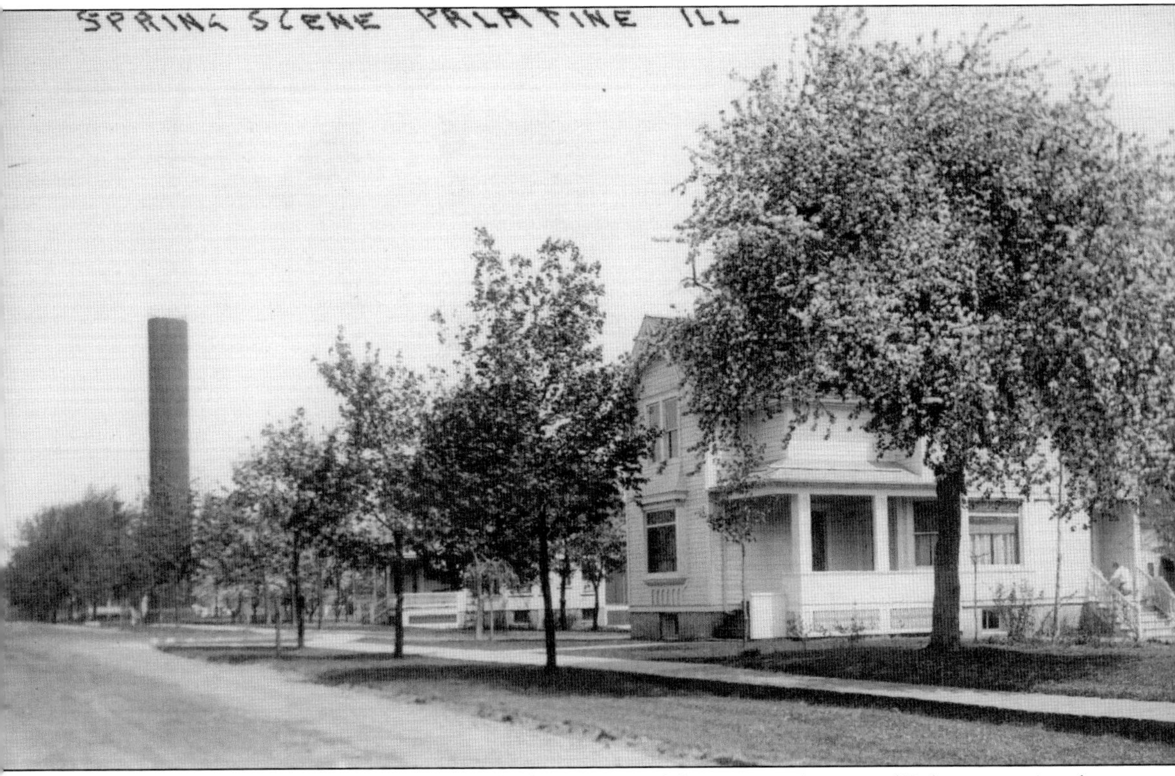

A SERIOUS PRANK. Vandals opened fire hydrants in widely separated parts of Palatine in April 1945, draining the village's entire water supply. The 100,000-gallon standpipe (on the left) was drained to the last drop. Residents who tried to draw water in the hours after midnight could not get a drop from their faucets in any part of the house.

The falling pressure sent the water and police departments on the hunt for the leaks, and they found the open hydrants. The vandalism was apparently the act of a group of high school–age boys, and their identities were pretty well known to police.

According to the newspaper, "Millions of dollars' worth of property was endangered in case of a fire and the act, far from being a kid trick, was an act of sabotage against a public works in wartime and is punishable as such."

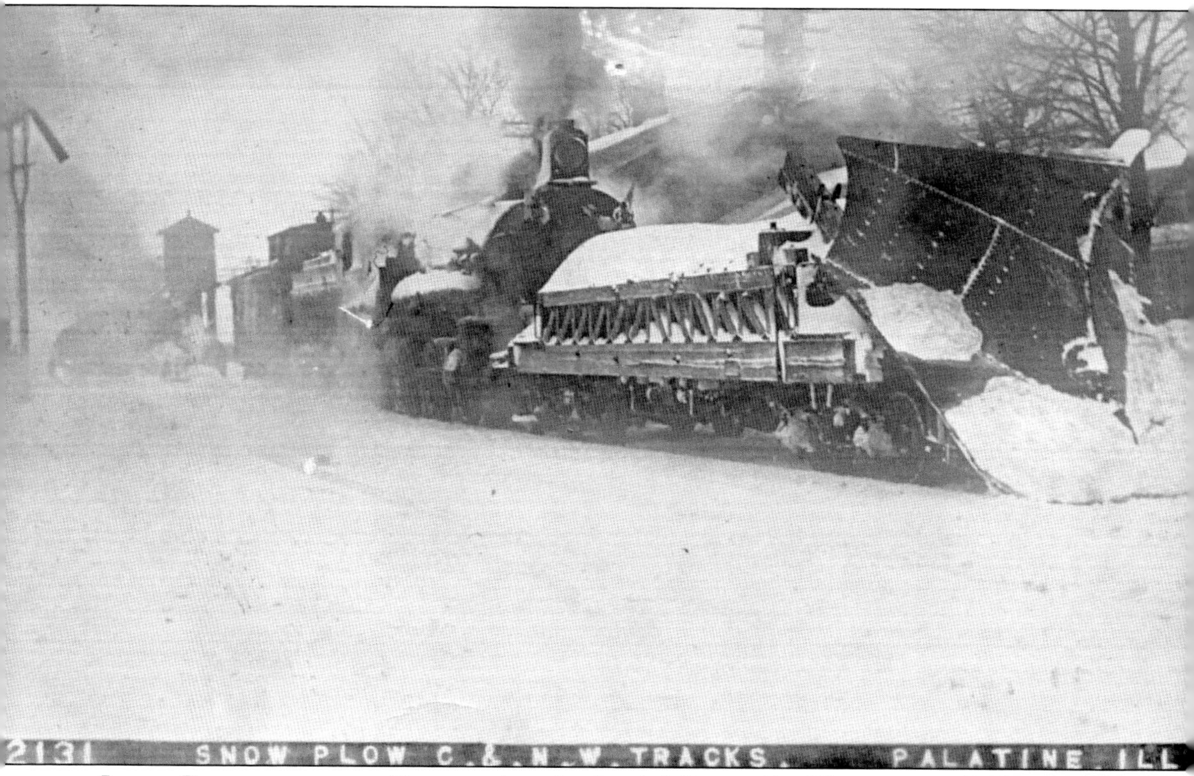

Julius Thurston to the Rescue. A train that left Janesville, Wisconsin, at 7:00 on a clear Saturday morning in March 1881 was struggling through a snowstorm with 65-mile-per-hour winds by the time it reached Crystal Lake. It finally came to a dead stop a mile and a half south of Palatine, and there it stood for 48 hours. Some snowdrifts were as high as the coaches.

The commissary department was not well supplied, and soon, the 30 men and four women were hungry and thirsty. They found several cans of milk on the train and were able to open them. A tea merchant offered his samples. Using a pair of lady's curling irons as tongs to hold an oyster can filled with snow in the stove, enough liquid was produced to make tea. That same method was used by an insurance salesman to boil a basketful of eggs he found in the baggage car.

In the evening, an angel named Julius Thurston, the baggageman at Palatine, brought a basket of provisions. He had spent two hours wallowing through drifts that were sometimes up to his shoulders. He reappeared at 11:00 the next morning with more food.

The time passed with singing, storytelling, snoring, and shoveling until 2:00 a.m. on Monday. The trainmen were helped with the shoveling by some male passengers, including a lawyer, a preacher, a merchant, an insurance man, and several traveling men.

The train was able to back down to the Palatine station. A snowplow with 80 shovelers managed to clear the track from Des Plaines back to Palatine. The train succeeded in reaching Chicago about noon on Monday.

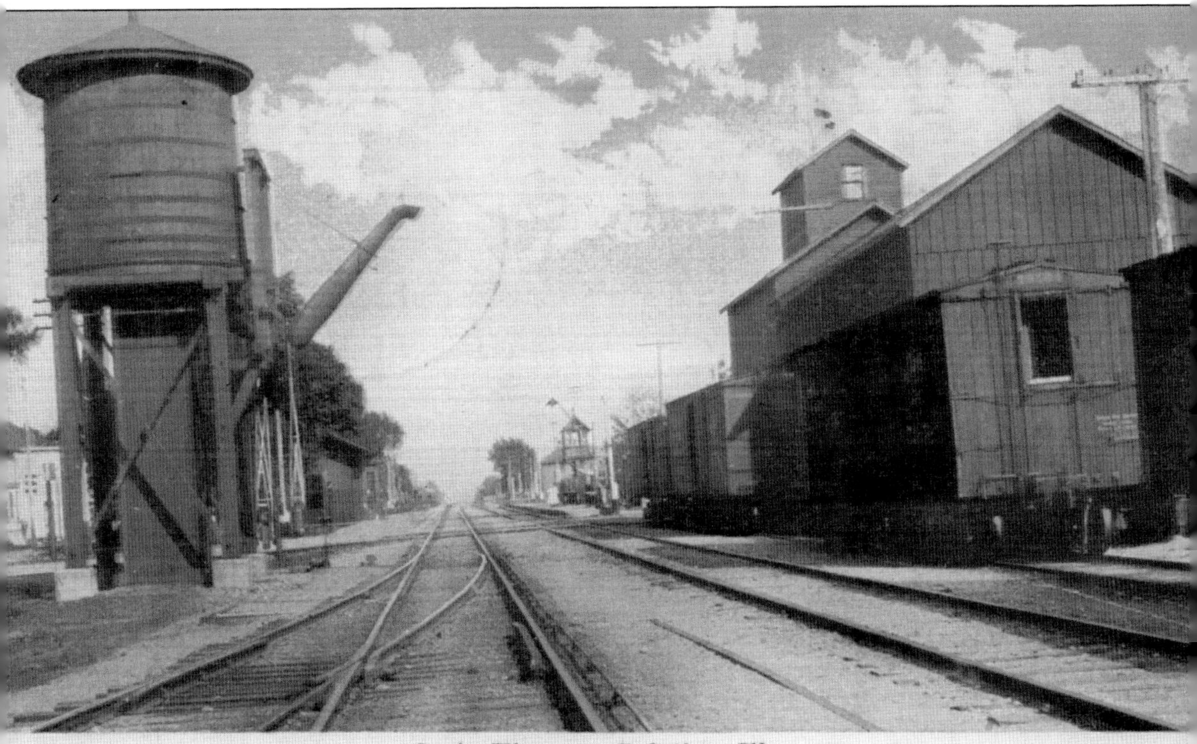

Grain Elevator, Palatine, Ill.

A Sunday Horror. At 5:00 a.m. on Sunday morning, April 19, 1887, a northbound train on a side track near the water tower (on the left) at the Palatine station was hit by a southbound train that ran wild. The trainmen saw the collision and jumped to safety. A total of six freight cars were smashed to pieces.

By 5:00 p.m., a large crowd had gathered to watch as a wrecking train from Chicago cleared the debris. Many people were standing under the water tank, which was 24 feet in diameter and probably contained 80,000 gallons of water.

There was suddenly a sharp pistol-like crack, and everybody ran away from the tower. It appeared that one of the bands from the tank had cracked. No serious results followed, so everyone went back to the spot. In less than three minutes, there was a crumbling noise and the structure fell. Five people were killed immediately, two others were fatally injured, and eight people were badly bruised.

An investigation into the accident concluded that the hoops that held the tank together were rusted and the shock of the accident loosened the hoops, causing the water tower to fall.

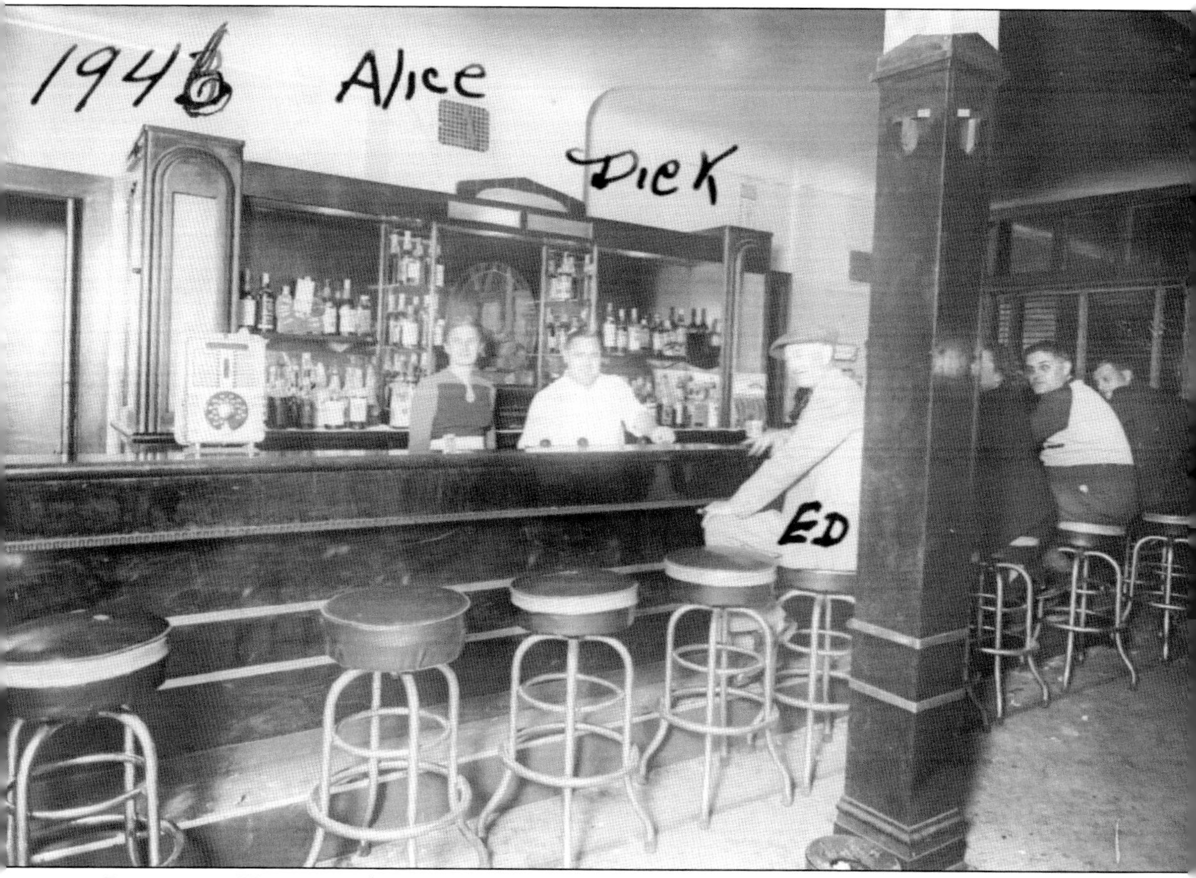

Dangerous Taverns. The tavern that is now Lamplighter was the location of two murders in earlier days.

One morning, a Palatine resident walked into Dick's Tavern (1930s–1940s) and shot owner Dick Sanford's wife, Alice, and the piano player Ed Batterman. The killer then shot himself. Both the gunman and Batterman died that night. Alice spent the rest of her life in a nursing home with a bullet lodged in her head. (The killer remains unidentified.)

In May 1962, when the building was Mac (Everett McCrea) and Al's (Zwurblis) Bar, a man entered and pulled a gun on McCrea's wife. The two men struggled, and both Everett and Louise McCrea were shot. Louise recovered, but her husband died on the scene.

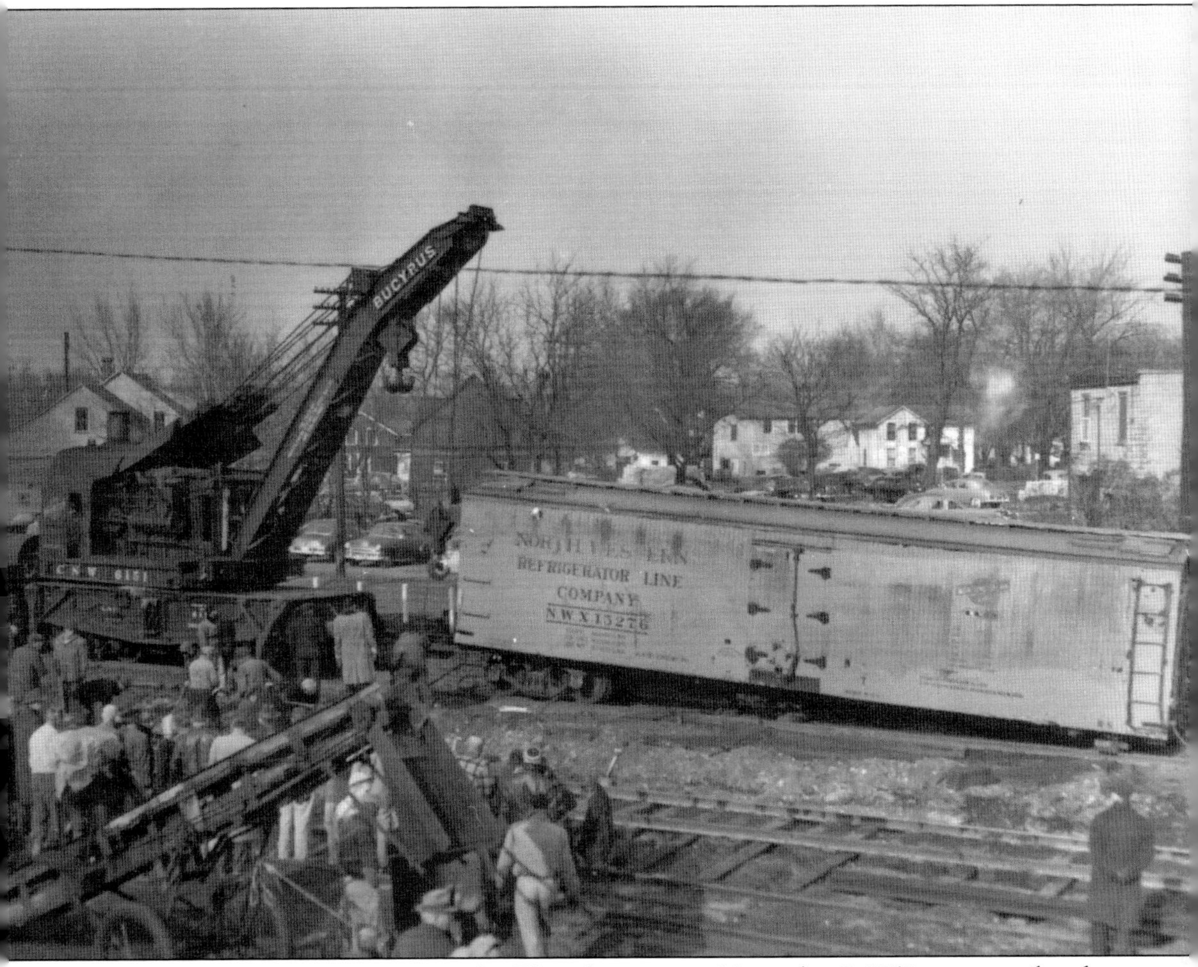

Massive Train Wreck in Palatine. On Thursday evening, November 9, 1950, twenty railroad freight cars piled up in the center of downtown Palatine. It was the worst train wreck of the Chicago & North Western Railroad in 50 years. All three tracks were blocked. A few automobiles were damaged. The station was spared. No motorist or person was close enough to the actual wreckage to be hurt, but if train No. 672 had been on time, it might have involved loss of life.

The wreck did result in a 24-hour water shortage in north Palatine because of a broken water main. Schools were closed, and local drugstores sold truckloads of bottled water. Volunteer National Guardsmen were called in, and the Palatine volunteer fire department stayed on duty. Commuters from the north were able to get to Chicago in the morning by using a Comfort Lumber Co. sidetrack, but trains from the south were backed up all the way to Des Plaines. The first priority was to clear one track.

Sightseeing traffic was so heavy on Friday, Saturday, and Sunday that the state police were pressed into service to keep cars moving. The local police kept people from getting close to the wreckage. Restaurants were so busy that they remained open 24 hours a day from Thursday evening until Sunday.

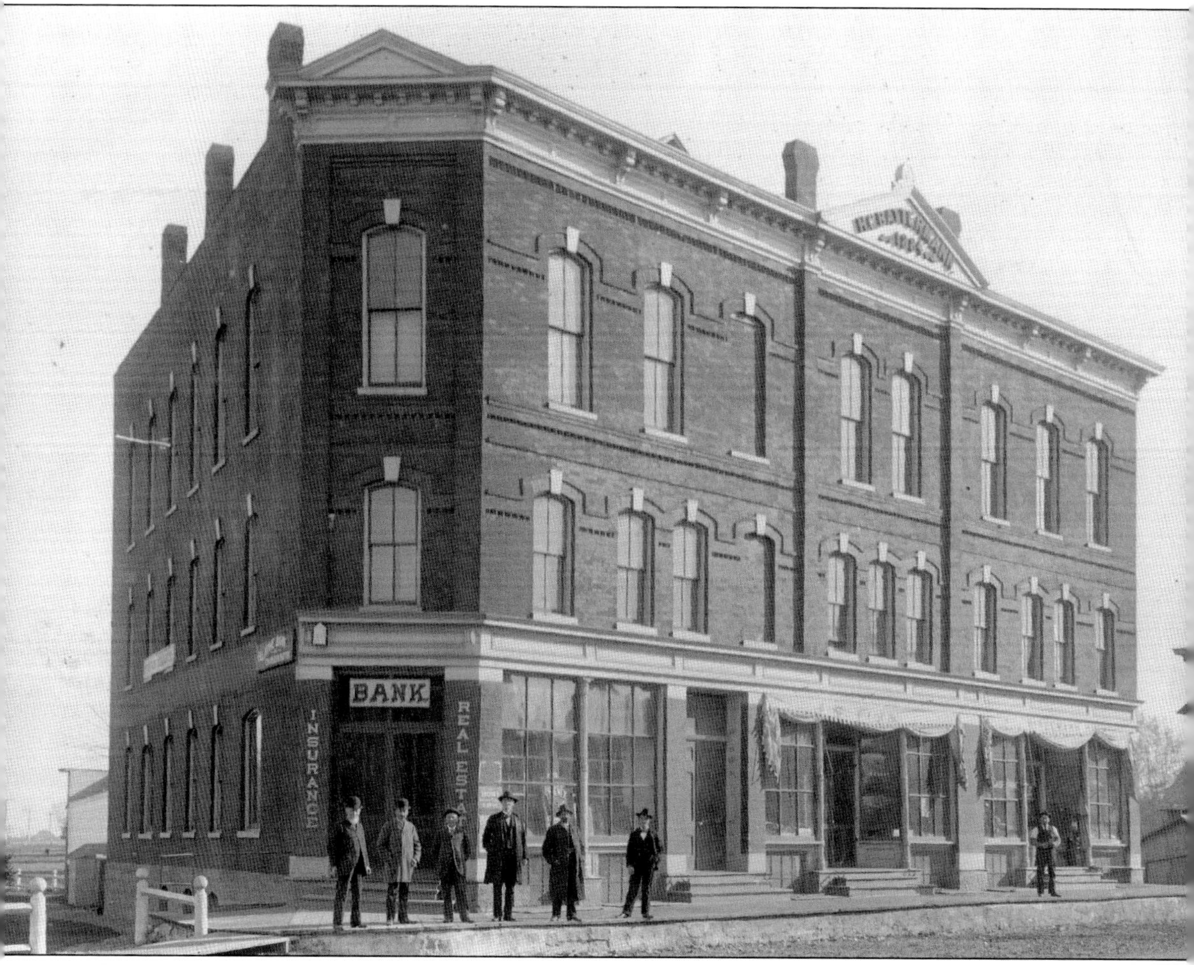

Patten Bank in Batterman Building, (from left to right) Henry C. Batterman, Charles Patten, Fred Gilbert, and Two Unidentified. An attempted robbery of Charles H. Patten's Bank of Palatine occurred in 1889. Fred J. Filbert, cashier, was lured out of his room and was struck on the head by the robber, who then threw Filbert under his desk. Henry Plagge, an aged farmer, entered the bank and, in a struggle with the man, a gun fired and struck the robber in the intestine. Plagge was also struck with the hammer, but was not seriously injured. Two men, having heard his cry of "Murder!" rushed in to help.

The robber was taken to the Cook County jail by train and died of his wounds the next day. Six months later, Fred Filbert died as a result of his head wound.

The newspaper later reported that the robber, supposedly William Lawton, was exhumed and identified as Dr. William Lewis of Chicago, who had been missing since the day of the attempted robbery. Relatives of Lewis claimed that the dead man was of unsound mind owing to the excessive use of morphine.

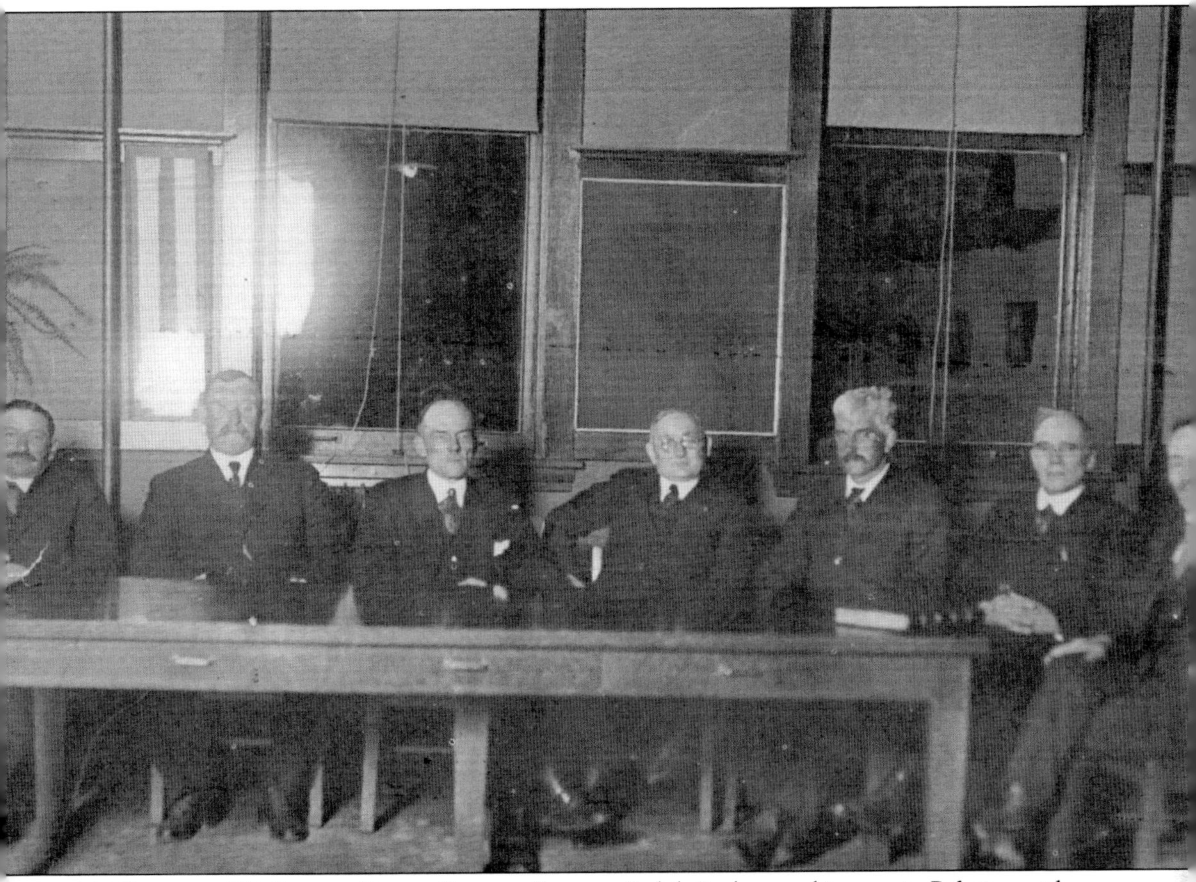

1920 District 211 Board, Ralph Peck in Center. Ralph Peck was a big man in Palatine with a successful law practice in Chicago. He was president of District No. 15 School Board and president of the District No. 211 High School Board after it was formed. He was the Palatine Township and Palatine Village attorney, president of the Palatine Township Republican Club, a trustee of the Methodist church, a Shriner, and an Odd Fellow and was active in other groups.

He was a vice president of the Mount Prospect National Bank and the receiver for the defunct PLZ&W Railroad in 1918. He ran for representative to Congress.

Peck was married to Caroline Kirchoff, who was well known for her whistling ability. He built the large house at 328 North Plum Grove Road that still stands.

On January 5, 1934, Peck paid a $2,500 fine and set off for the federal prison in Leavenworth, Kansas, to serve 18 months for embezzling $25,000 from the Palatine National Bank, of which he was president. The original indictment was handed down November 6, 1931. From then until his incarceration more than two years later, Peck appeared in court for the trial, was found guilty and sentenced, which he appealed. At that trial, he lost again, and the Supreme Court upheld the lower court's decision.

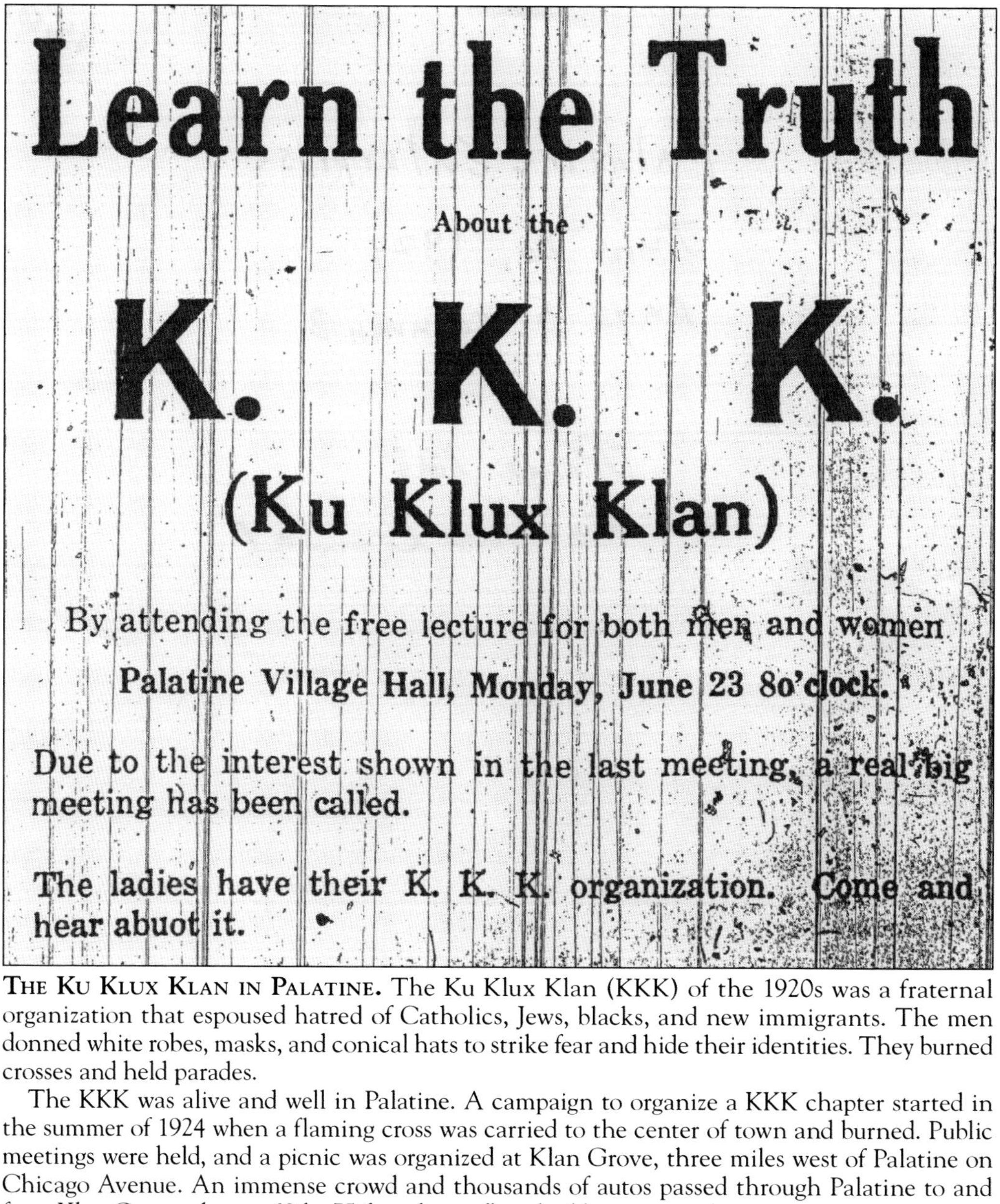

Learn the Truth

About the

K. K. K.

(Ku Klux Klan)

By attending the free lecture for both men and women

Palatine Village Hall, Monday, June 23 8o'clock.

Due to the interest shown in the last meeting, a real big meeting has been called.

The ladies have their K. K. K. organization. Come and hear abuot it.

THE KU KLUX KLAN IN PALATINE. The Ku Klux Klan (KKK) of the 1920s was a fraternal organization that espoused hatred of Catholics, Jews, blacks, and new immigrants. The men donned white robes, masks, and conical hats to strike fear and hide their identities. They burned crosses and held parades.

The KKK was alive and well in Palatine. A campaign to organize a KKK chapter started in the summer of 1924 when a flaming cross was carried to the center of town and burned. Public meetings were held, and a picnic was organized at Klan Grove, three miles west of Palatine on Chicago Avenue. An immense crowd and thousands of autos passed through Palatine to and from Klan Grove where a 60-by-75-foot dance floor had been erected.

The 1924 Cook County Fair, held on Dean's farm in Palatine, surpassed all previous years in amount of receipts. Labor Day was Klan Day, and thousands came. It was the only day of the fair when it rained.

When Owen Nangle was a boy, his mother hid him in a closet when crosses were burned on their lawn. His father was Catholic.

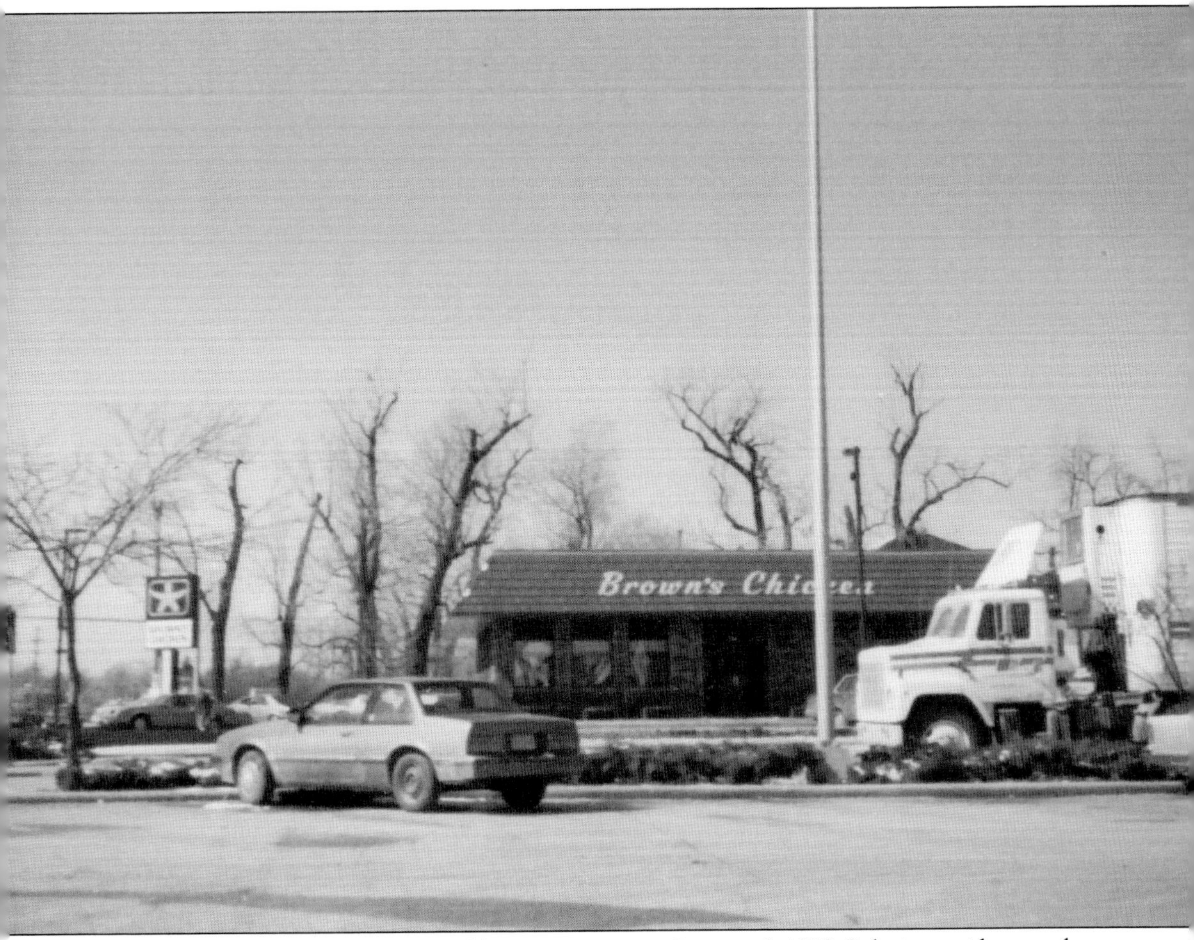

Brown's Chicken Massacre. On a cold, snowy morning, January 8, 1993, Palatine residents woke to the news of the terrible murders at Brown's Chicken on Northwest Highway. Seven victims were found in a cooler, including the couple who owned it and five employees. Television crews set up broadcasts on the corner of Smith Street and Northwest Highway as the community mourned and anxiously awaited news that the perpetrators had been caught.

It was a long wait. More than nine years later, a former girlfriend of one of the felons came forward with the names of two men, teenagers at the time of the murders. The men had eaten a chicken meal, and one of the police officers had the foresight to save the leftover chicken in an evidence locker. That provided DNA proof to convict Juan Luna. James Degorski was convicted due to the testimony of two former girlfriends. Both men were sentenced to life in prison without parole.

In a strange turn of events, a former Cook County jail guard was accused of beating Degorski in 2002. Degorski then won a nearly half-million-dollar settlement in a civil rights lawsuit.

A dry cleaner opened in the building where the massacre occurred but could not generate much business. So, the building was torn down and a bank now occupies the site.

Discover Thousands of Local History Books Featuring Millions of Vintage Images

Arcadia Publishing, the leading local history publisher in the United States, is committed to making history accessible and meaningful through publishing books that celebrate and preserve the heritage of America's people and places.

Find more books like this at
www.arcadiapublishing.com

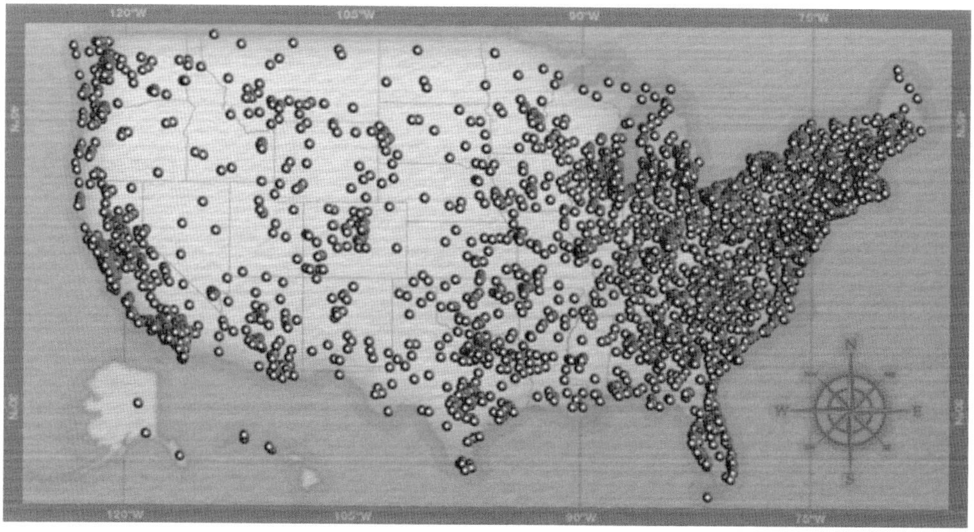

Search for your hometown history, your old stomping grounds, and even your favorite sports team.

Consistent with our mission to preserve history on a local level, this book was printed in South Carolina on American-made paper and manufactured entirely in the United States. Products carrying the accredited Forest Stewardship Council (FSC) label are printed on 100 percent FSC-certified paper.

MADE IN THE USA